Advancing from Stocks to Options Trading

Advancing from Stocks to Options Trading

Russell A. Stultz

Waterside Productions

Printed in the United States of America

First Printing, 2021

ISBN-13: 978-1-947637-28-3 print edition
ISBN-13: 978-1-947637-29-0 ebook edition

Waterside Productions
2055 Oxford Ave
Cardiff, CA 92007
www.waterside.com

THE OPTIONS TRADING WORKBOOK

Advancing from Trading Stocks to Trading Options

- Choosing Your Brokerage
- Funding Your Account
- Understanding Account Margin
- The Four Pillars of Wealth
- Day Traders and Swing Traders
- Trading Styles
- Using Price Charts and Chart Studies
- Using Option Chains
- Exploiting Time Value
- Using the Option Greeks
- Understanding Intrinsic and Extrinsic Values
- Exploiting Market Volatility
- American and European Expiration Styles
- Matching Trades to the Market
- Using Risk and Reward Ratios
- Using Probability
- Using Bracketed Trades
- Covered Calls
- Long and Short Puts and Calls
- Vertical Put and Call Spreads
- Iron Condors
- Strangles and Straddles
- Butterflies
- Calendar and Diagonal Spreads
- Developing Watch Lists
- Protective Stops and Profit Targets
- Rolling Out and Legging In
- Choosing a Suitable Option Strategy
- Using Rules-Based Option Trade Setups
- Option Trade Management Techniques
- Exploring Option Trades in Simulation
- Margin and Reg. T Calls

Table of Contents

Preface

I have traded stocks with mixed results for more than 35 years. And when I finally retired, I decided to supplement my retirement income through my trading activities. But I realized that I needed to learn much more about how to select the right stocks to be successful. A few friends who were doing quite well as traders suggested I enroll in a few courses from the Online Trading Academy. Although the tuitions they charged for their courses were several thousand dollars, I decided to begin by enrolling in a week-long technical analysis course. That course taught students how to analyze price charts to find trading opportunities. Looking back, the money I spent on the course tuition was the best financial investment I ever made.

That course taught me how to evaluate whether to buy or sell stocks based on the stock's underlying price charts. Referred to as *technical analysis*, it was by far the best course I ever sat through, including dozens of college courses. I learned how to use price charts and several popular *chart studies*. I saw how price charts provide vital information about how to determine where stock prices are most likely to go based on price trends, overbought and oversold conditions, and market volatility. I was so favorably impressed with that course, I wanted to learn more. I immediately enrolled in options, advanced options, and futures courses. All were excellent!

After taking multiple trading courses, I concluded that trading options made the most sense. I learned how options include mathematical indicators, called the *Greeks*, that make setting up an option trade and its outcome reasonably predictable. Because several Greeks symbols are used in the mathematical equations that compute option values, the name *Greek* stuck.

As you will see, this book describes how we use those values. And fortunately, they are not complicated. For example, *Theta* stands for time, *Vega* stands for volatility, and *Delta* stands for difference. And by combining my newfound charting knowledge with what I learned in my option courses, I quickly made enough income trading options to recover all the tuition I paid within a matter of weeks.

One instructor suggested that trading in isolation can be both difficult and extremely boring. Many people become discouraged and scrap their trading plans altogether. He suggested that some find it best to trade within a community of like-minded traders. "Meet at a Starbucks or Duncan Doughnuts for coffee. Gather around a table and share your trading ideas." Good idea, I thought. I passed around a sheet of paper hoping to find a half-dozen classmates who might like to meet. Several full sheets with names and email addresses were returned; Starbucks was out of the question. I was able to obtain permission to meet once each month in a large classroom at my church.

Our group met for the first time in 2013. We formed a trading club, decided to meet on the last Saturday morning of each month, and launched a club website. Today, our roster contains several hundred active market traders. Many are exceptionally successful option traders. In fact, many of our active option traders are multi-millionaires. And they willingly share several successful trading setups through well designed PowerPoint presentations. They show their price charts, describe the chart studies they use and why, which options they selected, and show their trade outcomes. This book includes several trades that were presented in our club meetings.

Most option traders succeed using a handful of the same familiar option trading setups. They are not complicated. They are all based on simple, readily available mathematical probabilities that are described in this book. Don't be alarmed by *math,* because it's just simple arithmetic. In other words, we use simple "trading rules" based on basic arithmetic. Although not every one of our trades return a profit, they do succeed most of the time.

This book shows you how options work. It introduces a variety of popular trading strategies that buy and sell call and put options. You will learn what call and put options are and when to use them. You'll learn when to buy or sell them separately or when to combine them. And once a trade is working, it must be managed. Trade management is an essential topic that is discussed at length in this book.

Most successful option traders I know began as stock traders. They evaluated company fundamentals including balance sheets, earnings and earnings growth, profitability, corporate debt, and new product announcements. They sought well-managed growth companies with superior products and good service and a loyal customer base. Then they examined price charts to see both historical and current buying and selling activity. The stocks they chose were based on what they saw on those price charts, especially the most recent price trends, i.e., upward, sideways, and downward trending prices called rallies, basing, and drops. They bought rallying stocks and *shorted* downward trending stocks.

Some of these stock traders learned how to make extra income by selling a call option for every 100 shares of stock they own — a simple option strategy called the *covered call.* This is essentially "free money!" A covered call is just one remarkably simple example of a way to earn extra income using options.

Today, many investors are learning how to trade options. Options trading volume has experienced remarkable growth over the past few years. For example, in 2018 option trading volume grew by an impressive 22 percent, dwarfing the trading volumes of the other three trading venues, i.e., *equities* (stocks, ETFs, and financial indexes), futures, and the foreign exchange markets.

In addition to option trade outcomes being reasonably predictable, there are other attractions including the ability to select from dozens of different *options strategies* (or setups). The diversity of strategies permits options traders to trade in any market condition: *bullish* (rallying), *bearish* (dropping), and *neutral* (moving sideways). There is nearly always something to trade, which is one of the many benefits provided by options.

For those who want to get started, they will find that options can be traded by people who have only a few thousand dollars in their brokerage account. Of course, the more they can invest, the greater their potential earnings: the difference between trading 100 shares or 1,000 shares of stock. Making a 50-percent profit on a $100 investment is not as rewarding as making 50 percent on a $1000 investment. But when a new option trader learns how options work, the trader can begin growing the money held within his or her brokerage account. And the return, or *financial leverage,* can be considerably more than that put at risk when trading a stock. For example, spending several hundred dollars on shares of stock might achieve a financial return of ten or twenty percent over a period of several months. In contrast, buying a few 100-share call options for a few hundred dollars and holding them for the same period might double an option trader's return on investment. And the option trader puts much less money at risk.

Experienced option traders use "trading rules" mentioned earlier. They know which options strategy to choose for the current market condition, the goal of the selected option strategy, and the corresponding level of financial risk. Option traders can also set profit targets and protective stops that trigger automatically when either a profit goal is achieved or to limit a loss to an acceptable amount.

Buying stock options with less money than it takes to buy the underlying stock itself provides enormous flexibility. Unless a trader is a dividend collector, when the price of a stock remains unchanged for several weeks, there is little incentive to buy or sell that stock. To earn a profit, stock traders need the stock's price to change. But option traders have strategies that permit them to profit when the price of the underlying stock remains unchanged (or moves sideways). One well-known market analyst claims that stock prices remain within a narrow price range about 80-percent of the time.

As mentioned, this book explains how options work and how to set up numerous popular option trades. They are popular because they usually work! Included are *options strategies* for different market conditions including both directional and unchanging price movements. There are also trades that leverage different levels of trading volumes, referred to as *market volatility.*

Finally, every option trade is a time-limited agreement between a buyer and seller; every option expires on a specific date. An option's market value, called the option *premium,* is affected by several factors. Just three of these include:

- The selected option price compared to the current price of the underlying *equity* (An equity is a financial instrument such as a stock or ETF.)
- The passage of time (An option's market value, or *premium,* declines with the passage of time.)
- Current market volatility (Changes in buying and selling volumes affect option premium values.)

DISCLAIMER

Trading and investing always involve risk. Any money traded or invested can be lost. You alone are responsible for any trading or investing activity that you undertake. Neither the author nor the publisher is licensed, qualified, or authorized to provide trading or investing advise nor will they assume any responsibilities for your actions. Hence, by reading this disclaimer and the information within this book, you understand that there is always risk involved in trading stocks, exchange traded funds, financial indices, bonds, option contracts, futures, and the foreign exchange currency market. The author and publisher make no representations or warranties for your trading success nor will they be held liable for your actions.

SECTION 1
FINANCIAL MARKETS, THEN AND NOW

What You Will Learn

1. Olive oil futures were traded in ancient Greece.
2. The French bought and sold agricultural debts in the 1100s.
3. The location of the first stock market system.
4. The first commercial company to issue publicly traded stock.
5. The London Stock Exchange, founded in 1802, prohibited stock trades due to fraud until 1825.
6. The New York Stock Exchange (NYSE) was founded in 1817 and quickly became larger than the London Stock Exchange. It is still the largest stock exchange in the world.
7. Alexander Hamilton, who served as Secretary of the Treasury from 1789-1795, encouraged the creation of American stock exchanges.
8. The NASDAQ stock exchange was created in 1971.
9. Charles Dow instituted the Dow Jones Industrial Avera1lge (DJIA).
10. Today, the DJIA lists the 30 largest U.S. stock companies.
11. The tulip bulb crash of 1637 in Holland, called *tulipmania*, is an example of what happens when a "market bubble" collapses.
12. Stock markets have experienced multiple crashes throughout history.
13. The stock market crash of 1929 was the worst in U.S. history.
14. Today, stock market circuit breakers are used to halt and moderate market crashes.

Introduction

Financial exchanges have been in existence in one form or another for more than two thousand years, although the first genuine stock markets that resemble todays were formed in the 1500s. But even before this, there were early markets that were similar in purpose to those that exist today. For example, the ancient Greeks were engaged in buying and selling olive oil futures during the lifetimes of Socrates and Plato. In the 1100s France had what they called a *courtier de change* system. The system encouraged investors to buy and sell agricultural debts throughout the country on the behalf of banks. In the 13th century Italian merchants and bankers in the cities of Venice, Pisa, Verona, Genoa, and Florence developed an exchange system in which they actively traded government securities.

Many believe that Antwerp, the commercial center of Belgium, instituted the world's first stock market system. The wealthy and influential Van der Beurze family lived there, which caused many to refer to these early stock markets as Beurzen.

While many early stock markets existed in Belgium and the Netherlands, markets also sprung up in Bruges, Flanders, Ghent, and Rotterdam in the 1400s and 1500s. Although the infrastructure and institutions resembled today's stock markets, none traded shares of privately held company stocks. Most transactions involved buying and selling properties and governmental and individual debts.

When riches and trade opportunities were first discovered in the East Indies, explorers sailed there by the hundreds. Unfortunately, many never made it home. Dozens of ships and fortunes were lost. Financiers were compelled to mitigate the risk by forming a corporation in 1600 called Governor and Company of Merchants of London trading with the East Indies. This was the famous East India Company, and it became the first company to use a limited liability structure that to some extent resembles today's modern exchange traded funds that include a "basket of stocks" that represent businesses that exist within a geographical region, an industry, or a market segment.

And it was the Dutch East India Company that became the world's first publicly traded company. It was the first to issue shares of company stock and bonds on the Amsterdam Stock Exchange in 1602. The company's stocks and bonds entitled each investor to a fixed percentage of the company's profits. Unfortunately, one in three ships returning from the East Indies were seized by pirates or lost in a storm. So instead of investing in the proceeds earned by a single ship and risking a total loss, investors began to purchase shares in multiple companies, almost like one of today's Exchange Traded Funds. Even if one ship was lost out of each three, by spreading the risk investors could still earn a profit. Combining the voyages worked well. Spreading the risk led to the formation of similar businesses throughout England, France, Belgium, and the Netherlands.

Unfortunately, the early days of an unregulated stock market was like the Wild West. In London, some businesses opened, issued stocks and shares for some risky new venture, and then disappeared. Many of these companies collected huge sums of money from investors and never made a single voyage. So these investors never received a single penny in dividends. Because these early transactions were unregulated, it made them extremely risky and subject to fraud. It became impossible to distinguish between legitimate and illegitimate business enterprises. As investors learned about these risky investments, they lost confidence, which stopped most of the market activity in its tracks. Due to the rampant fraud, the government of England became involved and prohibited the issuance of company stocks.

Despite this early prohibition on issuing stocks, the London Stock Exchange was officially formed in 1801. Companies were finally permitted to issue and sell shares of stock in 1825. The prohibition kept the London Stock Exchange from expanding into a global exchange. This provided a clear field for the fledgling New York Stock Exchange.

By taking advantage of the London Stock Exchange's draconian trading ban, the New York Stock Exchange (NYSE) was founded in 1817 — perhaps the most important event in financial history. Although the Philadelphia Stock Exchange already existed, the NYSE began trading stocks on its first day of operation. The trading volume soon became the world's largest. This led to the NYSE being the most powerful stock exchange in the country due to its location in New York, which is considered the center of U.S. trade and economics. But even with a late start, the London Stock Exchange became the dominant stock exchange in Europe.

Today, nearly every developed country in the world has a highly developed stock market. Dozens were started in the 19th and 20th centuries following the inception of the London and New York Stock Exchanges.

The Toronto Stock Exchange (TSX) was developed and began operations in 1861. The TSX is the largest in Canada and the third largest in North America by market capitalization. Stock companies based in Canada and the rest of the world are governed by the TSX. In fact, the TSX hosts the most oil and gas companies in the world — the primary reason for its high market capitalization.

Even war-torn countries like Iraq have their own stock markets. The Iraq Stock Exchange does not have a lot of publicly traded companies, but it is available to foreign investors. The Iraqi stock exchange was one of the few stock markets unaffected by the crash of 2008. Because stock markets exist around the world, trillions of dollars are traded each day, making these stock markets the engine of the capitalist world.

After slightly more than 200 years of dominance, the New York Stock Exchange finally faced its first challenger. The National Association of Securities Dealers and Financial Industry Regulatory Authority created the NASDAQ stock exchange in 1971. Instead of having a physical location, such as New York or London, all trades are submitted electronically on the NASDAQ exchange.

Originally, electronic trading gave the NASDAQ some major advantages over the other exchanges. Electronic transactions reduce the bid-ask spreads, where the Bid and Ask are a stock's buying and selling prices. The spread between the bid and ask is the domain of *market makers,* who match buy and sell orders to execute order transactions. Narrower bid to ask spreads achieve some minor reductions in the prices paid by traders. As you will learn later in this book, stocks having narrow bid to ask spreads in the pennies have higher trading volumes than those having wide bid to ask spreads that may exist in the dollars.

The competition between Nasdaq and the NYSE has led to many innovations in trading methods and technologies. In 2007 the NYSE expanded its reach by merging with Euronext, the largest financial exchange in Europe. This resulted in NYSE Euronext — the first transatlantic stock exchange.

Alexander Hamilton, Secretary of the United States Treasury

In the early years of the United States, the first Secretary of the Treasury, Alexander Hamilton, saw a need for the United States to quickly become an economic power. After an analysis of the European stock exchanges, he sought to establish a similar marketplace in the United States. During Hamilton's term from 1789 to 1795, he promoted the development of the marketplace through the creation of American stock exchanges.

The U.S. Treasury encouraged the trading of government securities. This occurred on the corner of Broad Street and Wall Street in New York City. Trading government securities eventually expanded to include trading company stocks. The stock market began to grow as companies began issuing stocks to finance the establishment and growth of their companies. This led to the reasonably brisk growth of the U.S. stock market, followed by a need for regulations and strict oversight.

Dow Jones Industrial Average and Other Major Indices

Stock market indices are an important part of our modern stock markets. The Dow Jones Industrial Average index is arguably the most important index in the world, although some would argue that the Standard and Poors 500 index, symbol SPX, is the most important financial index due to the number of listed stocks. The S&P 500 volatility index, symbol VIX, represents market volatility. High VIX values in the high 20s and above indicate larger than normal stock price volatility. In 2020 the VIX briefly rose into the 80s. High volatility signals an increase in risk due to unusually larger than normal price swings. VIX index options are also bought and sold. This is an indicator of risk. The Dow-Jones index was just one of the indices first created by Wall Street Journal editor Charles Dow, who also co-founded Dow Jones & Company. Dow's co-founders were Edward Jones and Charles Bergstresser, who were both American journalists.

The so-called Dow Averages were first published in 1885. The Dow Jones Industrial Average is made up of the 30 largest publicly owned American companies that play a key role in the American economy. The index started as a list of twelve companies involved in heavy industry, which is why it's called the "Industrial" Average.

Today, many of the companies listed on the index have little to do with heavy industry. Companies are added and removed from the index over time to reflect their influence on the U.S. economy. Notable companies currently on the DJIA include Apple, Boeing Aircraft, Facebook, Goldman-Sacks, IBM, Johnson & Johnson, McDonalds, Microsoft, etc.

When a company falls below the top 30 in market capitalization, it is removed and replaced. General Electric is just one example of a company that was on the DJIA list for many years and finally removed in 2013 due to its reduction in market capitalization.

Understanding the DJIA

The Dow Jones Industrial Average (DJIA) originally consisted of 12 companies: American Cotton Oil, American Sugar, American Tobacco, Chicago Gas, Distilling & Cattle Feeding, General Electric, Laclede Gas, National Lead, North American, Tennessee Coal and Iron, U.S. Leather, and U.S. Rubber. At the time these companies were among the titans of American industry. General Electric kept its place in the DJIA until 2013. Others have been broken up, acquired, and dissolved.

Charles Dow was an American journalist who founded a financial news bureau, originally called Dow, Jones & Co., with an investor colleague named Edward Davis Jones. Like any market observer, Charles Dow saw how stock prices tended to move like a wave in the same direction from day to day as investors reacted to events and expectations. He sought to put a number on that daily movement. So he chose 12 of the biggest and most influential corporations of the day. Each was a giant in its sector, and most reflected demand for the raw materials that fed the American economy, like coal, sugar, and oil.

Calculating the Dow Jones Industrial Average

In 1896 the Dow Jones Industrial Average was calculated each day by adding the closing stock prices of the 12 Dow stocks and then dividing by 12 to obtain the average. (Today, the Dow Jones Industrial Average includes 30 companies.)

Dow's *The Wall Street Journal* was first published on May 26, 1896, which included each day's DJIA index—considered the "gold standard" of stock market activity. The timing was ideal. The United States was emerging from a recession caused by the collapse in 1893 of the Philadelphia and Reading Railroads. Even with trouble in the railroad industry, economic activity was booming. Coal remained the dominant fuel for transportation, while demand for gas and electricity were rapidly increasing. Crops were a major export, while also essential to Americans.

Major Stock Market Crashes

Stock market crashes are an unavoidable side effect of any market where public sentiment plays a role. Most major stock markets have experienced crashes at some point in history. Stock market crashes are typically preceded by speculative economic *bubbles.* Because bubbles often burst, the term is considered appropriate and has been in use for many years. A stock market crash can occur when speculations are stretched far beyond the actual value of the underlying stocks.

There have been several major crashes throughout history, including Black Thursday or Terrible Thursday of 1929. Terrible Thursday was followed by Black Monday and Black Tuesday. The Dow Jones Industrial Average lost 50% of its value, sending America and much of the world into a deep economic depression and wiping out billions of dollars. In four years, the market lost 90% of its value.

Perhaps one of the more interesting market crashes of all time occurred in 1638 in Holland. Called *tulipmania,* in the mid-1630s tulip bulbs began to rise in value. Bulb speculators began buying the bulbs and drove the price of tulip bulbs up and into the hundreds of thousands of dollars. Investors were convinced that the price of these precious bulbs would continue to rise. A tulip bulb derivative market was created that resembled today's call options. Tulip bulb prices rose to as much as six times the average Dutchman's annual salary. Many investors were so convinced that the price would continue to rise that they began to mortgage their houses to obtain enough cash to buy bulbs. At one point tulip bulbs were valued between 4,000 and 5,500 gold florins — an amount of approximately $750,000 in today's currency.

But in 1637, the value of tulip bulbs began to fall rapidly. Thousands of Dutch investors became bankrupt and many lost their homes. All that was left was a few tulip bulbs that nobody would buy.

Other Major Stock Market Crashes

- Stock Market Crash of 1973-1974 (The Nixon shock & the devaluation of the U.S. dollar caused the market value to drop by 20%)
- Black Monday of 1987 (Programmed trading created investor panic and a 20% market decline.)
- The dot-com bubble of 2000 (Overbought tech stocks caused a 76.81% decline in the NASDAQ.)
- Stock Market Crash of 2008 (The greatest crash in history caused by illiquid bank loans; the Dow dropped more than 50% from $14,164.53 to $6,594.44).

Stock Market Circuit Breakers

In 2012 the NYSE created single-stock "circuit breakers." If the Dow drops by a specific number of points in a specific period of time, the circuit breaker automatically halts trading. This reduces the likelihood of a stock market crash, and when a crash does occur, it limits the damage of a crash.

The Chicago Mercantile Exchange (CME) and the Investment Industry Regulatory Organization of Canada (IIROC) also use circuit breakers. Both the NYSE and Chicago Mercantile Exchange (CME) use the following to determine how long trading will cease:

- 10% drop: If drop occurs before 2pm, trading will close for one hour. If drop occurs between 2pm and 2:30pm, trading will close for one half-hour. If the drop occurs after 2:30pm, the market stays open.
- 20% drop: If the drop occurs before 1pm, then the market halts for two hours. If the drop occurs between 1pm and 2pm, the market closes for one hour. If the drop occurs after 2pm, then the market is closed for the day.
- 30% drop: No matter what time of day a 30% drop occurs, the market closes for the day.

Today's Largest Stock Markets

The list of the top 10 largest stock markets in the world today indicates the changing roles of various countries throughout history. Today, the top 10 stock markets include markets in highly developed countries as well as markets in developing parts of Asia. Here are today's top 10 stock markets in the world ranked by market capitalization:

New York Stock Exchange	Hong Kong Stock Exchange
NASDAQ	Shanghai Stock Exchange
Tokyo Stock Exchange	Toronto Stock Exchange
London Stock Exchange Group	Frankfurt Stock Exchange
Euronext	Australian Securities Exchange

Other growing stock markets outside of the top 10 include the Mumbai Stock Exchange in Mumbai, India and the BM&F Bovespa stock exchange in Sao Paulo, Brazil.

There are also option exchanges throughout the world. The largest within the United States is the Chicago Board of Options Exchange (CBOE). Recall that the city of Chicago also hosts the Chicago Mercantile Exchange where futures transactions occur.

Section 1 Questions

1. Olive oil futures were traded in ancient ____________.
2. As early as the 12th century agricultural debts were bought and sold in the country of ___________.
3. Many believe that the first stock market system was developed in _________, _________.
4. The _______ _______ ________ _________ became the world's first publicly traded company in the year ______.
5. One out of three ships sailing from the East Indies were often lost to _________.
6. Why did the London Stock Exchange initially prohibit the sale of stocks? _____________________________
7. Which U.S. Stock Exchange was founded in 1817? _________________
8. The _____ ______ _______ ___________ is the world's largest stock exchange.
9. The ______________ stock exchange, which includes numerous tech stocks, was created in 1971.
10. The Secretary of the Treasury __________ _________, who served from 1789 to 1795, encouraged the creation of American Stock exchanges.
11. The Dow Jones Industrial Average (DJIA) was created by __________ ______ and originally listed a total of ____ different stocks.
12. Today, the DJIA lists the ___ largest U.S. companies based on their market ________________.
13. The TSX stands for the __________ ________ ___________.
14. The TSX's high market capitalization is due to the number of large _____ companies listed on that exchange.
15. ______ is the symbol used for the S&P 500 financial index.
16. The ______ is the S&P 500 volatility index, which is a tradeable index.
17. The first major stock market crash in the U.S. occurred in ________.
18. What is the purpose of stock market "circuit breakers?" ________________________________ ____.
19. CBOE is an abbreviation for the _________ _________ ____ ________ ___________.
20. The CBOE provides oversight for the U.S. __________ market.

SECTION 2
CHOOSING YOUR BROKERAGE

What You Will Learn

1. Countries depend on stock markets for the formation of business.
2. Equities, options, futures, and the foreign exchange are referred to as the *four pillars of wealth.*
3. The foreign exchange trades currency pairs. Also called the FX, it has the highest trading volume among all financial markets.
4. Market makers are responsible for matching buy and sell orders.
5. Fundamental analysis evaluates a company's financial information.
6. Technical analysists evaluate buying and selling trends on price charts in an attempt to determine a stock's directional price change.
7. Bracketed trades include protective stops and one or more profit targets.
8. OCO stands for one cancels other. When one stop triggers, the other is automatically cancelled.
9. Stocks, ETFs, indexes, precious metals, and real estate are all equities.
10. The location of the first stock market system.
11. Options are financial derivatives of stocks, ETFs, indexes, and futures.
12. Traders buy call options when they expect the price of a stock to rally.
13. Traders buy put options when they expect the price of a stock to drop.
14. Base and quote currencies, such as the Yen and Euro, are commonly bought and sold by FX traders.
15. Fundamental analysis is often used by buy and hold stock investors.
16. Technical analysis is used by shorter-term swing and option traders.
17. There are approximately 700 mathematical chart studies.
18. The ATR(14) shows a stock's 14-day average true price range.
19. The Bollinger Bands study plots trading volatility at two standard deviations above and below the 20-period Exponential Moving Average, i.e., EMA(20).
20. The Keltner Channel study plots the ATR(14) above and below the EMA(20).

Which Brokerage is the Best for Me?

You may already be a stock trader and have a relationship with a brokerage. And if you have a good relationship with your brokerage, confidence in your account manager, and have become a competent user of their trading application, your current brokerage will probably serve you well.

Or perhaps you know someone who is making a good income as an options trader and you want to learn more about what options are and how options can be used for a steady income. There are many retired people who make more income trading options than they earned when they were working in their full-time jobs. In any case, if you are reading this book, you probably know something about the benefits of options. If you do not already have a brokerage account and plan to start trading options, be sure to select a brokerage that provides an options-friendly trading application. Or if your current brokerage's trading platform does not support the functionality required to trade options, look around. Talk to some option traders to see which trading platform they use.

Most of us are familiar with names like Fidelity, Vanguard, Charles Schwab-TD Ameritrade, Interactive Brokers, E*TRADE, Merrill, and Trade Station to name some. But some of these do not provide full-featured options trading platforms. The author of this book has used seven different trading application and finally settled on thinkorswim from Charles Schwab-TD Ameritrade. Not only is it a good brokerage, their thinkorswim trading application includes an exceptionally robust options trading interface. They also have a rich network of branch offices throughout the U.S. and provide excellent telephone support for trading and education.

What to Look For

When either selecting a new brokerage or if not completely satisfied with your current brokerage, there are several things to consider.

Make sure the brokerage has prompt, courteous customer service. Find a few existing clients and ask them if they are satisfied with the brokerage's responsiveness to their needs. Ensure that you are satisfied with the answers to the following questions.

- Is the brokerage well established and financially solvent?
- Does the brokerage reimburse new customers for account transfer fees that may be charged by a previous brokerage?

- Does the brokerage pay an incentive fee when opening a new brokerage account?
- Are Personal Account Managers assigned to assist each new and existing client?
- Does the brokerage have a network of branch offices?
- Are the wait times for customer support acceptable?
- Does the brokerage offer 24/7 telephone support?
- Is the brokerage's website available 24/7 and reasonably intuitive and easy to use?
- Can you view and download trading transactions, monthly and year-end financial statements, and 1099s?
- Does the website let you submit messages and upload forms?
- Does it support funds transfers to and from your bank accounts?
- Does the brokerage have strong security on their website and trading applications?
- Does the brokerage's website and trading applications support the trading of stocks, options, futures, and forex?
- Is the execution speed fast when trading on the brokerage's website and trading applications?
- Are the brokerage's trade commissions and margin interest rates reasonable and competitive?
- Does the trading application have a "trading ladder" for day trading?
- Do dedicated support staffs exist for the trading platforms, trade and margin assistance, and education?
- Does the technical support staff have remote access to their customer's trading applications for support and training purposes?

You can also compare financial brokerages online. Many include rankings by features and detailed descriptions about benefits and features. The investopedia.com website includes some excellent brokerage descriptions. Check out the "Best Online Brokers" page on the investopedia.com website.

Funding Your Brokerage Accounts?

In addition to opening an account by transferring money from an existing brokerage account or simply depositing cash, many people transfer their 401K or IRA accounts into an IRA Rollover account. Once a deposit is made, account holders can begin investing their money in stocks, options, and perhaps futures. If you become a successful investor, you may be able to increase the value of your IRA Rollover account much faster than when it was managed by someone else.

IRA Rollover accounts have some SEC restrictions that do not exist in standard brokerage accounts. For example, SEC regulations prohibit individuals from entering unlimited risk trades in any qualified retirement account. An example would be to sell a put or a call option that might result in a major financial loss. These are called uncovered, or *naked,* puts or calls. Being covered by an equal number of shares of stock or by long calls or puts eliminates this extreme vulnerability that can happen if a large price swing occurs in the underlying equity. The danger associated with uncovered options is described in substantial detail later in this workbook.

Choosing Your Trading Application

As mentioned above, the author has used many different trading platforms from a variety of brokerages. He finally chose the thinkorswim trading platform from Charles Schwab-TD Ameritrade. It is feature-packed and the thinkorswim technical support is among the best. And there are thinkorswim versions that run on smart phones and tablets.

Within the past few years trading commissions have been discontinued by several brokerages including Charles Schwab-TD Ameritrade. Today, only the small option exchange fees charged by the Chicago Board Options Exchange (CBOE) are charged. Following is a partial list of thinkorswim's feature set.

- Create or import and save dozens of personal watch lists that fit your accounts.
- Import/export market data directly with Microsoft Excel.
- Display one or more price charts with access to hundreds of chart studies.
- Create and save "custom studies" that use your own parameters.
- Control the chart types and chart colors.
- Display or suppress volume graphs.
- Display and execute trades directly on price charts.
- Use drawing and text tools to annotate price charts.
- Use the thinkscript® scripting language to create custom chart studies.
- A feature-rich active trading ladder for day trading and futures trading.
- Create and save trade setups as order templates.
- Test option strategies with "back trades" using historical market data.
- Scan for stocks or options by price range, volume, volatility, chart studies, etc.
- Dynamically update personal watch lists as market conditions change.
- Display recent company news for a selected stock symbol.
- Send text and email alerts when a specified stock or option value occurs.
- Set thinkorswim's background color and text size.
- Display a market heat map to view key price movers.
- Display market analysist's upgrades and downgrades.
- Use market – and percentage-based stops, stop limits, and trailing stops.
- Access and view educational videos and Trader TV.
- Display all open and filled orders.
- Quickly cancel or cancel and replace unfilled orders.
- Permit technical support to access thinkorswim for examination and teaching.
- Import/export chart setups and custom chart studies with other thinkorswim users.
- Display dozens of public stock and ETF watch lists.

The above feature list is not the entire story. There are many other features that are not included in the list.

Retirement Accounts

As mentioned earlier in this section, many people transfer their 401K or IRA accounts into a Rollover IRA account within their brokerage. Once transferred and the account owner learns how to successfully trade options and/or futures, not to mention stocks and EFTs, they may be able to grow the value of their account much faster than when it simply held shares of stock and/or cash. However, transferring one's retirement account into a brokerage should only be done once the account owner is confident in his or her ability to manage and grow the account.

Margin and Margin Accounts

It is important to understand that buying and selling stocks usually uses what is called *account margin*. Short stock trades must be financed by cash and the value of the stocks and other equities held within each trader's brokerage account. Brokerages monitor the available margin in each trader's brokerage account. Stock values are discounted by brokerages for margin purposes. This can range from 50% to 85% of a stock's current market value, while cash is worth 100% of its value. Penny stocks, which typically have 5-character stock symbols, have no margin value and are avoided by most experienced traders.

If the account value is insufficient to finance a trade, the brokerage automatically rejects the trade. There are also times when an account's margin value declines due to a drop in the prices of the equities held with the account. When the value falls below what is required to support the current trades, the brokerage will issue a *margin call* which requires the account owner to either close one or more working trades or make a cash deposit to bring the account back within compliance.

Margin calls are designed to protect both the account holder and the brokerage from becoming vulnerable to a shortfall. If the account owner is unable to resolve the margin call by closing a vulnerable trade by selling stock or through a cash infusion, it could result in bankruptcy. A *Regulation-T Margin Call* is issued when a margin account makes a transaction that exceeds its available buying power. Generally, a Reg-T call is issued after an option assignment or auto-exercise of an option when there is not enough account equity to cover the loss. Although account margin rules are carefully monitored by brokerages, the Securities and Exchange Commission (SEC) has ultimate oversight responsibility.

It is important to note that account margin has a direct relationship with market volatility, specifically the S&P 500's VIX index described in Section 1. Often, an increase in the VIX index value increases risk and causes a trading account to exceed the brokerage's allowable margin value. When this happens, a margin call is triggered requiring the account holder to bring the account back within compliance by either selling stock or closing an option position that would have otherwise resulted in a profitable outcome.

Section 2 Questions

1. Can option trading provide a steady income? ______________________
2. Name three well-known brokerages:

   1) ________________________________
   2) ________________________________
   3) ________________________________
   4) ________________________________
   5) ________________________________

3. Do brokerages permit their clients to transfer and manage their retirement accounts? __________________________.
4. What does the SEC prohibit within a retirement account? ____________ ____________________ ______________________________________
5. Do all brokerages charge their clients trading commissions? ___________ ________________ _______________________________________.
6. How are trades financed within a brokerage account? ________________ _________________ ______________________________________
7. Why would a brokerage issue a margin call? _______________________ ___________________ ____________________________________
8. Who do margin calls protect? _______________________________ and ____________________ _________________.
9. What causes a Regulation-T Margin Call to be issued? ______________. _________________ ____________________________________.
10. Do both stock and cash held within a margin account have identical values? Explain: ________ ____
11. How does an increase in the value of the VIX index affect account margin? ____

Section 3
Trading Styles and the Four Pillars of Wealth

What You Will Learn

1. Day traders tend to make dozens of trades each day.
2. They create and save bracketed trade templates that include profit targets and protective stops.
3. Day traders use trading ladders and can submit a buy or sell order with a single mouse click.
4. A scalper is a trader who takes profits from small price moves.
5. Equities, options, futures and the foreign exchange are referred to as the four pillars of wealth.
6. The foreign exchange trades currency pairs. Also called the FX, it has the highest trading volume among all financial markets.
7. Market makers attempt to match buy and sell orders.
8. Fundamental analysis evaluates a company's financial information.
9. Technical analysists evaluate buying and selling trends on price charts in an attempt to determine a stock's directional price change.
10. Bracketed trades include a protective stop and one or more profit targets.
11. OCO stands for one cancels other. When either a profit or protective stop triggers, the other is automatically cancelled.
12. Stocks, ETFs, indexes, precious metals, and real estate are all examples of equities.
13. Options are financial derivatives of stocks, ETFs, indexes, and futures.
14. Market makers fill trades by matching buy and sell orders.
15. Base and quote currencies are used by FX traders.
16. Fundamental analysis is often used by buy and hold stock investors.
17. Technical analysis is used by shorter-term option and swing traders.

There are a variety of trading styles in use that involve the number and frequency of trades made and the trading tools involved. Here, the trading frequency and goals are discussed. You may decide to try day trading for a while. Day traders are *scalpers.* They constantly scalp relatively small price moves for profits. But after a week or two, the excessive action, demanding attention, and resulting stress may beat you down. While some traders may enjoy the action, which is akin to playing a video game or visiting a casino, others become fatigued and ultimately burn out. If this happens, it is time to do something different. But don't give up. You can still make a good living spending 45 minutes each day to find and trade a few decent trades.

When this works well, many people become *swing traders*, which is a natural progression. Although swing traders are close cousins to scalpers, there is substantially less stress. Although swing traders are looking for a stock prices to make a directional move, or price swing, they are more patient. Their trades can last for weeks all the way to years, as long as the price of the chosen stocks continue to trend in the right direction. Many traders eventually adopt the swing trading style because it is much less stressful, and the majority of their trades last substantially longer.

There are also *buy and hold* traders. These are usually people who buy a stock based on a tip from a friend, something they saw on a TV program, or something they read in the newspaper or on a website. Many do extensive research before choosing and buying a stock based on their research.

And some subscribe to one of the many websites that sell subscriptions by promising to reveal a "super stock." They produce videos that often waste valuable time by droning on and showing an endless series of companies like Apple, Google, Amazon, Shopify, and others whose stocks all increased in value by 1,000 percent. Showing history is not valuable news, but they all seem to do this as if what they are about to reveal will be another all-time winner. But what they are really doing, is selling subscriptions that may or may not be of any value.

There are some excellent stock research services. Many serious investors subscribe to stock analysis services like Investor's Business Daily (IBD). The IBD website, investors.com, ranks stocks based on a number of factors. One list includes the following description:

"A list of market-leading stocks generally showing strong earnings growth, positive institutional sponsorship and industry group relative strength as well as solid sales growth, profit margin and return on equity. The list takes overall market health into consideration and adds stocks in healthy market environments."

As a result of the research performed by IBD, many traders do quite well buying and selling stocks they find in the IBD lists.

Day Traders

People who make four or more trades on stocks and ETFs per day are classified as *pattern day traders.* A pattern day trader is a trader who has a margin account and executes four or more day trades over five consecutive business days. The number of day trades must constitute more than 6% of the margin account's total trading volume during the five-day period.

Those who consider themselves day traders are dedicated to their trading activities, which is a full-time job. Some successful day traders with sufficiently large margin accounts can make several thousand dollars in a single trading day. Seasoned day traders create and use several trade templates that most often include a buy or sell order, a stop loss, and one or more profit targets. Templates permit the day trader to submit several individual trades within a matter of minutes. Some of these templates may scale profits by including two or even three profit targets. Entering a trade with a stop loss and one or more profit targets is referred to as a *bracketed trade.*

Day traders use *trading ladders*, which is a trading interface that features green buy and red sell *rungs* that resemble parallel ladders. A typical trading ladder is shown in figure 3-1. A price is displayed next to each rung. When a price rung is clicked, a limit order is placed at the selected price. Notice the green

Buy Mkt and red Sell Mkt buttons. Market orders fill much faster than limit orders, especially when trading volume is good. Market orders are used for speed, as day traders want to get in and out quickly. The templates include a trade price, stop loss price, and profit target price. A single click on the price rung of the green ladder sends a buy order to the market; clicking the red rung sends a sell order to the market. Both include a profit target and stop limit order, which are also displayed on each working trade.

When the profit targets are greater in value than the stop loss, each trade's profit potential is greater than its possible loss. When the trader's price chart analysis is valid, the trader receives substantially more profit than he/she loses. If they set a 75-cent profit target and buy 100 shares of stock, when closed, they gross 75 dollars in profit. Fifty successful trades return $3,750 in profit less brokerage fees. Of course, there are always losing trades. But if the stop losses are set to 15 or 20 cents and only half the trades are profitable, the successful trades return much more profit than the unsuccessful trades lose. And odds are, a seasoned trader's price chart analysis is valid more than half of the time.

Examining the charts for price trends, price breakouts, buying and selling volumes, and the proximity to price support and resistance is important to how and where each trade is entered. This trader's chart analysis and template setup provides the edge needed to succeed more often than not.

Figure 3-1. A Typical Trading Ladder

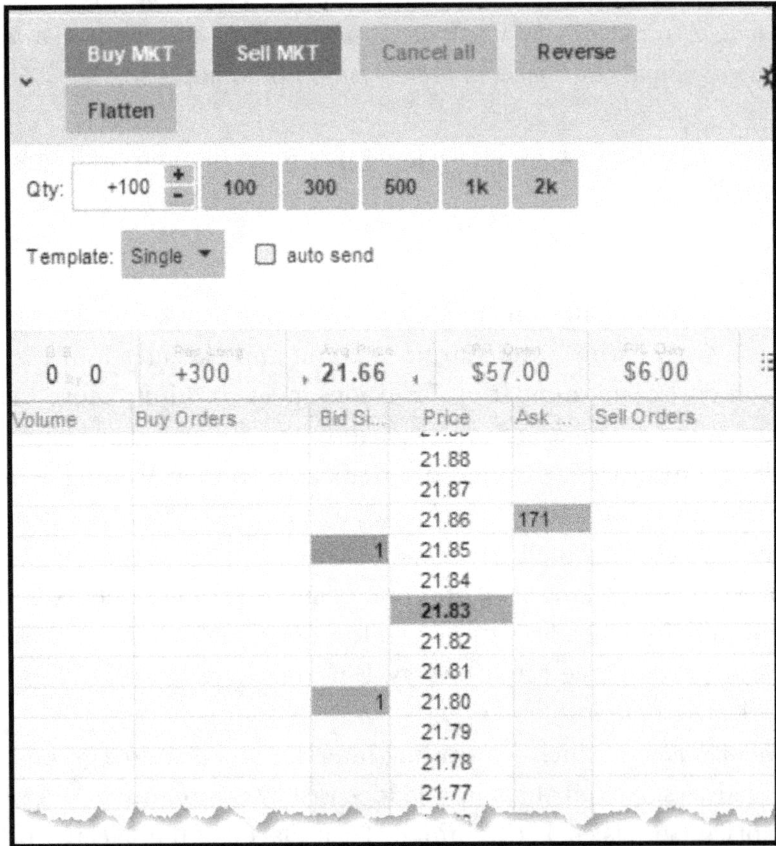

Swing Traders

Swing traders were mentioned above. These traders may also bracket each of their trades with profit targets and stop losses. And as the name implies, swing traders collect their profits from price swings. The difference is that swing traders may only enter a few trades each day or several trades in a week. But they spend more time validating their trade selections on the underlying price charts. The durations of their trades can be for several weeks, months, or perhaps even a year or two if the trader believes that the price of the chosen stock will continue to move in the right direction. There may be a few brief pullbacks, but as long as the upward trend is resumed, the swing trader will likely retain the trade.

Option traders are also swing traders. And option traders would rarely if ever enter as many trades as a typical day trader. Option traders use time to their advantage, because time has a major effect on option *premiums*—where premium is an option's market value. The durations of an option trade can range from several hours, a single day, or up to a few years. There are strategies that fit all of these timeframes. Option trades with different durations are discussed in detail within the pages of this book.

Market Capitalization

Market capitalization is not only a system, but also a term that relates to the size of a company. We often hear the terms *large cap*, *mid cap*, and *small cap* on financial programs on both television and talk radio. To clarify, these terms relate to the value of the outstanding shares of a company's stock held by investors including individuals, financial institutions, and perhaps a handful of mutual funds. The following table shows the relative sizes of large, mid, and small cap companies.

Company Size	*Market Capitalization*
Large Cap	More than $10 billion
Mid Cap	$2 Billion to $10 billion
Small Cap	$300 Million to $2 billion

Many investors are convinced that buying one or more small cap stocks provides a much greater opportunity for growth opportunities. And this is certainly true. Over the years the growth of many small cap stocks has outperformed large cap stocks by significant amounts. But the returns have also been riskier, because many small companies experience much higher market volatility than large, established companies. The stock price of a new company may increase rapidly and then plummet when investors begin selling to retain their financial gains.

The Four Pillars of Wealth

The four pillars of wealth include equities, options, futures, and foreign exchange. Each is briefly discussed. But because this is an options trading workbook, the discussion is brief. However, as a market trader you should be familiar with these terms and know the differences.

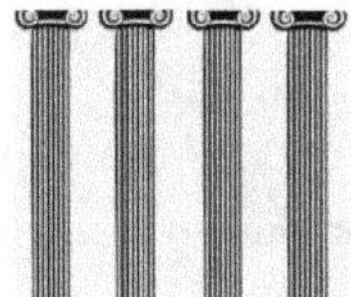

Equities

Every equity has an *intrinsic* value. Equities can include precious metals, real estate, stocks, collections of stocks, as in exchange traded funds and notes (ETFs and ETNs), bonds, and other marketable instruments that are regularly bought and sold.

Options

Many people who are new to options think of stock options. But options are also traded on several other financial instruments including ETFs, financial indices, and even futures contracts. Millions of ETF and financial index options are traded daily. The term *intrinsic* is used with equities.

Call and *put* options exist and are traded daily on thousands of stocks, ETFs, financial indexes, and futures contacts. A market trader may choose to buy a stock's call option instead of buying the stock itself, because the option can be purchased for a fraction of the cost of the stock itself. If the trader believes the stock's price will increase, or *rally*, the trader may choose to buy one or more calls. If the trader believes the stock's price is inflated and is likely to drop in price, the trader can buy one or more put options. Note that stock options represent 100 shares of stock. Buying five call options controls 500 shares of stock.

But the option may sell for a few dollars per share of a stock that is currently trading at $50 per share. So being able to control a few thousand dollars' worth of stock for several hundred dollars provides *financial leverage* to the option trader. Options also provide a lot of flexibility. A trader may expect a major price swing due to a pending earnings release, but he or she is undecided relative to the direction of the price move. They may buy a put and a call, called a "straddle." Then the buyer can sell the losing put or call and keep the profitable one. There are many such *strategies* that combine multiple puts, calls, or puts and calls. This book illustrates many in addition to explaining the goals, risks, and trade management techniques.

Option traders also use price charts to determine where the price of an equity is likely to go. However, option traders have an edge. In addition to having the same price charts that are used by both the day and swing traders, they also use what are called *option chains.*

Futures

As you read in the previous section, futures contracts have been around for centuries. Japan has a robust rice futures market that dates back hundreds of years. Within the United States, futures contracts are regulated by the Chicago Mercantile Exchange (CME).

Futures finance a large number of commodities including agricultural products, such as grains and livestock, oil and gas, precious and industrial-grade metals, currencies, treasury bonds, and much more. Futures are used by producers and processers, such as farmers and cereal manufacturers, to establish commodity values. Prices are negotiated based on a number of factors including product availability, quality, and current demand.

A farm co-op must negotiate a price for its crop before it risks the costs required to produce it. The processor, such as General Mills, must determine the cost of the grain and transportation in order to maintain a marketable sales price to its wholesalers and retail customers. Hence, a *futures price* is negotiated and settled upon between producers and processors in order to move forward. Approximately eighty percent of futures contracts exist between processors and producers. The remaining twenty percent of futures contracts are typically bought and sold by speculators. Like option contracts, futures contracts also have expiration dates. And futures prices may rise and fall based on product volumes, weather conditions, consumer demand, and a variety of other factors that affect supply and demand and trader sentiment.

Many traders buy and sell options on futures contracts. There are dozens of futures options called e-minis. Below are four that are traded on the financial indexes including the Dow Jones Industrials, S&P 500, Nasdaq, and Russell 2000. Although there are more e-minis from which to choose, four examples are included here. Notice how the number of shares included in the ES, NQ, and RTY e-mini option contracts are different than most 100-share stock option contracts.

Financial Index e-mini Futures	Symbol	Shares/Contract
S&P 500 index	ES	50
Nasdaq 100 index	NQ	20
Russell 2000 index	RTY	50
Dow Jones Industrial index	YM	100

There are some 40 e-minis. However, the trading volumes of most are substantially smaller than the four financial index options listed in the above table.

Foreign Exchange

The foreign exchange market, also called forex or simply FX, transacts trillions of dollars each day, while the daily stock market transactions are in the tens of billions. This makes the FX the largest trading venue in the world. The forex market is open 24 hours per day five days per week. It is dominated by institutional traders who compete for pennies while trading millions and tens of millions of *currency pairs*. Financial institutions and large banks regularly trade the foreign exchange.

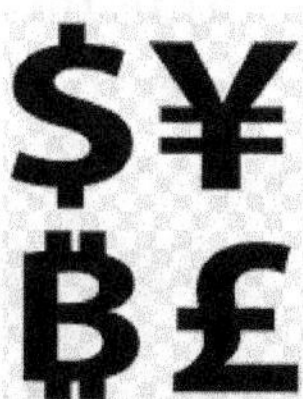

A popular pair is the Euro and US dollar, symbol EUR/USD. A few examples include the GBP/JPY (Pound Sterling/Japanese Yen) and the USD/BRL (US dollar/Brazilian Real). But there are many more from which to choose

The first symbol is called the base currency and the second symbol is called the quote currency. If the EUR/USD = 1.24000, the base currency (EUR) is worth $1.24000 US dollars. The trader must pay $1.24 for each Euro bought. If this exchange rate is maintained, the trader would receive $1.24000 when the Euro is sold. Here's a simple example of a forex transaction.

1. A trader believes the Euro will rally against the dollar (the quote currency).
2. The trader buys 10,000 Euros (the base currency) for $12,400 USD (quote currency).
3. The EUR rallies against the dollar to $1.25500 USD.
4. The trader closes the position with a sell order and profits $0.015 for 1.5 cents per Euro.
5. The trader's profit is $150.00 less commissions.

As you can see, the trader risked more than $12,400 on this trade for a $150 return—just 1.2%. To make a substantial amount of money on the forex market, the trader must be right. And millions of dollars must be exchanged.

Individuals (retail investors) buy or sell shares of stock, options, futures, or foreign exchange currency pairs with an expectation that the price of their investments will change and can be closed at some point for a profit. Most buy stocks in growth companies in which the stock price will appreciate based on sales growth and earnings. Of course, this is the goal; but often it is not the reality.

Order Submission and Fulfillment

Today, most active market traders deposit money in brokerage accounts and use the brokerage's Internet-connected, computer-based trading applications to open and close their trade orders. Electronic communications networks (ECNs) receive buying and selling orders from the brokerages for stocks, bonds, options, futures, and foreign exchange currency pairs.

Each exchange uses a group of authorized *Market Makers* who are responsible to receive and match each trader's buy and sell orders to consummate the trade transactions. There was a time when buy and sell orders were matched by a person, but out of necessity, this process has been automated due to the millions of orders that must be processed within minutes.

For a trade order to be filled, the prices must reside within the current Bid and Ask price range of the specified stock, option, futures contract, etc. There are *limit orders* and *market orders.* Limit orders establish a "limit price" that a trader is willing to accept. A market order fills almost immediately within a range of acceptable prices which are within the Bid and Call prices. Market orders give market makers more flexibility and are therefore easier to fill. Orders are filled when a reasonable match is found and the buying and selling volumes are sufficient. These transactions are automated and typically fill within a matter of seconds. When trade prices are outside the Bid-to-Ask price range, or when the trading volume is either weak or non-existent, an order may remain unfilled until it expires at the end of the day. There is also good till cancelled (GTC) orders that may exist for days to months until the trader decides to close it or it is closed by the brokerage according to its open order duration policy.

Deciding What to Trade

Fundamental Analysis

Buy and hold stock investors search for growth stocks. They tend to buy shares of a stock they plan to hold for an extended period. Most prudent long-term stock traders evaluate company fundamentals by analyzing income statements, earnings growth, profitability, product demand, new product announcements, etc. They also look at company price charts for price trends, trading volumes, and other indications that reveal the company's stock value and to identify whether to buy or short the stock. Buy and hold investors are not as interested in price chart analysis, called *technical analysis*, as they are the company fundamentals just described.

Technical Analysis

Both Day Traders and Swing Traders analyze price charts and use mathematical chart studies to determine buying and selling trends and "price swings." Recall the descriptions in section 4 of how day and swing traders constantly search for potential price breakouts. They evaluate price trends and use mathematical chart studies and the stock price's proximity to historical support and demand levels to find oversold or overbought stocks. This information determines the potential for a directional price move.

There are around 700 mathematical chart studies, but most seasoned traders use only about ten to perhaps a few dozen at most. Momentum study values are indications of a stock being oversold or overbought. Three common examples include the relative strength index (RSI), commodity channel index (CCI), and Stochastics oscillator. Bollinger Bands are used to evaluate trading volatility. The outside Bollinger bands are plotted at two standard deviations above and below a central 20-period exponential moving average plot, abbreviated EMA(20). When the outside Bollinger bands expand, volatility is high. When they contract, volatility is low.

Many traders also examine a stock's most recent 14-day price range. Called the Average True Range and abbreviated ATR(14). This study reveals a stock's average price range over the most recent 14-day period. It tells traders how a stock price is currently responding to recent buying and selling activity.

The Keltner Channel is another chart study that plots an equity's price range. This study uses a central EMA(20). Outer plots above and below the central EMA(20) plot exist at two times the ATR(14). Another study, called the trade the market squeeze (TTM_Squeeze), superimposes the Keltner Channel and Bollinger Bands. When the external Bollinger bands cross inside the Keltner Channel's ATR(14) bands, the price is said to be in a "squeeze." This signals a reduction in volatility which signals that a breakout back to normal levels of buying or selling volume is about to occur.

Unfortunately, the breakout may be caused by either an increase in buying or selling. The direction of the breakout is predicted using the Market Forecast study. This study evaluates buying and selling momentum for three different time periods in order to predict the dominant trading activity, i.e., buying or selling. When integrated into the TTM_Squeeze study, traders can anticipate the direction of the pending price breakout. This is used to as a basis for their selection of either a bullish or a bearish trade strategy.

Using Protective Stops and Profit Targets (Bracketed Trades)

Experienced traders often use what are called bracketed trades with stocks, options, futures, and foreign exchange (forex) trades. Bracketed trades include protective stop orders and profit targets. Protective stop orders are typically set to trigger if the price of a stock drops by 8% to perhaps 15%. (Recall the terms *long* for buy and *short* for sell.) Profit targets are typically set to trigger if the price of a long stock rises by 50% to perhaps 70%. Bracketed trades are also used with short stocks, options, and futures.

Some traders use reward-to-risk ratios such as 3:1 or 2:1. For example, the protective stop is set to trigger when the price of a stock drops $1.00 and the profit target triggers when the stock rises by $3.00. Some find the 3:1 ratio stops out too often from normal price swings. When this happens, they use a reward-to-risk ratio of 2:1 to reduce the number of times their trades are stopped out unnecessarily.

Watch Lists

A lot of the information provided so far in this section applies to traders of all kinds. And most long-time option traders also trade stocks or probably started their market trading activities as stock traders. And all traders constantly search for stocks with prices that are either in favor and rallying or have lost favor and are dropping. All have heard stories and read articles about people who bought several hundred shares of Apple, Google, or Amazon stock when they were selling for a few dollars per share and became millionaires by simply holding their stock until they were worth hundreds of dollars per share.

These stories lead many people to look for the "golden stock." Although most will never find the golden stock, many can do quite well with a good string of smart trades on stocks, ETFs, and financial indexes that each return hundreds, thousands, and even tens of thousands of dollars. In order to find stocks with good upside potential takes a little work. Successful traders are constantly studying the market looking for opportunities. Many seek out emerging markets and new technologies in hopes of finding a few rising stars. When this book was written, several innovative breakthroughs were prominent.

- 5G telecommunications devices
- Cloud storage and networking
- Electric car companies
- New, long-lasting battery technology
- Self-driving LiDAR technology
- Transportation as a Service (TaaS)
- Robotics and Manufacturing Automation

- Artificial Intelligence
- New power generation technologies

Traders frequently search the Internet for trading ideas. Once they find stocks of interest, they store the symbols in a watch list. When that list is saved to a trading application, the application automatically adds dynamically updated price and earnings information. If you don't already have a list of stocks and ETFs of interest, you should create one. In fact, you may create several that list stock and ETF symbols for different market sectors. Examples might include a watch list for microchip makers, airlines, automotive companies, block chain currency ETFs, home builders, precious metal ETFs, and perhaps networking and cloud computing companies to just name a few.

While stock trader watch lists are usually restricted to affordable stocks that fit their budget, option traders can buy and sell options on expensive stocks like Amazon (AMZN) and Alphabet (GOOG) even though these stocks are priced in the thousands of dollars per share. This is because both have affordable options. So trading options is not as financially restrictive as trading stocks.

The watch in figure 3-2 includes columns for the stock symbol, company name, last price, price change, earnings per share, the ATR(14), and the 52-week high and low.

Figure 3-2. A Typical Watch List

Symbol	Last	Description	Net Chng	ATR	EPS	52High	52Low
AMT	232.99	AMERICAN TOWER CORP COM USD0.01	+.79	5.23	4.23	272.20	174.32
AMZN	3352.15	AMAZON COM INC COM	+21.15	82.09	41.83	3552.25	1626.0318
ANET	321.91	ARISTA NETWORKS INC COM	+1.93	7.29	8.93	323.835	156.63
BMRN	85.22	BIOMARIN PHARMACEUTICAL COM	+.41	2.54	4.48	131.945	68.25
CGNX	87.02	COGNEX CORP COM	+.80	2.09	1.06	88.15	35.20
CRM	238.89	SALESFORCE.COM INC COM	+.91	5.1	3.81	284.50	115.29
EQIX	754.29	EQUINIX INC COM	+7.38	17.0	5.08	839.77	477.87
GLW	37.42	CORNING INC COM	+.14	0.97	.54	38.84	17.44
IFNNY	41.135	INFINEON TECHNOLOGIES AG ADR SPONSOR...	+.7475	1.11	.3146	43.550	11.000
ILMN	428.91	ILLUMINA INC COM	+.27	14.99	4.31	453.68	196.78
MCHP	145.44	MICROCHIP TECHNOLOGY COM	+1.70	5.19	1.26	155.36	53.15
NVDA	543.64	NVIDIA CORP COM	-2.93	15.92	6.12	589.0699	180.6807
PANW	379.85	PALO ALTO NETWORKS INC COM	-2.64	12.16	-3.11	390.07	125.47
REGN	498.98	REGENERON PHARMACEUTICALS INC COM	+.14	15.79	27.28	664.64	377.44
SBAC	273.86	SBA COMMUNICATIONS CORP COM USD0.01 ...	-.38	6.82	-.14	328.369	205.20
SPLK	170.24	SPLUNK INC COM	-2.02	5.66	-4.97	225.8944	93.92
SQ	240.38	SQUARE INC COM CL A	+2.66	10.36	.67	246.49	32.33
SWKS	178.95	SKYWORKS SOLUTIONS INC COM	-.15	7.71	6.35	189.70	67.90
TSM	127.78	TAIWAN SEMICONDUCTOR MANUFACTU ADR ...	-.37	4.49	3.174	136.13	42.70
VRTX	215.26	VERTEX PHARMACEUTICAL COM	+1.55	7.05	10.29	306.08	197.47

Watch lists are typically linked price charts and option chains. When linked, clicking a stock symbol automatically displays the corresponding option chain and price charts for speed and convenience.

Once armed with a few watch lists, you are ready to begin evaluating stocks and options. Begin by selecting a stock of interest, examine its price charts, and then check its option chain. Many traders learn to display multiple price charts that each cover a different timeframe. For the best visibility in how a stock's price behaves over time, use candlestick charts and consider displaying all four of the following price charts:

Chart Term Lengths	*Candle Durations*
Long-Term Chart	3-years with 1-week candles
Intermediate-Term Chart	1-year with 1-day candles
Short-Term Chart	20-days with 1-hour candles
One-Day Tick Chart	50 trades (or ticks) per candle

Most trading platforms permit you to select and enlarge an individual chart to full screen for improved viewing. Be sure to become familiar with a handful of useful chart studies and add them as needed. For example, you can add the trading volume bars, the 20-period exponential moving average plot, abbreviated EMA(20), and perhaps add a momentum oscillator that shows current trading volumes. Consider the Moving Average Convergence-Divergence (MACD) oscillator. There are several others you can examine including the Relative Strength Index (RSI), the Commodity Channel Index (CCI), the Stochastics Oscillator, and the Awesome Oscillator.

Many traders add the SMA(50) plot to their charts, where SMA stands for *simple moving average.* This signals exceptional price deviations from the norm. This tells you when an underlying stock or financial index is either above or below its normal price trajectory. Some traders use this plot in combination with perhaps an EMA(20)—the 20-period exponential moving average. A crossover is viewed as a signal to trigger either a buy or sell order. For example, a buy order is signaled when a rising SMA(20) plot crosses over the SMA(50) plot. A sell order is signaled when the EMA(20) plot drops below the SMA(50) plot. Chart study crossovers are commonly used when analyzing price charts.

Figure 3-3 illustrates two moving average crossovers. The first crossover signals a sell order and the second a buy order. Notice how both signals accurately predict the directional price moves.

Figure 3-3. Two EMA(20)-SMA(50) Crossovers.

Account Margin

The funds we deposit into our brokerage accounts may include cash and perhaps a variety of financial instruments. When moving funds from one brokerage to another, we often transfer stocks, bonds, and even working trades. The cash and each financial instrument have value. Once the account is open, brokerages permit the account holders to use their assets as collateral to buy stocks and other financial instruments. While account holders can usually use 100% of the cash value within their accounts, brokerages hold back a portion of each account's value for safety. For example, the brokerage may permit a trader use 50% to 70% of the value of the stocks held within the trader's account to purchase additional stocks or for financing options, futures, and/or forex trades.

NOTE penny stocks, also called "pink sheet" stocks, have no margin value. These stocks are poorly regulated and often unaudited Therefore, penny stocks are often quite risky and avoided by most savvy traders.

If a person owns $200,000 worth of Apple and Microsoft stock and their brokerage permits them to use 50% of the stock value to purchase additional securities, they can borrow up to $100,000 of the stock's current value to purchase additional securities, such as buying shares of a different stock, a call or put option, or perhaps a futures contract.

Option Trading Levels

Option traders are granted options trading levels based on years of options trading experience, the ability to pass a brokerage-administered options test, or both. Following is a typical list of four options trading levels and the types of option trades permitted for each:

Level 1 — The sale of covered calls and cash-secured put options
Level 2 — The purchase of put and call options
Level 3 — Option spreads including vertical puts, calls, and iron condors
Level 4 — Naked calls and puts.

Portfolio Margin

Brokerages also grant *portfolio margin*, which is available to experienced level 4 option traders who have a minimum account value of $125,000. Portfolio margin (PM) accounts permit the use of up to 85% of stock value in compliance with S.E.C. guidelines. A PM account's value must remain above $100,000. Account values change with risk caused by market volatility. It is important to understand this dynamic. Most trading platforms display each account's current margin status. To evaluate your margin risk, you can call a member of your brokerage's support staff to learn how to examine your current margin status.

Margin Calls

When an account holder exceeds the allowable borrowing limit, the brokerage issues a *margin call.* The trader is required to sell stock or another security to bring their account value back within compliance. They may also be required to deposit more cash into their account to bring it back within compliance. In conclusion, it is essential to understand how a margin accounts works. Be sure you know your brokerage's rules and how to evaluate your current account margin status. Otherwise, you may encounter what can become a serious financial shortfall.

Section 3 Questions:

1. What is a *scalper*? ____
____
2. Can day trading be stressful? ____
____
3. Why do you think swing trading to be less stressful than day trading? ______________
____.
4. What is a *pattern day trader*? ______________________. ______________________
______________________.
5. A "trading ladder" is well suited to which trading style? ____________ ______________
______________________.
6. Day traders use templates that include three elements. First is the entry price. The other two are a protective ______ ______, and a __________ target.
7. Swing traders also bracket trades with __________ __________ and profit __________.
8. Three terms are used to describe a company's capitalization, including: __________ cap, ___________ cap, and __________ cap.
9. List the "four pillars of wealth": ______________, ______________ ______________, and ______________.
10. Call and put options are traded on stocks, ETFs, financial indexes, and ____________ contracts.
11. Spending $50 on a $1,000 stock is referred to as ____________ ______________.
12. The abbreviation CME stands for the ____________ ____________ ____________.
13. Futures contracts are negotiated between producers and ____________.
14. Currency pairs are traded on the ______________ ______________.
15. The abbreviation GTC stands for ________ ________ __________.
16. Name two types of financial analysis used by traders: ______________ ______________
17. Watch lists are often linked to _________ _________ for further analysis.
18. What do the abbreviations SMA and EMA stand for? ____________ __________ _________ and _________ ____________ __________
19. A moving average crossover is seen as a buy or sell ____________.
20. Portfolio margin is available to _________ _______ ________.

SECTION 4
UNDERSTANDING HOW OPTIONS WORK

What You Will Learn

1. Options are financial derivatives of stocks, ETFs, futures, and financial indexes.
2. Options are bought and sold for a fraction of the cost of a corresponding stock, ETF, futures contract, or financial index.
3. Options are governed by a number of option exchanges including the Chicago Board of Options Exchange (CBOE).
4. Option traders buy and sell put and call options.
5. Option trades are set up on mathematical tables called option chains.
6. Option values, called premium, are listed in an option chain's Mark column.
7. Every option trade is between a buyer and seller.
8. All options are time-limited with a fixed expiration date.
9. The Options Clearing Corporation (OCC) settles expired options.
10. Option prices fluctuate with a variety of factors including price changes in the underlying stock, market volatility, the passage of time, etc.
11. Understanding the Option "Greeks" is key to option analysis.
12. Options have intrinsic and extrinsic value.
13. Understand the difference between a credit and a debit spread.
14. Examine some basic option trades that include buying and selling calls, puts, and vertical spreads.
15. Match an option strategy to your bullish, bearish, neutral market bias.

What are Options?

Options are time-limited financial derivatives of equities, such as stocks, exchange traded funds and notes, financial indexes, and futures contracts. Like stocks, option contracts are bought and sold, or "traded," through brokerages who subscribe to the services of one or more options exchanges. Market makers collect and match buy and sell orders from individual and institutional traders and fill the orders. As part of their service, market makers may also take buy and sell positions in orders to complete order executions.

Financial Leverage

Financial leverage is a major advantage that is available to option traders. An option trader can buy one or more 100-share call or put stock options for a fraction of the cost of buying or shorting the underlying stock itself. And if the stock price rallies, the price of the call options will also increase. If the price drops, the price of the put options increase. If a trader simultaneously buys a call option and sells a put option on a rallying stock, the option can earn substantially more money than if the trader had just bought stock.

This is just one of the many advantages of financial leverage offered by options. And it is one of the main reasons for the recent increase in options trading volume.

Section 5 includes a substantial amount of information on how option trades are constructed. It describes how traders use price charts and option chains. It includes several examples of bullish, bearish, and neutral option strategies. And it illustrates how puts, calls, and a variety of *vertical spreads* that include two or more options are constructed.

The Options Contract

Your brokerage has access to several different options exchanges. These include the Chicago Board Options Exchange (CBOE), the NYSE Arca, the International Securities Exchange, the Boston Options Exchange, the Eurex Exchange, and the Montreal Stock Exchange. Most brokerages provide trading platforms that use "Best" in order to choose the exchange with the best Bid to Ask offer. Like stocks, option values fluctuate with the market price of the underlying equity. Every option trade is a contractual agreement between a buyer and seller. Each option has a specific expiration date, much like an auto or homeowners insurance policy. As an option approaches its expiration date, the remaining time value begins to drop rapidly. On option expiration day, the option's value plummets to zero when the market closes.

The market (or Mark) value of an option is also called the option's *premium.* Like insurance policies with declining premium values due to the passage of time, option premium values also depreciate with the passage of time.

Option values are listed within financial tables called *option chains.* The use of these tables is described in detail within this book. Here, you learn how to use option chains to analyze, select, and trade options. Like stocks, options can be bought or sold. Called a *spread,* you can also buy an option and sell a different option at the same time.

As mentioned above, option contracts exist between a buyer and a seller and are governed by well-established option trading rules. Most of us trade options through a financial brokerage that uses electronic communications networks over which orders are processed on stocks, options, futures, and currency exchanges. Specifically, option contracts are managed by one of the above-mentioned options exchanges and the Options Clearing Corporation (OCC). The OCC is responsible for clearing all option contracts upon expiration. The OCC auto-exercises all short (sold) options that expire in the money (ITM) by even one penny. In the money and out of the money call and put options and option strike prices are illustrated in figure 4-1 and discussed in substantial detail later in this section. For now, the price of an

ITM call option is less than the price of the underlying equity, while an ITM put option is greater than the price of the underlying equity. And there are only two kinds of options: call options and put options. Once you understand what call and put options are and how they work, which is revealed in this section, your grasp of options will increase exponentially.

Option sellers avoid holding ITM options through expiration because this requires the option sellers to settle with the buyers. (Read more about Assigning and Exercising ITM Options later in this section.) There are also out of the money options, abbreviated OTM.

Most option contracts represent 100 shares of the underlying equity, although there are some futures and "mini" options that have 10-, 20-, and 50-share option contracts. Unless otherwise noted, the examples in this book use the common 100-share stock option contract.

Options Pricing

Like time-limited insurance policy premiums, the value of option premiums becomes worthless upon the option's expiration date when the market closes, which is 4 p.m. EST. All options have time value, also referred to as *extrinsic value*. Extrinsic value is the difference between the market price, or premium, of an option and its *intrinsic value*. Extrinsic and intrinsic values are described in substantial detail later in this section.

In addition to declining in value with the passage of time, the option's extrinsic value varies with several other factors including the changes in the price of the underlying stock and the current trading volume occurring in the underlying equity to name a few. The intrinsic value of an option is an option's relative worth based on the option's *strike price*. Strike prices are described in detail below. We can think of an option's intrinsic value as the difference between the strike price of an option and the current price of the underlying equity, which is commonly the price of the stock. Unlike insurance policy premiums, which have a linear decline in value with each passing day, an option's value is based on several variables that constantly fluctuate due to many factors that include changes in market *volatility*, the underlying stock's price, trading volume, the number of working option contracts, the time remaining till expiration, and the option's *strike price* relative to the current stock price. You can examine an option chain and the prominent option variables in figure 4-1. The option variables are listed and described in the Exploring Option Values paragraph below.

When examining figure 4-1, see how an option chain displays a series of strike prices in a central Strike column. The strikes are arranged from low-to-high prices and correspond to possible prices of the underlying equity. The strike price that is closest to the current price of the underlying equity is referred to as the *at the money* strike price, abbreviated ATM.

The shaded regions of the option chain are *in the money* (ITM) strike prices, while the strike prices with white backgrounds are said to be *out of the money* (OTM). Also notice how the mark values of both call and put options increase as the strike prices move *deeper in the money*. Examine figure 4-1 to see how the call premium values in the Mark column increase as the corresponding strike prices move down and deeper into the money. Also see how the put option values in the Mark column increase as the corresponding strike prices move up.

The Option Chain

The option chain illustrated in figure 4-1 is a financial table that displays a substantial amount of information. Option traders use option chains to analyze, select, configure, and ultimately trade option contracts.

The central column displays a list of option strike prices for the corresponding equity. The equity is a stock, ETF, financial index, or futures contract. While the term stock is used in this book to represent the equity, it could be one of the other financial instruments just mentioned.

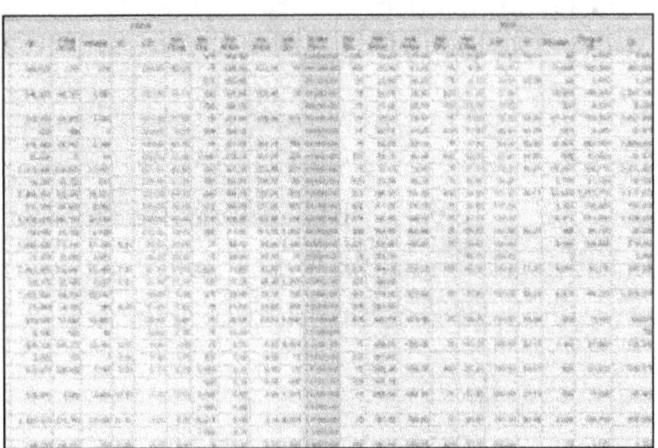

The central strike price column includes those prices at which options are bought or sold. For example, the McDonald's stock option chain includes 200, 205, 210, etc. strike prices in $5 increments. An option trader may choose to buy or sell one or more $200 put or call options. However, the trader's goal is to choose an option strike price that will return a profit. It is possible to choose a strike price that is vulnerable to substantial risk. But if you follow the advice in this book, you are more likely to choose strike prices that should succeed more often than they fail.

Buying and Shorting Stock

You should also know that stocks, ETFs, and even futures contracts are also bought and sold on option chains. If you want to buy a stock, click the stock value in the Ask price cell at the top of the chain for each 100 shares of stock you want to buy. Click the Bid price cell to short 100 shares of stock. You can adjust the number of shares on the order bar and then click Submit to view order confirmation information prior to final submission.

You can also submit bracketed trades. This is done by adding a profit target and a stop loss to your order before submitting it to the market. You can ask your brokerage's technical support staff to walk you through this and other order types.

What's in the Option Chain?

Examine the McDonalds' stock option chain contained in figure 4-1. Be aware that other columns can be added or removed by the user. Some columns, like Strike, Bid, and Ask, are permanent. But the Mark, Vega, Theta, Extrinsic, Intrinsic, and Open Interest columns are optional. There are several other available option value columns like Last, Probability ITM, Probability OTM, and Probability Touching to name just a few.

But adding too many columns creates clutter and makes option chains difficult to use. Most option traders include only those columns that are required to evaluate their option trade setups. Most of the option chains shown in this book include Delta, Theta, and Open Interest in addition to the default Strike, Bid, and Ask columns.

- Bid — The option's current selling price
- Ask — The option's current buying price

- Mark — The option's *market value* midway between the Bid and Ask values
- Delta — A value that shows the option's price change for each $1.00 change in the value of the underlying stock, ETF, etc.
- Theta — The daily drop in an option's value, also called *time decay*, which increases dramatically as an option approaches expiration
- Vega — An option's sensitivity to volatility; a .05 Vega changes the option's Mark value by 5 cents in response to a 1% change in Implied Volatility (IV%).
- Intrinsic Value — The market price, or premium, of an option less its extrinsic value. Out of the money options do not have intrinsic value.
- Extrinsic Value — The difference between an option's market price, or its current premium value, and the option's *intrinsic value.*
- Open Interest — The number of option contracts that existed when the market opened in the morning. Traders look for high Open Interest values for liquidity.

Other columns that can be added to an option chain include:

- Gamma — A secondary *Greek* that determines the value of Delta; gamma values increase when closer to the money and as an option approaches expiration.
- Probability OTM (out of the money) — The calculated probability of the option's strike price remaining out of the money through option expiration.
- Probability ITM (in the money) — The probability of the option's strike price becoming in the money prior to expiration. Note that Delta and Probability ITM are within 1 or 2 percent. For convenience, most option traders use the value of Delta.

Gamma Risk As mentioned in the above list, the gamma Greek is a secondary value used to compute the values of Delta. Many option traders simply check the Delta values to determine the current effect of gamma. Although it is not shown on the option chain in figure 4-1, you can add a gamma column to your option chain. Gamma is highest at strikes near or at the money as an option approaches its expiration date. A gamma 0.02 and a $1.00 price change in the underlying stock causes the value of Delta to change the option's premium by 2 cents. If Delta's value is .40, a .02 gamma causes a .008-cent change in the value of Delta for each $1.00 increase or decrease in the price of the underlying. The term *gamma risk* describes how gamma can change option prices due to its rising influence on Delta values, especially as an option approaches expiration and at strikes that are either close to or at the money.

NOTE: The terms *long* and *short* are commonly used jargon for buying and selling. Long is synonymous with buy and short is synonymous with sell. A *long call* is the same as a bought call option; a *short put* is the same as a sold put option. When you encounter these terms, it's important to understand their meanings.

As described earlier, swing traders make their incomes from directional price swings. Swing traders buy stocks that they believe will rally and they sell (or short) stocks that they believe will drop in value. When their trading bias is validated by the directional price move, they close their working trades for profit. When their bias is wrong, they close their trades before they suffer a major loss. This is commonly done using a protective stop loss. Profit targets and stop losses are discussed in substantial detail in Section 7.

Option chains make option trading outcomes substantially more predictable. This book goes into the reasons this is true and describes why and how to choose, set up, enter, and close a variety of option trades for profit. Option trades can also be modified by simultaneously closing a current option trade and opening a new one that expires at a later date. This process is called *rolling out*, which is done regularly by most experienced option traders. The processes of rolling out, up, and down are also described in Section 7.

As mentioned above, option chains are used to evaluate option premiums, to locate high-probability option trade setups, and then to submit the trade setup to the market. A typical McDonald's stock option chain is illustrated in figure 4-1, below. Spend some time examining it before continuing.

Looking at figure 4-1, you can see the option strike prices in the central column. Each option chain displays a central column that includes an option's *strike prices.* Option traders can select and either buy or sell *call* and *put* options at the listed strike prices. This is done by clicking on the corresponding Bid column value to sell or the Ask column value to buy. When entering a trade that includes two or more options, you can hold down the Ctrl key and click a Bid (sell) value and then an Ask (buy) value at two different strikes. An option trade can contain as many as four different option strike values. But be aware that complex, four-strike option trades are often difficult to fill. Therefore, many traders break four-strike option trades into two orders and submit each separately. This makes the orders much easier to fill. This is discussed again in the practice sessions contained in Section 8.

Notice how the strike prices range from low at the top of the table to high at the bottom. The incremental values or strike *widths* between these strike prices vary. Two dollar and 50-cent strike price increments exist in figure 4-1. You will see how the strike price increments are smaller for inexpensive stocks and become larger as stock prices increase in value. There are also *penny increment options,* with one-penny strike widths. As you will see, the incremental values between strikes vary within the option chain examples included in this book.

Important Notes

1. The option strike price that is closest to the price of the underlying stock or ETF is said to be "at the money."
2. Call strike prices that are greater than the price of the underlying equity and put strike prices that are less than the price of the underlying equity are "out of the money." Out of the money values have a white background.
3. Call option strike prices that are less than the price of the underlying equity and put option strike prices that are greater than the price of the underlying equity are "in the money." In the money values have a shaded background.

As you read earlier, stock markets are an indispensable part of today's global economy. Countries around the world depend on stock markets for the formation of businesses and economic growth. Since 1602 and the issuance of stock and warrants in the Dutch East Indies Company, companies have been issuing shares of stocks to raise capital. The capital is used to finance the company's ability to hire employees, to buy essential furnishings and fixtures, and to acquire the space required to conduct company operations. Without the necessary capitalism and the ability to operate in a free market, it would be impossible for entrepreneurial independent businesses to exist.

Because every option has a specific expiration date, option traders construct their trades based on the amount of time remaining until expiration. This can range from hours to a few years which depends upon the strategy used by the trader.

Each option has a premium which ranges in value according to the option's *strike price,* which is a price that is either the same as, greater than, or less than the price of the underlying stock. As you read above, the strike price closest to the current stock price is called the *at the money* strike price. But option traders can buy and sell options that are both greater than and less than the at the money price. Option prices and how we select them is discussed in substantial detail throughout this book.

Stock quote and option quote for MCD on 2/7/21 10:22:34

LAST	LX	Net Chng	BID	ASK	Volume	Open	High	Low
212.58	N	1.55	212.59	212.99	2600218	212.59	214.18	212.01

UNDERLYING EXTRA INFO

Yield	PE	Div	Div.Freq	Div.Date	52High	52Low	Shares	Beta
2.43%	33.69	1.29	Q	2/26/21	231.91	124.23	7.45E+08	0.6296

19 FEB 21 (12) 100				CALLS										PUTS				$21.06 (±6.722)	
Mark	Delta	Extrinsic	Intrinsic	Theta	Vega	Open.Int	BID	ASK	Strike	BID	ASK	Mark	Delta	Extrinsic	Intrinsic	Theta	Vega	Open.Int	
20.2	0.95	0.11	20.09	-0.04	0.04	28	17.9	22.5	**192.5**	0.06	0.13	0.095	-0.02	0.095	0	-0.02	0.02	152	
17.625	0.96	0.035	17.59	-0.03	0.03	39	15.25	20	**195**	0.07	0.15	0.11	-0.03	0.11	0	-0.02	0.03	3524	
15.4	0.92	0.31	15.09	-0.06	0.06	28	13.1	17.7	**197.5**	0.11	0.23	0.17	-0.04	0.17	0	-0.03	0.04	297	
13.225	0.87	0.635	12.59	-0.08	0.08	362	11.6	14.85	**200**	0.26	0.37	0.315	-0.08	0.315	0	-0.05	0.06	3863	
10.575	0.87	0.485	10.09	-0.07	0.08	34	10.1	11.05	**202.5**	0.39	0.5	0.445	-0.11	0.445	0	-0.06	0.07	301	
8.325	0.82	0.735	7.59	-0.08	0.11	176	7.75	8.9	**205**	0.62	0.76	0.69	-0.16	0.69	0	-0.08	0.1	438	
6.3	0.74	1.21	5.09	-0.1	0.13	229	6.05	6.55	**207.5**	1.05	1.34	1.195	-0.25	1.195	0	-0.1	0.13	446	
4.425	0.63	1.835	2.59	-0.11	0.15	1578	4.25	4.6	**210**	1.67	1.95	1.81	-0.36	1.81	0	-0.11	0.15	1915	
3.04	0.5	2.95	0.09	-0.11	0.16	740	2.83	3.25	**212.5**	2.6	3.05	2.825	-0.5	2.825	0	-0.12	0.16	344	
2	0.38	2	0	-0.11	0.15	840	1.85	2.15	**215**	4.1	4.5	4.3	-0.64	1.89	2.41	0.11	0.15	134	
1.165	0.26	1.165	0	-0.09	0.13	1208	0.99	1.34	**217.5**	4.25	6.3	5.275	-0.9	0.365	4.91	-0.04	0.07	89	
0.765	0.18	0.765	0	-0.08	0.11	13590	0.7	0.83	**220**	7.6	8.45	8.025	-0.87	0.615	7.41	-0.07	0.09	231	
0.55	0.13	0.55	0	-0.07	0.09	317	0.45	0.65	**222.5**	9.75	10.65	10.2	-0.95	0.29	9.91	-0.03	0.04	5	
0.34	0.09	0.34	0	-0.05	0.06	2234	0.3	0.38	**225**	11.35	14	12.675	-0.97	0.265	12.41	-0.03	0.03	15	
0.175	0.05	0.175	0	-0.03	0.04	113	0.06	0.29	**227.5**	13.75	17.1	15.425	-0.92	0.515	14.91	-0.07	0.06	1	
0.215	0.05	0.215	0	-0.04	0.04	4207	0.2	0.23	**230**	15.65	19.7	17.675	-0.97	0.265	17.41	-0.03	0.02	143	
0.175	0.04	0.175	0	-0.03	0.04	2753	0.17	0.18	**232.5**	17.8	22.1	19.95	-1	0.04	19.91	-0.01	0	0	
0.105	0.03	0.105	0	-0.02	0.02	208	0.02	0.19	**235**	20.2	24.7	22.45	-1	0.04	22.41	-0.01	0	0	
26 FEB 21 (19) 100 (Weeklys)																		$23.72% (±9.06)	
5 MAR 21 (26) 100 (Weeklys)																		$24.65% (±11.369)	

Figure 4-1. A Typical Option Chain for McDonalds Stock (MCD)

Exploring Option Values

As discussed earlier, option prices rely on a number of different variables. In fact, several complex mathematical equations exist that constantly update option values based on:

- Price of the underlying stock, ETF, financial index, or futures contract
- The option's strike price relative to the option's current at the money price
- Current market volatility (buying and selling volume)
- The number of option contracts that exist, called *Open Interest*
- The amount of time remaining until option expiration.

All these items affect option values. They are constantly changing with buying and selling activity, the passage of time, and price fluctuations in the underlying stock. Fortunately for option traders, every good trading platform and several websites include option chains that are constantly updated.

Below is a brief list of option chain columns and descriptions. The values are per share. Multiply by 100 to derive the total value for each option contract.

- *Bid* — Selling price
- *Ask* — Buying price
- *Mark* — Premium value (midway between Bid and Ask)
- *Theta* — Exiting time value per day
- *Vega* — Volatility influence
- *Delta* — The amount option premium changes in response to each $1.00 change in price of the underlying. Delta also used to measure probability of ITM
- *Open Interest* — Existing option contracts when market opened
- *IV%* — Implied Volatility; high values increase premium values
- *±23.903* — The current dollar value to remain OTM through option expiration

Options also have *intrinsic* and *extrinsic* values plus several others. Following is a discussion about these two important values. Although most option traders are familiar with intrinsic and extrinsic values, many option traders rarely display these values on their option chains.

Intrinsic Value

Intrinsic value is an estimate of an asset's value, which is usually calculated by financial analysts who attempt to determine the net worth of some asset. These computations can be quite complex, especially when there are numerous variables to consider. In the case of an option's intrinsic value, the calculation includes several variables such as the financial performance of the underlying company, the current price of the company's stock and its current trading volume. Valuation models exist that often include numerous factors based on the company's past and projected performance and its standing within its market sector. Fortunately for option traders, they can display a list of intrinsic values that correspond to each strike price contained within the corresponding option chain.

Extrinsic Value

Extrinsic value is the difference between an option's market price, i.e., its premium value, and the option's intrinsic value. As mentioned, both intrinsic and extrinsic values are available on option chains, although rarely displayed. An option's total value is the sum of its extrinsic and intrinsic values. Because an option's value decreases with time, the option's extrinsic value decreases as the option approaches it expiration date. The value that remains is the option's intrinsic value. However, once an option expires all of its value is lost and the option becomes worthless.

Another way to determine an option's extrinsic value is to subtract the option's current premium value listed in an option chain's Mark column and the current price of the underlying stock. Hence, intrinsic value of all *in the money* options is the difference between the stock's current price and the option's strike price. Clearly, a definition of *in the money* (ITM) is needed. Call options that exist at strike prices that are less than the price of the stock, called the *at the money* (ATM) price, and put options that exist at strike prices that are greater than the price of the stock are both referred to as being *in the money* (ITM). Assuming a $20.00 stock price, the following table lists in, at, and out of the money options and includes their abbreviations, which by now should be familiar.

Stock Price	***$20.00 per Share***	***Strike Price Description***
Call or Put Strike Price	$20.00	"At the Money" (ATM)
Call Strike Prices	Greater than $20	"Out of the Money" (OTM)
Call Strike Prices	Less than $20	"In the Money" (ITM)
Put Strike Prices	Greater than $20	"In the Money" (ITM)
Put Strike Prices	Less than $20	"Out of the Money" (OTM)

An option's extrinsic value increases with a corresponding increase in buying and selling volume, or volatility. Finally, only extrinsic value exists for options that are out of the money. As you will see, when you display intrinsic value columns on an option chain, 0.00 exists in the OTM value rows.

The passage of time also reduces extrinsic values. In fact, extrinsic values decrease much faster in the final weeks and days of an option's life. This is reasonable as the price of the underlying stock has less time to make a significant move. This favors option sellers who own OTM options, while punishing option buyers. While the option sellers let the options expire worthless for profits, the buyers usually sell to close their options to collect what little residual value may remain. Hence, shorter times are the seller's friend and the buyer's enemy.

Following is a clarifying example that illustrates how options use both intrinsic and extrinsic values relative to the price of a stock. In this example, the stock is trading at $50 and the $55 call option has an intrinsic value of $5.00. If the $55 call option's premium is $6.00, then $1.00 in extrinsic value exists.

Stock Value	*$50.00*
Call Option's Strike Price	$55
Call Option's Intrinsic Value	$55
Call Option's Extrinsic Value	$1.00
Call Option's Premium (or Mark) Value	$56.00

Call and Put Options

There are only call options and put options. And like stocks, option traders can either buy or sell them. When bought, they are called *long calls* or *long puts*; when sold, they are called *short calls* or *short puts.* (Stock traders also use the terms long and short for buying and selling.)

NOTE: For simplicity and as previously mentioned, "stock" is used as the underlying equity for the option trades described in this book. But as you should recall, options also exist on ETFs, ETNs, financial indexes, and futures.

Options can be traded at the strike prices listed on the corresponding option chain. The option's price can be greater than, less than, or equal to the underlying stock price. And as you now know, the option's price is called its *strike price.* Option strike prices correspond to the current price of the underlying stock. As you saw in the option chain illustrations, the option chain is used to set up and execute an option trade.

It's important to understand that options are bought and sold at different prices depending on an option trader's market bias. Option prices can be at the money (ATM), out of the money (OTM), or in the money (ITM). The trader's bias is formed by where he or she expects the underlying stock's price to go.

Here are a few simple examples of how put and call options are selected based on the trader's bullish, bearish, or neutral bias.

The trader expects the stock price to rally (bullish):

Buy one or more long-term calls that expire in 90 or more days. If the stock's price rallies and the calls move deeper ITM, they may be sold for a profit. The longer term is used to minimize the effect of time decay during the first several weeks or months. Many traders sell call options that expire in a year or more.

Sell one or more short-term puts that expire in a month to six weeks. When sold, the seller collects a credit. As the short puts approach expiration, time decay reduces the premium value. A buy-to-close order may be used to exit the trade for less than originally received. (Sell for a dollar, buy back for a quarter.) Option sellers frequently keep OTM short options until they expire worthless. This permits the seller to retain all of the initial credit that was collected when the puts were originally sold.

The trader expects the stock price to drop (bearish):

Buy one or more long-term puts that expires in 90 or more days. If the stock's price drops and the puts move deeper ITM, the puts may be sold for a profit. This should be done before time decay begins to erode the put options' price for a loss. Several weeks or months is typical to avoid a substantial loss from time decay.

Sell one or more short-term OTM calls that expire in a month to six weeks. If the stock drops as expected, the calls will move farther OTM and the premium will drop in value, both from the stock's price drop and the option's loss in premium value as the calls move farther OTM. The trader may either buy to close his/her short options for substantially less than initially received or the calls may be retained until they expire worthless in order to keep all of the initial credit received when the options were originally sold.

The trader expects the stock price to remain within a narrow range (neutral):
Sell one or more calls or puts that expire in a matter of days to perhaps six weeks. If the stock price remains virtually unchanged, time decay will reduce the option premium throughout the life of these short-term options. The trader may submit a buy-to-close order when enough profit exists, or the short calls and/or puts can be kept through option expiration.

Put and call options are often sold at the same time. Simultaneously selling both puts and calls is a popular option strategy called a *short strangle.* This strategy collects premium from both short put and call options, which can be quite rewarding. But if the underlying stock price begins to move against either the put or the call, the vulnerable option should be closed to avoid a loss. The put or call that remains can be kept as long as it remains safely OTM.

As you can see on any option chain, option prices correspond to the price of the underlying stock. Options are said to be *at the money*, *out of the money*, or *in the money* Option premiums increase as strike prices move deeper in the money.

CAUTION: If a short option is permitted to become ITM, it can be exercised by the option's buyer. Hence, short options can become vulnerable to substantial losses. For this reason, brokerages establish trading levels, which are based on an option trader's experience and knowledge. Only those option traders with the highest trading levels are permitted to trade *uncovered* options. Covering requires that short option be secured (or "covered") by shares of stock or by an equal number of long options. These setups are discussed in more detail later in this book. It is important to understand that short, uncovered options can potentially blow out your account if they move into the money and become subject to exercise (described in the next paragraph). However, there are devices, such as protective stops and long, covering positions, and rolling to a different strike price and a later expiration date that can mitigate this exposure.

Exercising or Assigning ITM Options

When either a put or call option is bought, the buyer has the right to exercise his or her option if the strike price of the option moves ITM. For example, if ten short $50 call options move ITM to $55, the option buyer can *exercise* or "call" the stock away from the option seller. When exercised, the option seller must deliver 1,000 shares of stock, now worth $55 per share, to the option buyer. The option buyer is required to pay the option seller the original $50 option's strike price for stock that's now worth $55 per share.

ITM short put options are also subject to being exercised by the buyer of the puts. When puts are assigned to the seller, the buyer "puts" the underlying stock to the seller, who must pay for the stock at the option's original strike price. If ten $50 put options are ITM by $5.00 per share, the put buyer must pay $50,000 for stock that is now worth $45,000. The put seller suffers a $5,000 loss less the premium credit originally received when the trade was initially entered. This trade permits the put buyer to collect

$50,000 for stock that's now worth $45,000 for a $5,000 profit less the few hundred dollars in premium that was paid when the buyer originally bought the ten $50 put options.

Another Option Chain

Figure 4-2 is another simple option chain. This one shows Marine Max, Inc. (HZO) stock options. Notice that HZO stock is currently priced at $41.83 as shown below LAST.

Other values include:

- The Net Change shows that the stock price has declined by $1.24.
- The option expiration date is 19 Mar 21 — 48 days until option expiration.
- The 100 indicates the number of shares in each option contract.

Figure 4-2. Another Typical Option Chain.

Stock quote and option quote for HZO on 1/30/21 16:46:31														
LAST	LX	Net Chng	BID		ASK		Size	Volume	Open	High	Low			
41.83	N	-1.24	41.69	P	42.5	P	1 x 2	7E+05	44	44	40.3			
19 MAR 21 (48) 100		CALLS									PUTS		77.61%	±$9.709
Mark	Delta	Theta	Vega	Open.Int	BID	ASK	Strike	BID	ASK	Mark	Delta	Theta	Vega	Open.Int
19.65	0.96	-0.01	0.01	0	17.7	21.6	22.5	0	5	2.5	-0.11	-0.1	0.03	0
17.3	0.94	-0.02	0.02	4	15.6	19	25	0	4.9	2.5	-0.13	-0.1	0.03	2
13.3	in the money calls			0	11.5	15.1	30	0.5	out of the money puts				03	41
8.95	0.77	-0.04	0.05	5	8.2	9.7	35	1.4	2.55	2	-0.23	-0	0.05	37
5.4	0.62	-0.04	0.06	16	5.2	5.6	40	3.1	3.8	3.5	-0.38	-0	0.06	103
3.1	0.44	-0.04	0.06	199	2.5	3.7	45	6.1	6.5	6.3	-0.56	-0	0.06	26
1.675	0.28	-0.04	0.05	547	1.3	2.05	50	9.5	11.1	10	-0.68	-0	0.05	2
1.275	out of the money calls			8	0.95	1.6	55	13.7	in the money puts				.04	0
0.85	0.15	-0.03	0.04	101	0.5	1.2	60	18.5	19.5	19	-0.81	-0	0.04	0
0.8	0.13	-0.03	0.03	1	0.2	1.4	65	23	25.6	24	-0.78	-0.1	0.04	0
16 APR 21 (76) 100														

- The 77.61% ±$9.709 at the far right of the option's expiration date is HZO stock's current *implied volatility* value (IV%) compared to historical volatility, which is the average volatility for the past 12-month period.
- The ±$9.709 is a mathematical calculation based on the current volatility value. This value is an instantaneous mathematical derivation of how much the current price may fluctuate during the 48 days that remain throughout the life of these HZO options.

NOTE: As previously discussed, high IV% values increase option premium values. This encourages traders to sell options for the increased premium value. Low IV% values reduce premium values, which encourages traders to buy options while they are relatively inexpensive.

HZO's options have strike price increments of $5.00 except for the $22.50 and $25.00 strikes. The total number of strike prices and increments increase for high-priced stocks. For example, incremental strike prices values can be as high as $50 to $100 for expensive index options like the NASDAQ 100 financial index, symbol NDX. Depending on which options you plan to trade, most trading applications permit users to adjust the total number of strike prices centered on the central ATM strike.

Looking at figure 4-3, notice how the ITM call and put option values are shaded while the OTM call and put option values have white backgrounds. The HZO stock price labeled LAST is currently $41.83. The – 1.24 Net Chng tells the trader that today's HZO stock price has dropped by $1.24.

Prior to selecting an option trade, most seasoned traders check company news and examine price charts in order to develop a rational trading bias. As previously mentioned, the trader can have a bullish, neutral, or bearish bias based on his/her analysis.

Recall how every option *contract* is a time-limited agreement between one or more buyers and sellers. The time to option expiration can vary widely ranging from one or more days, to weeks, months, and even a few years. Experienced option traders choose different expiration dates based on whether they are buying or selling options. There are a few logical reason to sell short-term options and buy long-term options. One includes the fact that risk increases when a stock's price is given more time to increase or decrease. It is fairly intuitive to understand how prices usually change less in a few days to a week than they do in several weeks to a few months.

And there are dozens of different option strategies from which to choose based on your market bias. It is possible to buy or sell a single option or combine as many as four different options in a single trade. You can even include multiple expiration dates, called *calendar spreads* and *diagonal spreads.* Although this may sound complicated, several clarifying examples are provided within the pages of this book. You will see how options work, how to minimize your trading risk, and how option values behave in response to the following events:

- Changes in the price of the underlying stock
- The passage of time
- An increase or decrease in the current market volatility.

You also learn how to manage an option trade so you can either recover entirely from a losing trade or minimize a potential loss. You will soon learn that option trades are much more flexible than stock trades, because option traders have a much larger diversity of strategies from which to choose. And one of the goals of this book is for its readers to understand how to select which strategies fit a current market condition. As all seasoned traders know, the market can be full of surprises. It may be rallying today and dropping tomorrow, rallying at market open and dropping by mid-morning. All traders are caught by these unexpected market moves. But option traders have more tools at their disposal in order to deal with these random changes. And they typically have less money at risk.

Choosing the Time till Expiration

As a rule, we buy options that expire in 90 or more days and sell options that expire in a matter of days to perhaps a month to six weeks. The effect of the option's daily loss in time value is displayed in the Theta column for each strike price.

The loss in time value increases with each passing day as the option approaches its expiration date. Although the following examples refer to an option chain that expires in 34 days, most experienced option traders usually buy options that expire in three or more months to reduce the ever-increasing daily loss in the option's time value. They depend on the price movement of the underlying equity to offset the daily losses in time value.

Buying Call Options

Looking at the option chain in figure 4-1, if we believe the underlying stock will rise in price, we might choose to buy a call option. In this example, we would probably buy one or more 220 call options, which is close to the *at the money* strike price. If the stock price increases as expected, the call option's strike price will move down and *in the money*. As the stock price increases, the call option's strike price moves even deeper in the money. This increases the option's premium value. When satisfied with the increase in the call option's premium value, we can sell to close the call option to collect the profit.

Buying Put Options

Looking at figure 4-3, the value inside the Last cell at the top of the option chain shows $210.45 per share as the value of Arista Networks stock. If we believe the underlying stock will drop in price, we could buy one or more put options. If we buy one or more 210 put options and the stock price drops as expected within a few days, the put option's strike price moves up and into the money. The $210 put option could then be sold for a profit.

Using options, you are able to buy 100 shares of ANET $220 options for $6.20 per share, or $620 for each 100-share option contract. This option trade gives you control of $21,045 worth of stock for just $620. This is an example of the financial leverage provided by options: the ability to control more than $21,000 worth of stock for only 2.95% of the stock's value.

Figure 4-3. An Option Chain for Arista Networks Stock

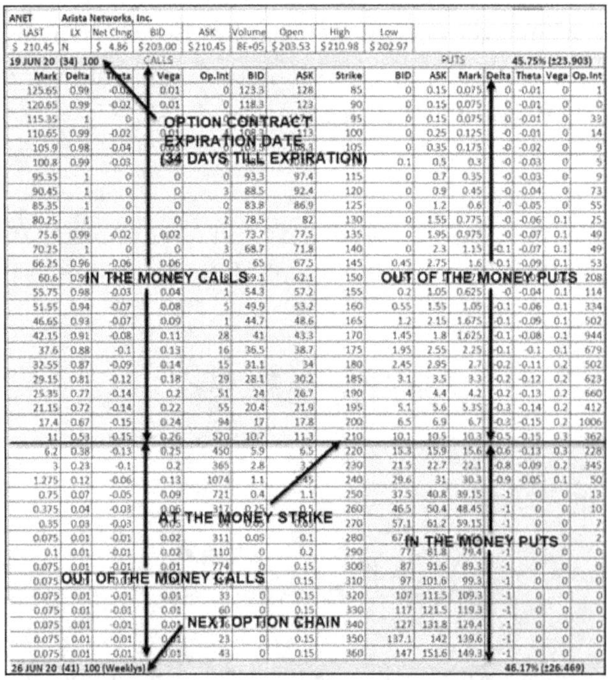

ANET Arista Networks, Inc.

LAST	LX	Net Chng	BID	ASK	Volume	Open	High	Low
$ 210.45	N	$ 4.86	$203.00	$210.45	8E-05	$203.53	$210.98	$202.97

19 JUN 20 (34) 100 — CALLS — PUTS — 45.75% (±23.903)

Mark	Delta	Theta	Vega	Op.Int	BID	ASK	Strike	BID	ASK	Mark	Delta	Theta	Vega	Op.Int
125.65	0.99	[illegible]	0.01	0	123.3	128	85	0	0.15	0.075	0	-0.01	0	1
120.65	0.99	-0.02	0.01	0	118.3	123	90	0	0.15	0.075	0	-0.01	0	0
115.35	1	0	[illegible]	[illegible]	[illegible]	[illegible]	95	0	0.15	0.075	0	-0.01	0	33
110.65	0.99	-0.02	[illegible]	[illegible]	[illegible]	113	100	0	0.25	0.125	0	-0.01	0	14
105.9	0.98	-0.04	[illegible]	[illegible]	[illegible]	[illegible]	105	0	0.35	0.175	-0	-0.02	0	9
100.8	0.99	-0.03	[illegible]	[illegible]	[illegible]	[illegible]	110	0.1	0.5	0.3	-0	-0.03	0	5
95.35	1	0	0	0	93.3	97.4	115	0	0.7	0.35	-0	-0.03	0	9
90.45	1	0	0	3	88.5	92.4	120	0	0.9	0.45	-0	-0.04	0	73
85.35	1	0	0	0	83.8	86.9	125	0	1.2	0.6	-0	-0.05	0	55
80.25	1	0	0	2	78.5	82	130	0	1.55	0.775	-0	-0.06	0.1	25
75.6	0.99	-0.02	0.02	1	73.7	77.5	135	0	1.95	0.975	-0	-0.07	0.1	49
70.25	1	0	0	3	68.7	71.8	140	0	2.3	1.15	-0.1	-0.07	0.1	49
66.25	0.96	-0.06	0.06	0	65	67.5	145	0.45	2.75	1.6	-0.1	-0.09	0.1	53
60.6	[illegible]	[illegible]	[illegible]	[illegible]	[illegible]	62.1	150	[illegible]	[illegible]	[illegible]	[illegible]	[illegible]	[illegible]	208
55.75	0.98	-0.03	0.04	1	54.3	57.2	155	0.2	1.05	0.625	-0	-0.04	0.1	114
51.55	0.94	-0.07	0.08	5	49.9	53.2	160	0.55	1.55	1.05	-0.1	-0.06	0.1	334
46.65	0.93	-0.07	0.09	1	44.7	48.6	165	1.2	2.15	1.675	-0.1	-0.09	0.1	502
42.15	0.91	-0.08	0.11	28	41	43.3	170	1.45	1.8	1.625	-0.1	-0.08	0.1	944
37.6	0.88	-0.1	0.13	16	36.5	38.7	175	1.95	2.55	2.25	-0.1	-0.1	0.1	679
32.55	0.87	-0.09	0.14	15	31.1	34	180	2.45	2.95	2.7	-0.2	-0.11	0.2	502
29.15	0.81	-0.12	0.18	29	28.1	30.2	185	3.1	3.5	3.3	-0.2	-0.12	0.2	623
25.35	0.77	-0.14	0.2	51	24	26.7	190	4	4.4	4.2	-0.2	-0.13	0.2	660
21.15	0.72	-0.14	0.22	55	20.4	21.9	195	5.1	5.6	5.35	-0.3	-0.14	0.2	412
17.4	0.67	-0.15	0.24	94	17	17.8	200	6.5	6.9	6.7	-0.3	-0.15	0.2	1006
11	0.53	-0.15	0.26	520	10.7	11.3	210	10.1	10.5	10.3	-0.5	-0.15	0.3	362
6.2	0.38	-0.13	0.25	450	5.9	6.5	220	15.3	15.9	15.6	-0.6	-0.13	0.3	228
3	0.23	-0.1	0.2	365	2.8	[illegible]	230	21.5	22.7	22.1	-0.8	-0.09	0.2	345
1.275	0.12	-0.06	0.13	1074	1.1	[illegible]	240	29.6	31	30.3	-0.9	-0.05	0.1	50
0.75	0.07	-0.05	0.09	721	0.4	1.1	250	37.5	40.8	39.15	-1	0	0	13
0.375	0.04	-0.03	0.06	317	0.25	0.5	260	46.5	50.4	48.45	-1	0	0	10
0.35	0.03	-0.03	[illegible]	[illegible]	[illegible]	[illegible]	270	57.1	61.2	59.15	-1	0	0	7
0.075	0.01	-0.01	0.02	311	0.05	0.1	280	67	[illegible]	[illegible]	[illegible]	[illegible]	0	2
0.1	0.01	-0.01	0.02	110	0	0.2	290	77	81.8	79.4	-1	0	0	0
0.075	0.01	-0.01	0.01	774	0	0.15	300	87	91.6	89.3	-1	0	0	0
0.075	[illegible]	[illegible]	[illegible]	[illegible]	[illegible]	0.15	310	97	101.6	99.3	-1	0	0	0
0.075	0.01	-0.01	0.01	33	0	0.15	320	107	111.5	109.3	-1	0	0	0
0.075	0.01	-0.01	0.01	60	0	0.15	330	117	121.5	119.3	-1	0	0	0
0.075	0.01	-0.01	[illegible]	[illegible]	[illegible]	[illegible]	340	127	131.8	129.4	-1	0	0	0
0.075	0.01	-0.01	[illegible]	23	0	0.15	350	137.1	142	139.6	-1	0	0	0
0.075	0.01	-0.01	0.01	43	0	0.15	360	147	151.6	149.3	-1	0	0	0

26 JUN 20 (41) 100 (Weeklys) — 46.17% (±26.469)

OPTION CONTRACT EXPIRATION DATE (34 DAYS TILL EXPIRATION)
IN THE MONEY CALLS
OUT OF THE MONEY PUTS
AT THE MONEY STRIKE
IN THE MONEY PUTS
OUT OF THE MONEY CALLS
NEXT OPTION CHAIN

Uncovered (or Naked) Short Options

Only those traders having the highest options trading level granted by their brokerage can sell uncovered options. The risk associated with selling uncovered puts or calls was briefly mentioned in Section 3. Selling call and/or put options that become ITM can lead to a major financial loss. Experienced option traders rarely permit the strike price of their short options to move into the money. There is a minor exception when a trader wants to pick up a stock during a temporary drop in its price, but this is rare and can be quite risky if the trader is wrong about the stock's price recovery. Most option traders prefer to close their short options and take the loss, because as you read in the exercising and assigning ITM options paragraph, being exercised can cost thousands of dollars.

An exception exists when a trader would like to own stock that is currently dropping in price. The trader must be bullish and believe that the stock will recover quickly and resume its upward price trajectory. The trader decides to sell a $98 put on a $100 stock. When sold, we'll assume the put seller receives $4.00 per share in option premium. If the stock drops below $98 price of the short put to $97, the stock becomes ITM by $1.00. When exercised, the trader would receive the stock for $98.00 per share that's now worth $97 per share. Because the trader originally received $4.00 in premium, the stock can be sold for $97 per share. The $3.00 in residual premium becomes profit, less any overhead in commissions and exchange fees. But since the trader is bullish on the stock and expects to rally, he/she retains the stock and uses it to produce income by selling a series of covered calls. Covered calls are described in the next paragraph.

The above short term option trade is just one simple example of what option traders do hundreds of times per week. And there are dozens of other option setups, or option strategies that are used regularly. Many are equally as simple.

The Covered Call

A covered call is often the first option trade used by people who own shares of stock and then discover options. For example, one trader owns 300 shares of MasterCard stock, symbol MA that are currently trading at $331.58 per share. In this covered call example, the trader examines the option chain in figure 4-4. The options expire in 38 days. A far OTM, reasonably "safe" call option strike price at a Delta .19 is selected. This strike is used because the trader plans to sell a series of MasterCard covered calls every month or two throughout the year. The trader can sell up to three MasterCard option contracts which are covered by the 300 shares of stock.

The trader decides to sell three $360 call option contracts for $3.12 per share in premium for a total credit of $936 less a few dollars in exchange fees. The MasterCard stock is currently $28.42 below the short call's $360 strike price. Even if the stock rallies above $360 per share and the option is exercised and called away, which is highly unlikely, the trader would receive $8,526 from the sale of the stock plus the $936 credit in premium for a total profit of $9,462.

Now instead of the option expiring worthless according to plan, assume the MasterCard stock rallies a dollar to two above the $360 strike price. Because it became a dollar or two ITM, the buyer of the three $360 calls exercises the options and calls them away for a small profit. Our covered call seller earned a credit of $936.00 in premium less about $3.00 in option exchange fees when the three short calls were initially sold. This added to the $28.42 in profit from the sale of the stock earns the $9,462 shown in the previous paragraph.

Covered calls are popular, but there is always a chance that the option might become ITM and be called away. Be sure to calculate the risk based on the Delta value of the short call's strike. Most prudent traders use Delta values at or close to .25. But to be even safer, consider Delta values of .20 down to .15.

Figure 4-4. Three Covered Call Option Trades on 300 Shares of MasterCard Stock

Stock quote and option quote for MA on 2/9/21 11:43:13

LAST	LX	Net Chr	BID	BX	ASK	AX	Size	Volume	Open	High	Low
331.58	D	-5.45	331.5	N	331.6	Q	4 x 2	1737932	335.95	336.22	330
Last Size	Yield	PE	Div	Div.Freq	Ex Div.	52High	52Low	Shares	Beta		
100	0.53%	52.05	0.44	Q	1/7/21	367.25	200	994454904	1.176		

19 MAR 21 (38) 100				CALLS							PUTS		31.50% (± 27.314)	
Mark	Delta	Theta	Vega	Open.Int	BID	ASK	Strike	BID	ASK	Mark	Delta	Theta	Vega	Open.Int
97.6	0.91	-0.12	0.14	2	96.8	98.4	235	0.13	0.57	0.35	-0.02	-0.03	0.04	92
92.275	0.92	-0.11	0.13	12	91.9	92.65	240	0.14	0.5	0.32	-0.02	-0.03	0.04	214
87.275	0.92	-0.1	0.13	5	86	88.55	245	0.31	0.44	0.375	-0.02	-0.03	0.05	96
82.425	0.92	-0.1	0.13	36	81.9	82.95	250	0.29	0.7	0.495	-0.03	-0.04	0.06	308
77.55	0.92	[illegible]	[illegible]	[illegible]	77.05	78.05	[illegible]	0.48	0.55	0.515	-0.03	-0.04	0.07	[illegible]
30.675	[illegible]	[illegible]	[illegible]	[illegible]	[illegible]	[illegible]	[illegible]	[illegible]	[illegible]	[illegible]	[illegible]	[illegible]	0.3	[illegible]
26.7	0.75	-0.14	0.34	209	26.45	26.95	310	4.65	4.85	4.75	-0.23	-0.13	0.33	2762
22.9	0.71	-0.15	0.37	174	22.7	23.1	315	5.85	6.05	5.95	-0.28	-0.14	0.37	1233
19.525	0.65	-0.16	0.4	377	19.2	19.85	320	7.35	7.5	7.425	-0.34	-0.15	0.4	624
16.15	0.6	-0.16	0.42	597	16	16.3	325	9.1	9.35	9.225	-0.4	-0.16	0.42	485
13.275	0.54	-0.16	0.43	832	13.15	13.4	330	11.2	11.5	11.35	-0.46	-0.16	0.43	886
10.8	0.47	-0.16	0.43	4853	10.65	10.95	335	13.7	14	13.85	-0.53	-0.16	0.43	838
8.6	0.41	-0.15	0.42	711	8.5	8.7	340	16.55	16.85	16.7	-0.6	-0.15	0.42	408
6.85	0.35	-0.14	0.4	644	6.7	7	345	19.65	20.05	19.85	-0.66	-0.14	0.4	380
5.3	0.29	-0.13	0.37	1787	5.2	5.4	350	23.1	23.55	23.325	-0.72	-0.13	0.36	364
4.1	0.24	-0.12	0.34	1869	4	4.2	355	26.8	27.35	27.075	-0.78	-0.11	0.32	158
3.125	0.19	-0.11	0.3	3294	3.05	3.2	360	30.95	31.45	31.2	-0.82	-0.1	0.28	71
2.395	0.16	-0.09	0.26	324	2.33	2.46	365	35.1	35.75	35.425	-0.87	-0.08	0.23	28
1.82	0.12	-0.08	0.22	2615	1.77	1.87	370	39.5	40.2	39.85	-0.9	-0.07	0.19	17
1.405	0.1	-0.07	0.19	356	1.36	1.45	375	44.1	44.8	44.45	-0.93	[illegible]	0.15	83
[illegible]	[illegible]	[illegible]	0.16	[illegible]	[illegible]	[illegible]	[illegible]	[illegible]	[illegible]	48.35	-1	[illegible]	[illegible]	[illegible]
0.235	0.02	[illegible]	0.05	6	0.02	0.45	[illegible]	92.85	94.1	93.475	-1	0	0	8
0.315	0.02	-0.03	0.06	35	0.04	0.59	430	97	99.7	98.35	-1	0	1.83	2
26 MAR 21 (45) 100 (Weeklys)														

Finally, many option traders include *good till cancelled* (GTC) limit stop orders that are constructed to return a profit when the short call's premium value drops by 50% to 65%. The option's premium drops in value from the passage of time as long as it remains OTM through expiration.

Vertical Spreads

Vertical spreads are among the most popular option strategies in use today. There are vertical put spreads and vertical call spreads. Each sells and buys an equal number of option contracts either above or below the other. Here are four common examples:

1. Sell an OTM short put and buy a long put two or more strikes below.
2. Sell an OTM short call and buy a long call two or more strikes above.
3. Buy an ATM long call and buy an OTM short call two or more strikes above.
4. Buy an ATM long put and sell an OTM short put two or more strikes below.

These four examples have the following names:

1. Bull put spread—Used by bullish traders who expect a price rally.
2. Bear call spread—Used by bearish traders who expect a price drop.

3. Bull call spread—Used by bullish traders who expect a price rally.
4. Bear put spread—Used by bearish traders who expect a price drop.

Most traders place the short OTM options at strikes having Delta values at or farther OTM than two standard deviations (67.28%). Although many place their short calls and puts at a strike having a Delta .30 value, consider being slightly more conservative by placing your short options at a strike having a Delta value of .25. This provides a 75% probability of the vulnerable short strike remaining OTM through expiration.

The strike width of these spreads, i.e., the number of strikes between the short and long options, should be carefully considered. In the case of the popular bull put spread, increasing the strike width returns more premium. But increasing the spread width also increases risk. Here are a few examples of what can happen.

Both puts expire ITM: The price of stock XYZ has been trending up and is now selling for $60 per share. The strike widths on XYZ's option chain are in $1.00 increments. Kim decides to enter a bull put spread and sells five OTM $53 puts and buys five OTM $51 puts two strikes below. Kim collects the difference in premium of 40 cents per contract for a total credit of $200 in option premium. Kim's bullish bias is wrong. XYZ's stock drops to $50 and the short and long puts both expire ITM. Kim loses the $2.00 per share difference between the $53 and $51 strike prices of the short and long puts. This is a loss of $200 for each of the five option contracts. The $1,000 loss is offset by the initial $200 credit received for a total loss of $800.

The short put expires ITM, the long put remains OTM: Again, the strike width on XYZ's option chain is $1.00 between strikes. But Kim decides to place the long put four strikes farther OTM and sells five $53 puts and buys five $49 puts for a credit of 70 cents per share in premium. Kim receives a credit of $350 in premium when the five bull put spread orders are filled. Kim's bullish bias is wrong and XYZ's stock price drops to $50. This is $3.00 below the short put and $1.00 above the long put. While the OTM long put expires worthless, the $53 short put has expired $3.00 ITM for a major loss. Kim is assigned 500 shares of the XYZ stock for $53 per share and must pay $26,500 for the stock. The loss would be offset by the $350 credit received when traded. And Kim can sell the XYZ stock for around $49 per share for a total of $24,500. Kim's total loss comes to $26,850 less $24,850 or approximately $1,650 assuming she can sell XYZ for $49 per share.

When considering a short vertical spread, whether a put spread or a call spread, the second example explained how a desire to earn more premium by using a wider spread can lead to unnecessary risk. As one of my option trader friends says, "pigs get slaughtered." Do not let yourself surrender to temptation that can lead to increased risk. And be sure to monitor and exit your trades whenever necessary. It's usually less expensive to close a failing trade then to let it expires ITM for a major loss.

Rolling a trade is a common option maintenance strategy that you use as a recovery tool when a trade begins to unravel. As previously mentioned, rolling is discussed at length in Section 7 as one of the essential trade management techniques commonly used by option traders.

Now that you've read how spread width can increase risk, five different vertical spread examples are provided. You can use these as trading models. Be sure to test your option strategies in simulation, or "paper trading." This will help you learn how to set up and manage a variety of option strategies before using the funds in your brokerage account.

1. **Bull Put Spreads:** A bull put spread, also called a short vertical put, is used when a trader expects the price of the underlying stock to either rally or remain within a narrow price range. Bull put spreads were used in the above examples that illustrate how spread width affects risk. This bull put spread is a bullish to neutral credit spread that includes an OTM short put and an OTM long call put one or more strikes below. The bull put returns a credit because the premium received from the short put option is greater than the premium paid for the long put option below. The wider the spread between the short and long options, the greater the credit. This is because the long option is farther OTM. The premium can be improved by increasing the number of strikes, called the *strike width,* between the short and long put options. As you can see in figure 4-5, the Mark value received from the $26 strike returns $1.03 per share in premium while the Mark value paid for the $24 long put is $0.60 cents. This is a net difference of $0.43 cents. The spread returns $43 per 100-share option contract when filled. Selling 10 vertical put spreads returns $430 in premium less the option exchange fees. These fees typically range between 50 cents to $1.00 per option contract, depending on the trader's arrangement with his/her brokerage. The fees charged by brokerages often rely on trading volumes.

LUV	Southwest Airlines Company												
LAST	LX	Net Ch	BID	BX	ASK	AX	Size	Volume	Open	High	Low		
29.2	N	1.46	29.13	P	29	P	20 x 3	26819663	28.5	29.33	28.2		
19 JUN 20 (30) 100		CALLS							PUTS		73.72% (±5.035)		
Mark	Delta	Theta	Op.Int	BID	ASK	Strike	BID	ASK	Mark	Delta	Theta	Op.Int
5.8	0.82	-0.03	2	5.7	5.9	24	0.55	0.65	0.6	-0.16	-0.03	108
5.35	0.81	-0.03	0	5.2	5.5	24.5	0.65	0.75	0.7	-0.18	[illegible]	26
4.9	0.79	-0.03	3073	4.8	5	25	0.75	0.85	0.8	-0.21	-0.03	5730
4.6	0.76	-0.03	6	4.5	4.7	25.5	0.85	0.95	0.9	-0.23	-0.03	57
4.2	0.74	-0.03	127	4.1	4.3	26	1	1.05	1.03	-0.26	-0.03	423
3.8	0.71	-0.03	107	3.7	3.9	26.5	1.1	1.2	1.15	-0.28	-0.03	2053
3.5	0.68	-0.03	115	3.4	3.6	27	1.25	1.35	1.3	-0.32	-0.03	124
3.15	0.65	-0.03	16876	3.1	3.2	27.5	1.5	1.6	1.55	-0.35	-0.04	2977
2.88	0.61	-0.04	684	2.8	3	28	1.6	1.75	1.68	-0.38	-0.04	37
2.58	0.58	-0.04	76	2.5	2.7	28.5	1.9	2	1.95	-0.42	-0.04	37
2.33	0.54	-0.04	118	2.3	2.4	29	2.05	2.2	2.13	-0.46	-0.04	104
2.1	0.51	-0.04	170	2.1	2.2	29.5	2.3	2.55	2.43	-0.49	-0.04	2
1.88	0.48	-0.04	9880	1.9	1.9	30	2.6	2.8	2.7	-0.53	-0.04	2894
1.63	0.44	-0.03	54	1.6	1.7	30.5	2.9	3.1	3	-0.56	-0.04	1
1.45	0.41	-0.03	750	1.4	1.5	31	3.2	3.4	3.3	-0.6	-0.03	0

Buy for $0.60

Sell for $1.03

Figure 4-5. Setting up the Bull Put Spread on an Option Chain

2. **Bear Call Spreads:** A bear call spread is used when the trader expects the price of the underlying stock to decrease or remain within a narrow price range for the life of the option. This option strategy includes an OTM short call and an OTM long call one or more strikes above. This is also a credit spread because the 88-cent premium received from the short call is greater than the 30-cent premium paid for the farther OTM long call. This trade returns 58 cents per share in premium. Like short put spread, the premium can be increased by increasing the *strike width* between the short and long call options.

Figure 4-6. Setting up a Bear Call on an Option Chain

LUV Southwest Airlines Company

LAST	LX	Net Ch	BID	BX	ASK	AX	Size	Volume	Open	High	Low
29.2	N	1.46	29.13	P	29	P	20 x 3	26819663	28.5	29.33	28.2

19 JUN 20 (30) 100 CALLS PUTS 73.72% (±5.035)

Mark	Delta	Theta	Op.Int	BID	ASK	Strike	BID	ASK	Mark	Delta	Theta	Op.Int
5.8	0.92	-0.03	2	5.7	5.9	24	0.55	0.65	0.6	-0.15	-0.03	108
3.15	0.65	-0.03	16876	3.1	3.2	27.5	1.5	1.6	1.55	-0.35	-0.04	2977
2.88	0.61	-0.04	684	2.8	3	28	1.6	1.75	1.68	-0.38	-0.04	37
2.58	0.58	-0.04	76	2.5	2.7	28.5	1.9	2	1.95	-0.42	-0.04	37
2.33	0.54	-0.04	118	2.3	2.4	29	2.05	2.2	2.13	-0.46	-0.04	104
2.1	0.51	-0.04	170	2.1	2.2	29.5	2.3	2.55	2.43	-0.49	-0.04	2
1.88	0.48	-0.04	9880	1.9	1.9	30	2.6	2.8	2.7	-0.53	-0.04	2894
1.63	0.44	-0.03	54	1.6	1.7	30.5	2.9	3.1	3	-0.56	-0.04	1
1.45	0.41	-0.03	750	1.4	1.5	31	3.2	3.4	3.3	-0.6	-0.03	0
1.13	0.34	-0.03	189	1.1	1.2	32	3.9	4.1	4	-0.66	-0.03	0
1	0.31	-0.03	9356	1	1.1	32.5	4.2	4.5	4.35	-0.69	-0.03	1307
0.88	0.28	-0.03	72	0.8	1	33	4.6	4.8	4.7	-0.73	-0.03	26
0.5	0.18	-0.02	7931	0.5	0.6	35	6.2	6.4	6.3	-0.84	-0.02	688
0.3	0.12	-0.02	4742	0.3	0.4	37.5	8.5	8.7	8.6	-0.91	-0.01	798

Sell for $0.88

Buy for $0.30

Although widening the distance, or width, between strikes returns more premium when a credit spread is sold, as you now know, it also increases risk. In this trade example, if the trader permits both options to expire ITM, he/she would lose $3.50 per share, or $350 per option contract. However, if the option is allowed to expire in between the short and long strikes, i.e., within "landing zone," the short option would likely be exercised for a major loss. When this happens, the option buyer pays the option seller $33/share for the airline stock and the option seller's brokerage delivers 100 shares of the seller's stock to the option buyer for each option contract.

3. **Bear Put Spreads:** A bear put spread, also called a *long put spread,* is another vertical spread that is used when the option trader identifies a downward-trending stock like a hotel, cruise line, or airline stock during the COVID19 pandemic or perhaps Boeing immediately following the two crashes of the 737 Max airliners. The long put within these trades usually expires in 90 or more days, while the short put may expire much sooner. Of course, this depends entirely on the net premium that must be paid. The purpose of the short put is to finance a portion of the premium that must be paid. As with most bullish and bearish strategies, for the trade to succeed, the trader's bearish bias must be confirmed by the anticipated price drop. Traders with limited funds have an incentive to sell longer-term short puts for their increased premium values. And the short put strike prices are typically selected farther OTM to prevent them from becoming assigned before the long put has enough time to rise sufficiently deep into the money. Once the premium of the long put is sufficient, the trader can close the bear put for profit.

   If the trader's bearish bias is wrong, which would be difficult to imagine for the transportation and aircraft stocks and the price of the underlying stock rallies, the long put would be sold. The short put could either be retained through expiration or bought when the initial credit received is sufficient.

4. **Bull Call Spreads:** A bull call spread is used when the trader expects the price of the underlying stock to rally. Also called "the poor man's covered call," the bull call anchors an OTM short call in the same way that 100 shares of stock anchors each short call option that is sold in the covered call strategy. The long call options are placed at or very close to the money and a short call is placed at a strike having a Delta value at or below .30. Some traders use two standard deviations (68.27%) or a .30 Delta. To be slightly safer, having a Delta value of .25 is recommended.

   Like the bear put, the bull call is also a debit spread and is typically given ample time for the underlying stock to rally in accordance with the trader's bullish bias. Many traders use what is termed as a *diagonal* bull call spread. The diagonal spread uses two expiration dates. The trader may choose to include a long call that expires in six months to perhaps a year and a short call that expires in four to six weeks. Once the short call is profitable, it can be rolled to a later expiration date for a credit in premium. (The *roll* buys-to-close the current short-term short call option and simultaneously sells the same number of call options that expires at a later date and perhaps at a slightly higher strike.) This process can be repeated several times until the series of short calls offsets the initial cost of the long calls and returns a profit.

If the long call becomes sufficiently ITM for profit, the bull call trade would be closed for a substantial profit. Once closed, another bull call spread would likely be considered.

There are numerous reasons to roll working option trades. Rolling one trade into another is often done as a normal part of a long-term trading strategy. But options are frequently rolled as a maintenance technique to recover from a losing trade or to minimize a loss.

The term *diagonal* was introduced above to describe an option strategy that includes two different expiration dates. Diagonal spreads include two or more options that skip several expiration dates. There are also *calendar* spreads that include options that expire on consecutive expiration dates. Diagonal and calendar spreads are discussed again in item 6 below.

5. **Iron Condors:** The iron condor is a neutral option strategy that combines a bull put vertical spread and a bear call vertical spread. The object is to collect option premium from both the call and put spreads. Iron condors are used when a trader expects the price of the underlying stock to remain within a narrow price range. Some refer to this as a stock that is moving sideways. Because both the bull put and bear call spreads are credit spreads, that is, they both return a credit in option premium when traded, the iron condor is quite popular. If the stock price rallies or drops and threatens one of the vertical spreads, the vulnerable spread is closed, and the other is retained. Because iron condors are credit spreads, options that expire within a matter of several days to perhaps a few weeks are used.

Figure 4-7. An Iron Condor Setup Example

LUV Southwest Airlines Company

LAST	LX	Net Ch	BID	BX	ASK	AX	Size	Volume	Open	High	Low
29.2	N	1.46	29.13	P	29	P	20 x 3	26819663	28.5	29.33	28.2

19 JUN 20 (30) 100 CALLS PUTS 73.72% (±5.035)

Mark	Delta	Theta	Op.Int	BID	ASK	Strike	BID	ASK	Mark	Delta	Theta	Op.Int
5.8	0.82	-0.03	2	5.7	5.9	24	0.55	0.65	0.6	-0.16	-0.03	108
5.35	0.81	-0.03	0	5.2	5.5	24.5	0.65	0.75	0.7	-0.18	-0.03	26
4.9	0.79	-0.03	3073	4.8	5	25	0.75	0.85	0.8	-0.21	-0.03	5730
4.6	0.76	-0.03	6	4.5	4.7	25.5	0.85	0.95	0.9	-0.23	-0.03	57
4.2	0.74	-0.03	127	4.1	4.3	26	1	1.05	1.03	-0.26	-0.03	423
3.8	0.71	-0.03	107	3.7	3.9	26.5	1.1	1.2	1.15	-0.28	-0.03	2053
3.5	0.68	-0.03	115	3.4	3.6	27	1.25	1.35	1.3	-0.32	-0.03	124
3.15	0.65	-0.03	16876	3.1	3.2	27.5	1.5	1.6	1.55	-0.35	-0.04	2977
2.88	0.61	-0.04	684	2.8	3	28	1.6	1.75	1.68	-0.38	-0.04	37
2.58	0.58	-0.04	76	2.5	2.7	28.5	1.9	2	1.95	-0.42	-0.04	37
2.33	0.54	-0.04	118	2.3	2.4	29	2.05	2.2	2.13	-0.46	-0.04	104
2.1	0.51	-0.04	170	2.1	2.2	29.5	2.3	2.55	2.43	-0.49	-0.04	2
1.88	0.48	-0.04	9880	1.9	1.9	30	2.6	2.8	2.7	-0.53	-0.04	2894
1.63	0.44	-0.03	54	1.6	1.7	30.5	2.9	3.1	3	-0.56	-0.04	1
1.45	0.41	-0.03	750	1.4	1.5	31	3.2	3.4	3.3	-0.6	-0.03	0
1.13	0.34	-0.03	189	1.1	1.2	32	3.9	4.1	4	-0.66	-0.03	0
1	0.31	-0.03	9356	1	1.1	32.5	4.2	4.5	4.35	-0.69	-0.03	1307
0.88	0.28	-0.03	72	0.8	1	33	4.6	4.8	4.7	-0.73	-0.03	26
0.5	0.18	-0.02	7931	0.5	0.6	35	6.2	6.4	6.3	-0.84	-0.02	688
0.3	0.12	-0.02	4742	0.3	0.4	37.5	8.5	8.7	8.6	-0.91	-0.01	798

Buy for $0.60

Sell for $1.03

Sell for $0.88

Buy for $0.30

There are two other popular option strategies that sell an uncovered option with a short vertical spread on the other side of the option chain. Called the *twisted sister,* this bullish option strategy combines a short OTM naked put with a bear call spread. The other, called a *jade lizard,* is a bearish option strategy that combines an uncovered short OTM naked call with a bull put spread. These strategies are used by advanced level traders who want to increase the premium received by avoiding having to pay for one of the long options. Note that the names *twisted sister* and *jade lizard* are not in the least descriptive. And, as you read earlier, only those traders having the highest option trading permission can trade these due to the uncovered call and put options.

6. **Diagonal and Calendar Spreads:** The vertical spread option strategies described in items 1 through 4 above are often constructed using two different expirations. This was alluded to in the bull call and bear put discussions. Option traders frequently buy long-term options that expires in 90 or more days and sell an equal number of short-term options that expires in a matter of days to perhaps a few weeks to a month. Calendar spreads are separated by a single expiration, while diagonal spreads are separated by two or more expiration dates. To avoid confusion, some use the term *diagonal* for any vertical spread that uses two different expiration dates.
7. **Other Option Strategies:** There are numerous additional option strategies with names like *butterflies, strangles, straddles, synthetics, ratio spreads,* and *collars.* I include 78 option strategies in my books:
   The Option Strategy Desk Reference
   The Only Option Trading Book You'll Ever Need, 2nd edition
   Both are available from Amazon
   All 78 option strategies are described including setups, bullish or bearish bias, risk graphs, and trade management techniques for each.

Credit and Debit Spreads

Option trades such as vertical bull put spreads that return a credit in premium when filled are commonly called *credit spreads.* Option trades that require option traders to pay money when filled are called *debit spreads.* A few examples of a debit spread include buying a call or put option or a bull call spread. Many option traders favor a series of short-term credit spreads such as the bull put spreads, bear call spreads, and the iron condors described above. Some qualified option traders that are permitted to sell uncovered calls and puts make huge incomes selling naked short-term puts and calls, where *naked* is a jargon for *uncovered.*

Using Probability for a Successful Option Trade Outcome

How far out of the money should we place our short call or put options to prevent them from becoming ITM prior to the option's expiration? One of the benefits that attract people to options is the abundance of options math that is contained within each option chain. The next paragraph describes how we use the options math, called *Greeks,* in addition to the Bid, Ask, Mark, and Open Interest columns to determine what, when, and how to trade. Using a Delta .25 was discussed in a few of the preceding vertical spread examples. Here, we briefly describe how option traders use the Delta Greek to determine the probability of how vulnerable each option's strike price is to become in the money during the life of the option.

Although some trading platforms can display a Probability ITM and a much more conservative Probability Touching column within the option chains, most option traders simply use Delta values. The value of Delta is always very close to the corresponding Probability ITM value. (There is also Probability OTM, which is the reciprocal of probability ITM).

When a short option is sold, regardless whether it's a put or a call, most traders would like to have at least a 75% chance of having it remain OTM through expiration. Therefore, most traders use Delta values at or quite close to .25. This provides a 75% chance of having the corresponding strike price remain out of the money through the option's expiration. The 75% odds of success are quite good, especially when the Las Vegas casinos make millions of dollars each day with 54.5% odds of winning against their clientele.

Although the .25 Delta value is considered by many to mean the corresponding strike has a 75% probability of remaining OTM through expiration, some traders use .30. Others use one standard deviation—a value of 68.27%. (Standard deviations are frequently used in statistics.) As you should have seen in the preceding trade setup illustrations, the short option strikes all included Delta values very close to .26 to .28.

Option Expiration "Styles"

There are two option expiration styles: American and European. The American-style option expiration can be exercised by the option buyer any time an option becomes in the money. If an American-style option remains out of the money through expiration, the option expires worthless. This permits option sellers to retain the premium originally collected when the option was sold.

European-style expiration options cannot be exercised prior to the option expiration date. However, if an option trader permits a European-style option to expire in the money, even by one penny, it is immediately auto-exercised by the Option Clearing Corporation (OCC). While most options are American style, the financial index options have European-style expirations. This includes the S&P 500, Nasdaq 100, and Russell 2000 symbols SPX, NDX, and RUT.

Trading Volatility

Trading volatility is a measure of the current buying and selling volume. Volatility, labelled *Vega*, is among the most influential variables that affect option prices. When volume (or volatility) is high, option prices increase in value; when trading volume is low, option prices decline. Seasoned option traders consider a stock's current buying and selling volume compared to historical trading volume. Volatility values are referred to as *implied volatility* (IV) and *historical volatility* (HV). You may recall that HV is a measure of the average trading volume for the most recent 12 months. Both IV% and HV% values are important and are available on most trading platforms.

When implied volatility and option premiums are relatively high, seasoned option traders prefer selling short-term options that expire within a few days to perhaps a few months. Many traders sell several short-term puts and calls every few days for steady incomes. Hence, some traders collect more premium by selling a dozen or more short puts and calls each month than others who buy and hold long-term options for several months.

When option premiums are relatively low as a result of a low implied volatility value, option traders prefer to buy longer-term options that expire in three months to perhaps a year. This is because low IV% values contribute to low premium values which reduces the initial cost of the trade. The trader expects the volatility to return to historical volatility levels which increases option premium values. A favorable change in the price of the underlying stock combined with an increase in volatility usually results in a substantial rise in premium value. When this happens, the option can be closed for profit.

This is an example of how risk and reward have a direct correlation. When IV is high, trading volume boosts option premium values. High buying or selling volume also produces correspondingly stronger moves in the price of the underlying stocks. Conversely, when IV% values are relatively low, the corresponding weak trading volume reduces option premium values. This contributes to small changes in the price of the underlying stock and correspondingly minor changes in an option's premium value. Hence, low trading volume results in relatively small moves in the price of the underlying stock, which is seen as a sideways move on the stock's price chart.

Another volatility measure is IV Rank. IV Rank ranges from 0.0% to 100%. Some trading platforms display IV Rank values on price charts as a *chart study.* The IV Rank value is easier to understand than the IV%. The IV Rank tells traders where the absolute current volatility resides relative to the last 12-month historical volatility range. The formula for IV Rank is:

$$\text{IV Rank} = \frac{100 \times (\text{current IV level} - \text{52 week IV low})}{(\text{52 week IV high} - \text{52-week IV Low})}$$

An IV Rank calculation example is shown here:

52-Week IV High = 46
52-Week IV Low = 12
Current IV level = 30
100 x (30 – 12) = 1800
46 – 12 = 34
IV Rank =1800/34 = 52.94

Section 4 Questions:

1. An option is a time-limited derivative of an equity such as a ________________, ________________, ________________, etc.
2. There are two kinds of options: call options and _______ options.
3. The abbreviations for in the money and out of the money are _______ and ________.
4. Financial ______________ is a major advantage of trading options.
5. Most option contracts on stocks represent __________ shares of stock.
6. The exiting time value of an option is also referred to as ___________ value.
7. Changes in market ______________ affects the price of an option.
8. Each option chain has a vertical column of option ___________ prices.
9. The prices of both put and call options increase as they become deeper ____ ______ ___________.
10. Option values are examined on a mathematical table called an ____________ ____________.
11. You can buy and short stocks, ETFs, and even futures contracts on an ___________ ___________.
12. Out of the money options do not have any ____________ value.
13. The difference between an option's market price and its current premium value is called the option's _________ _________.
14. Open interest shows the number of option ___________ that existed when the market opened in the morning of the current trading day.
15. Gamma risk increases as an option approaches its __________ _______.
16. Long refers to ________ while short refers to ________.
17. Trades that contain four different option strikes are often difficult to __________.
18. The incremental values between strike prices is called the strike _________.
19. The acronym ATM stands for _____ _____ ________.
20. _____ strike prices that are greater than the ATM strike price are OTM.
21. Name three variables that affect option prices: __________________, ____________________ and ______________________.
22. The Mark is midway between the _________ and the _________.
23. __________ is the amount the option premium changes in response to a $1.00 change in the underlying.
24. Delta is also used as a measure of ________________.
25. A trader might buy _____ options when bullish on a stock.
26. When bearish on a stock, the trader might buy a _________ option.
27. Another word for an uncovered short option is a ______________ short option.
28. A trader owns 500 shares of stock and sells five OTM call options. This is a __________ ________ strategy.
29. The bull put vertical spread is a credit spread that sells OTM put options and buys an equal number of put options farther _______.

30. An iron condor combines a bull put spread and a __________ __________ spread.
31. Diagonal and calendar spreads use two different ____________ dates.
32. Credit spreads collect premium when entered. Traders are required to pay for ___________ spreads.
33. A Delta value of .25 has approximately a _____% probability of remaining OTM through option expiration.
34. The ______________ option expiration style cannot be exercised prior to expiration.
35. The abbreviation IV stands for Implied Volatility. HV is ___________ volatility.
36. IV Rank ranges from 0.0% to _____%.

Section 5
Using Price Charts

What You Will Learn

1. Experienced traders use price charts to determine current market conditions.
2. Japanese candlestick charts are the most popular chart type in used today.
3. The meaning and use of a tick chart
4. A red candle represents the period's price drop from the top to the bottom.
5. The base of a green candle represents the period's opening price.
6. A use of chart studies
7. Some uses of simple and exponential moving average plots
8. Recognizing buy and sell signals on price charts
9. The use and interpretation of Bollinger bands, the Keltner channels, and trading momentum studies
10. A price chart's support level is at the bottom of a price chart.
11. Demand and supply zones are considered more reliable than chart patterns.
12. Market makers fill trades by matching buy and sell orders.
13. Base and quote currencies are used by FX traders.
14. Fundamental analysis is often used by buy and hold stock investors.
15. Technical analysis is used by shorter-term option and swing traders.
16. There are approximately 700 mathematical chart studies.
17. The ATR(14) shows a stock's average price range over the most recent 14 trading days.
18. The Bollinger Bands study plots trading volume

Price Chart Setups

Experienced traders use price charts to determine what is currently happening to the one or more stocks and other similar financial instrument of interest. There are several chart types including line charts, bar charts, area charts, and candlestick charts. Candlestick charts were developed in the early 1700s by Japanese rice futures traders. They were adopted by market traders in the U.S. in the 1990s and have become the most popular in use today. A typical price candle can represent a week, day, hour, minute, or even what is called a *tick*, where a tick can be set to represent a specific number of trades, such as 25 or 50. The body of a candle is usually colored green to indicate a price increase and red to indicate a price drop. The bottom of a green candle shows the opening price and the top shows the closing price. The tips of lines that resemble candle wicks, called the *shadows*, represent the high and low price for the current time value or tick.

Figure 5-1 illustrates two typical candles. Notice the amount of information each candle provides. The width of each candle corresponds to the selected time period, such as a week, day, hour, etc. The body of each candle is green or red to indicate the direction of the price. The tips of the candle wicks or *shadows* show the high and low for the selected time period.

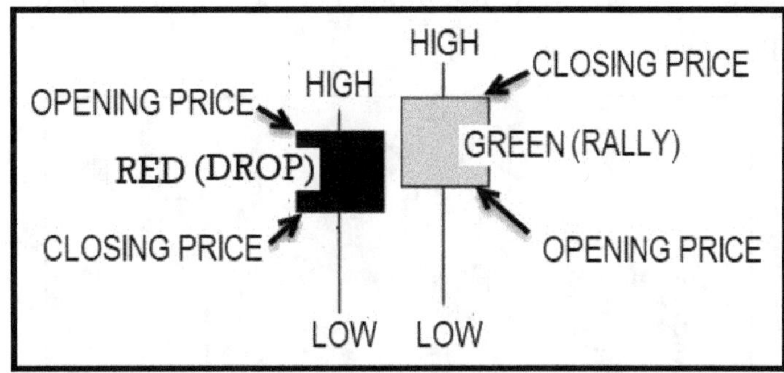

Figure 5-1. The "Candles" in a Candlestick Chart

We examine price charts to determine if the stock of interest has been trending upward, downward, or is stuck within a narrow price range, referred to as *moving sideways*. Perhaps the stock has experienced some strong selling action and is presently near a historical support level at the bottom of the chart. Or the stock may be overbought and the price candles are now near the top of the price chart close to resistance where traders stop buying a stock and begin selling.

Many traders use price chart patterns such as double tops, double bottoms, head and shoulders, cup and handle, and bull or bear flags. There are many more from which to choose. You can examine several popular price chart patterns on the stockcharts.com web site.

Among the most popular patterns is the double bottom near a historical support level at the bottom of a price chart. The double top is equally popular. It exists near a historical resistance level near the top of the price chart. The double bottom pattern near support levels is seen as an indication of oversold stocks. This encourages new buying or perhaps entering long calls bull put spreads. The double top pattern near a historical resistance level is seen as an indication of an overbought stock. This pattern encourages shorting the underlying stock, buying puts, or selling a short vertical call spread that includes one or more OTM short calls below an equal number of long calls.

The trader often begins with a watch list of qualified stocks. The watch list should include only those stocks that are affordable and that have good daily trading volumes that exceed a million shares. Most traders look at price charts for an established price trend. Many traders display multiple price charts to see how the stock price has changed over the last few years. This often includes one week per candle, one day per candle, and one hour per candle charts. Tick charts are examined to see current trading activity. Volume bars show buying and selling action.

Demand and Supply Zones,

Figure 5-2 illustrates a typical "demand zone" where a stock is currently oversold and near a price support level. Notice the double bottom chart pattern is also present to indicate a potential price breakout. There is also a recent low, a brief buying rally, followed by selling (profit taking). When the stock becomes oversold and the price drops again, it sets up ideal conditions for another rally. This is an ideal time for stock traders to buy the underlying stock. As mentioned earlier, option traders consider buying calls or perhaps selling bull put spreads.

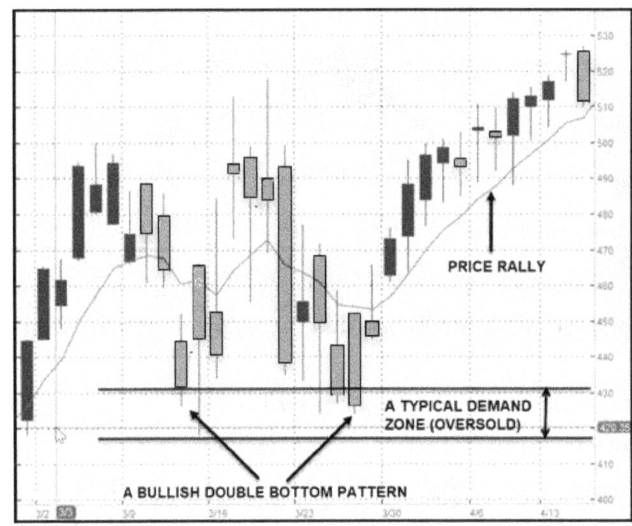

Figure 5-2. A Demand Zone and the Double Bottom Chart Pattern

Although a lot of traders look for chart patterns like those described on the stockchart.com website, demand zones like the one shown in figure 5-2 tend to be much more reliable. Also look for *supply zones* at the top of your price charts to find bearish trading opportunities, where stocks are often overbought. The supply zones are usually accompanied by double top chart patterns, which are a mirror image of the double bottom pattern shown in figure 5-2.

A Few Popular Chart Studies

Most seasoned market traders, regardless of what and how they trade, regularly analyze price charts before entering a trade. It is important to know what has happened, what is currently happening, and, more importantly, what is likely to happen. In addition to looking at the formations made by looking at lines, bars, or a series of candles for the price trend, most traders are also interested in the buying and selling volumes, or trading volatility, average daily price swings, buying and selling momentum, and several other measures that help the trader consider whether to buy, sell, or look elsewhere.

There are approximately 700 price chart studies. Some are quite useful, while others may not be. Most trading applications include several dozen of the most popular chart studies. Most trading platforms include links to chart study descriptions. If you see a study that intrigues you, read the narrative that describes how it is used. Here are a few studies to consider.

Moving Averages— Simple and exponential moving averages have been in use and quite popular for many years. Traders use short-term and long-term moving average plots and watch for moving average plot crossovers as trade signals. For example, a price rally is forming when the nine-period simple moving average plot, abbreviated SMA(9), crosses above an EMA(20) plot. (EMA abbreviates exponential moving average.) If the SMA(9) continues its upward trajectory and crosses an SMA(50) plot, many traders see this as a trade signal. Being bullish, the trader would consider buying the stock or perhaps a few call options. Or the trader might consider selling a bull put vertical spread that was described in Section 4.

The trader may short a stock, buy a few put options, or perhaps sell a bear call spread when an EMA(20) plotline trends downward and crosses over the SMA(50). Note that simple moving averages are linear, while exponential moving averages (EMAs) are weighted toward the most recent price points.

Figure 5-3. Moving Average Crossover Signals

ATR(14)— ATR stands for *Average True Range.* The 14 indicates a 14-day trading period in which the average daily price range of the subject stock is summed and divided by 14. An ATR(14) value of $2.25 means the stock price has ranged by $2.25 over the most recent 14 trading days. Traders use the ATR(14)

value to estimate how much the price is likely to rise or fall over the next several days. Of course, events can occur that cause major increases or decreases that exceed the current ATR(14) range.

Bollinger Bands— The Bollinger Bands is another popular chart study. It includes three key plotlines. A 20-period simple moving average, the SMA(20) forms the central plot. Two exterior plotlines exist two standard deviations above and below the central SMA(20) plot. These external plots show the expansion and contraction of trading volatility. The exterior bands widen with an increase in trading volatility and contract with a decrease in trading volatility.

Keltner Channel— The Keltner Channel resembles the Bollinger Bands plot. It uses the same SMA(20) central plot as the Bollinger Bands. The exterior bands are 1.5 times the ATR(14) above and below the SMA(20). The Keltner Channel and Bollinger Bands are sometimes overlaid to signal a price breakout. When the exterior Bollinger Bands compress inside the 1.5 ATR(14) plotlines, the combined studies are said to be in a "squeeze." This is viewed as a signal for a price breakout, which occurs when volatility returns to normal values. However, whether the price of the stock will rally and drop is not shown.

The TTM_Squeeze— This study was developed by a trader named John Carter, where TTM stands for "trade the market." The study combines the Bollinger Bands and Keltner Channel studies. It was developed to signal a potential price breakout. The study also includes a plotline that's based on the Market Forecaster study, which signals the probable direction of the price change, either upward or downward.

Figure 5-4. Bollinger Bands Squeeze inside the Keltner Channel

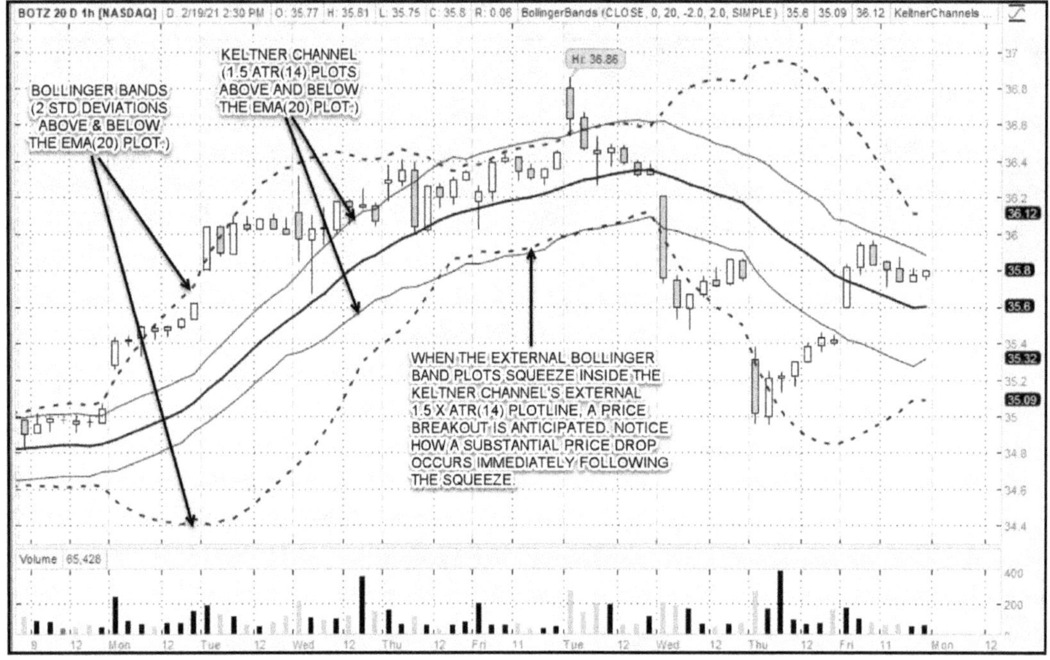

Momentum Studies— There are numerous momentum studies, often referred to as *momentum oscillators,* that are used to determine whether a stock is currently overbought or oversold. These studies are based on the relative velocity of price changes. A commonly used momentum study that was developed in the 1970s was named the relative strength index abbreviated RSI. Four other popular momentum oscillators include the commodity channel index (CCI), the Stochastics Oscillator, the Awesome Oscillator, and the Moving Average Convergence-Divergence (MACD). The MACD is quite popular and used by many chart analysts, although some traders have adopted the Awesome Oscillator because it contains a moving average crossover line and a series of colored momentum bars.

These momentum oscillator studies measure the relationship between the closing price and the price range over a predetermined period. Many traders favor the stochastics indicator because it is easy to understand and has a high degree of accuracy in knowing when to buy or to sell. Momentum oscillators are displayed at the bottom of price charts. They include plots and numerical values that correspond to oversold and overbought conditions. Three different momentum oscillators are illustrated in figures 5-5 through 5-7. You can see how to use them online. However, because these momentum studies are quite similar, try a few and then choose the one you like the best, such as the stochastics oscillator or MACD. But use only one. Displaying multiple oscillators occupies extra screen space and serves little purpose.

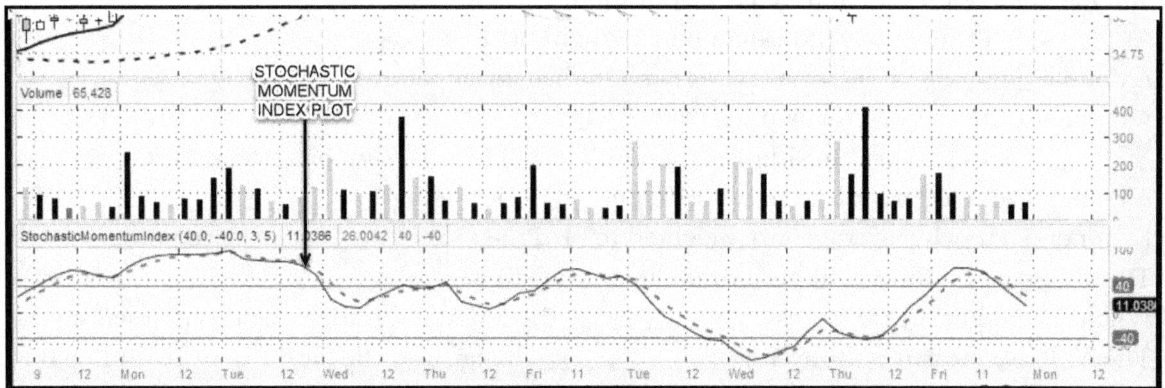

Figure 5-5. The Stochastic Momentum Index

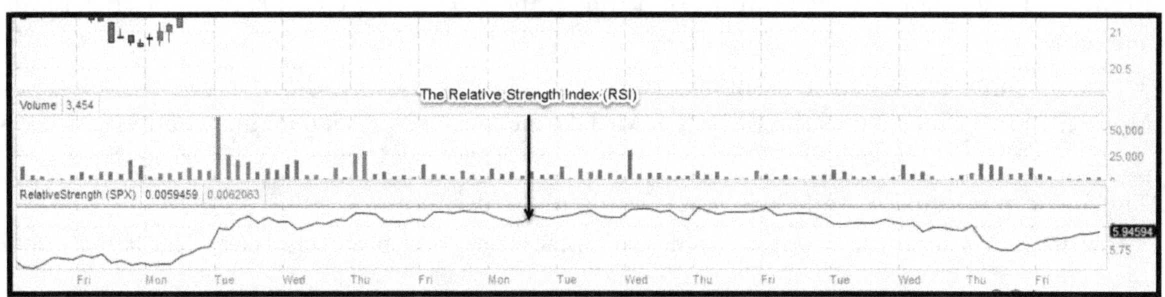

Figure 5-6. The Relative Strength Index (RSI)

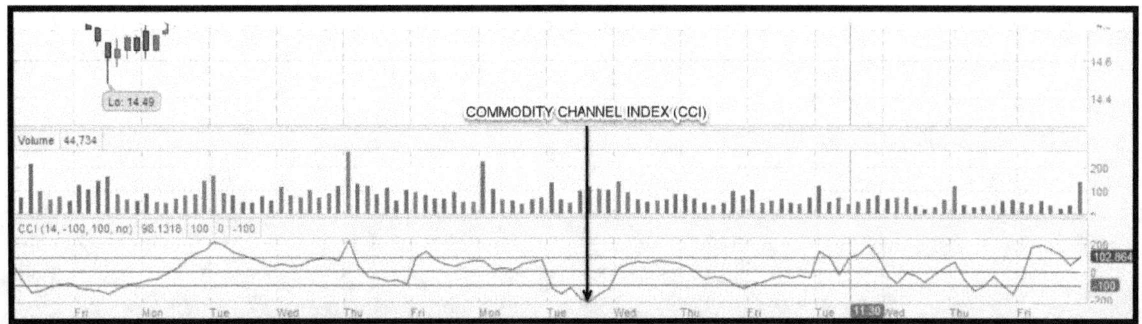

Figure 5-7. The Commodity Channel Index (CCI)

Section 5 Questions

1. To see what is currently happening to the overall market or to a specific stock, traders examine __________ __________.
2. Japanese candlestick charts were first used in the early 1700s with ________ futures.
3. Today, the __________ ___________ chart is among the most popular in use today.
4. Tick charts measure s specific number of __________.
5. The top and bottom of a candlestick's ____________, also called its wick, measures the high and low value for the established time duration.
6. A _________ candle body indicates an increase in price.
7. A double _____________ chart pattern is a bullish chart pattern.
8. A demand zone is located at a price chart's ___________ level.
9. ________ zones and price resistance are both located near the top of a price chart.
10. A demand zone is an indication of the underlying stock being _________.
11. Exponential moving averages are weighted toward the most __________ price points.
12. The abbreviation for the 50-period simple moving average is _________.
13. When the 50-period SMA crosses ___________ the EMA(20), traders see this as a sell signal.
14. The ATR(14) measures the average ______ ______ change over the most recent 14 trading days.
15. The ________ is used as the central plot for both the Bollinger bands and the Keltner Channel studies.
16. Bollinger bands plot trading volatility over time while the Keltner channel tracks a stock's average daily __________ _________.
17. The TTM_Squeeze is used to a signal a price ___________.
18. Momentum studies such as the RSI, CCI, MACD, etc. are used to determine whether a stock is ________ _________ or _______ _______.
19. The Awesome Oscillator and Stochastics Oscillator are two more _____________ ___________.
20. How many momentum studies should you place on your price charts at the same time? ________.

Section 6
Trading Rules

What You Will Learn

1. Trading rules are used by every experienced options trader.
2. Rules dictate which strategies are best suited to the current market conditions.
3. Developing and using watch lists
4. What to include and what to ignore within watch lists
5. The importance of trading volume
6. The use of the 14-day average true price range, i.e., the ATR(14)
7. The use of dividend and earnings release dates
8. More about the VIX or *fear factor*
9. How to use implied volatility with your option trade selections
10. How to choose expiration dates that suit each option strategy's goals
11. When to buy options and when to sell them
12. The importance of using familiar option strategies

Rules-Based Option Trading

Every experienced option trader uses trading rules to select and construct his or her option strategy. The rules dictate which strategies are most suitable for the current market conditions.

The market is rallying: buy long-term calls; sell short-term puts.

The market is dropping: buy long-term puts; sell short-term calls.
The market is moving sideways: buy an iron condor.

These are just a few simple responses to the listed market conditions. But there are several other rules that option traders must consider. These include market volatility, time till expiration, a stock's average price range, an option's open interest value, and more.

Developing and Using Watch Lists

Most seasoned traders develop several watch lists of stocks, ETFs, financial indexes, and futures. They may be separated by industry, price range, or some other category. Traders who subscribe to stock market advisories, like Investor's Business Daily, often have watch lists dedicated to the IBD 50 and IBD's initial public offering (IPO) stock list. These stocks have been carefully vetted by their team of analysts based on company growth, earnings, institutional acquisitions, etc. As a stock trader, some of the stocks may seem too expensive to consider. But as an options trader there are strategies that can be used even for stocks and financial indexes that are trading for thousands of dollars per share. Finally, be sure to avoid stocks with poor trading volumes below one million shares per day. Volume is important to order fulfillment, because traders want their buy and sell orders to fill as quickly as possible.

Many of the sample trades included in Section 4 employed some basic rules that helped the option trader choose reasonably safe strike prices. Here, trading rules are viewed relative to the information and tradable symbols within your personal watch lists.

- Price of the underlying equity (Examine only those stocks that are affordable.)
- Daily trading volume (Consider at least one to two million shares per day.)
- Earnings per share (profits for bullish trades, losses for bearish trades)
- 52-week high and low (room to rally or drop for a bullish or bearish strategy)
- Large or small ATR(14) values that are well suited to your trading strategies.
- Directional trend on the price charts; look for price rallies, basing, or drops.
- Price position (proximity to support or resistance — near a recent low or high)
- Earnings report dates are sometimes accompanied by a brief price rally or drop.
- Dividend dates; dividend distributions often produce a small price drop.
- Company announcements (mergers and acquisitions, new product releases, patents, lawsuits, lay-offs, stock buy backs, company director changes, etc.)
- Business Sector (health of the business sector to which the company belongs)
- Implied Volatility versus Historical Volatility (High IV% increases premium values.)
- Current VIX Value (High volatility index values increase option premiums and increase margin stress.)

The S&P 500 volatility index, symbol VIX, is often referred to as the *fear factor.* When the VIX is in the mid-20s or above, option premium values begin to increase dramatically due to a corresponding increase in risk. This risk results from greater than usual price swings in stocks, ETFs, and financial indexes. Account margin risk also increases with increases in the value of the VIX index. This often leads to an increase in account margin calls which must be dealt with by the brokerage account holders. Otherwise, the brokerage will take corrective action to bring accounts back within compliance. This can include the brokerage margin department disposing of stocks or option positions to reduce the risk to an acceptable level.

Choosing an Option Strategy

Once a trader develops a directional bias based on these and perhaps a few other considerations, he or she may be ready to choose a compatible options strategy. This involves choosing a qualified equity (we'll continue to use "stock"), opening the option chain for that stock, choosing a compatible expiration date or date(s), and checking the selected option chain's IV% for compatibility with the trader's bullish, bearish, or neutral trading bias.

Following are lists of option values to consider when buying and selling options.

Buying Options:

- Relatively low IV% or IV Rank ≤ 20% when buying options. Low IV% reduces the cost of option premiums. This reduces the cost of buying options. When IV% increases, the option premiums also increase which is a primary goal when buying options. (Buy when the option price is low and sell when the option price is high.)
- Each strike price's Open Interest should be at or above 10 per option; use an Open Interest value ≥ 300 for a 3 – or 4-strike option strategy such as an iron condor or a butterfly. (The butterfly strategy is introduced later in Section 8.) A vertical spread, such as a bull put, should have an Open Interest value of at least 10 at each of the two strikes. More is always much better for increased liquidity and required to fill open trade orders.
- Bullish trades: Long put Mark values should increase as the price of the underlying decreases causing the long put to move deeper ITM. Bearish trades: Long call Mark values should increase as the price of the underlying increases and the long call moves deeper ITM.
- Expiration of long options should be ≥ 90 days; some traders buy LEAPS options that expire in 12 months to perhaps two years. This minimizes the initial reduction in option premium caused by Theta, i.e., the passage of time. LEAPS stands for *long term equity anticipation security.*
- Bid to Ask Spreads are narrow for heavily traded stocks and options. This is also an indication of good liquidity and promotes the fast trade execution.

Selling Options

- Relatively high IV% or IV Rank ≥ 60% when buying options. High IV% values increase option premiums. When the IV% value decreases to historical levels, the option premiums will also decrease. This is a primary goal when selling options. (Sell options when the premiums are high; buy options when premiums are low.)
- Each strike price's Open Interest should be at or above 10 per option contract; ≥ 300 for a 3 – or 4-strike option strategy. A vertical spread, such as a bull put or bear call, should have an Open Interest value of at least 20 at each of the two strikes. More Open Interest is always better for increased liquidity and faster order execution.

- Bullish trades: Short put Mark values will decrease as the price of the underlying increases. Bearish trades: Short call Mark values will decrease as the price of the underlying decreases. The trade returns a profit when the Mark values of these short options decline in value.
- Short Option's Delta value should be at or below ±0.25 for a 75% probability of remaining OTM through expiration. The Delta values of long puts and short calls are negative; the Delta values of short puts and long calls are positive.
- Expiration of short options should be ≤ 56 days (8 weeks). When selling options, traders want the premiums to decrease in value. Selling an option for $1.00 and buying to close the option for 50 cents or less is a common practice.
- Bid to Ask Spreads are narrow for heavily traded stocks and options. This is also an indication of good liquidity and promotes substantially faster trade execution.
- ±Values, shown to the right of the IV% at the top of each option chain, is the current calculation of how far OTM a strike price should be to prevent assignment (or being exercised). For example, if the price of a stock is $100 and ±$10.50 is displayed to the right of the IV% value, a short option's strike price should be placed at $11.00 or more from the current ATM value. Of course, this changes with time, so choose some extra width for safety.

Option Strategies

Most option traders have their favorite option strategies. Some are satisfied with a small handful of strategies that they use most of the time. Because the trader is intimately familiar with each of his/her favorite strategies, costly trading mistakes are avoided. And even when they are not successful, the trader knows how to manage them in order to minimize the loss.

Knowing how these favorite strategies work is important for several reasons. First, it helps the trader select an underlying stock that is a good fit for his or her chosen strategy. This would include the current stock price, recent stock movement, and buying and selling volumes. And the trader also knows how to use the option chain and select an appropriate expiration date(s) for the chosen strategy. Moreover, the trader knows which strikes to use based on previous trade experience.

Assume the trader has had success with the vertical spreads described in Section 4, i.e., the bull put when bullish, the bear call when bearish, and the iron condors when neutral. These are all quite popular, commonly used trades. The trader may begin by examining his/her watch list and the corresponding price charts to find a stock that is trending upward, another that has been moving sideways and remaining within a narrow price range, and perhaps a third that is trending downward. A trading fit exists for all three of these popular strategies.

The next section examines a few trade setups and introduces and describes the display and use of risk graphs. It also describes some common trade management techniques that are used by most experienced option traders. These techniques are important to understand and use, especially when a trade experiences an unwanted setback.

Section 6 Questions

1. Every experienced option trader uses ___________ _________.
2. The rules dictate which __________ __________ to use based on the current market conditions.
3. Developing and using one or more ___________ _________ is a useful practice.
4. Some traders subscribe to stock market _____________ such as Investor's Business Daily.
5. Dividend distributions often produce small price ________ in the underlying stock.
6. Earnings reports are sometimes accompanied by a brief price ___________ or __________.
7. Stocks included on your watch lists should have an average trading volume of at least _____ _________ shares per day.
8. A narrow Bid-to-Ask spread is an indication of _________ trading volume.
9. Traders check the IV% on an option chain before selecting a compatible bullish, bearish, or neutral _________ __________.
10. Low IV% values or ranks reduce __________ values.
11. Option trades fill faster when Open Interest values are ___________.
12. Expiration of long options should be greater than _______ days.
13. LEAPS stands for _____ ______ _________ __________ _________.
14. Short put Mark values decrease as the price of the underlying stock ___________.
15. Short option's Delta value should be at or below ±0.25 for a _____% probability of remaining OTM through expiration.

Section 7
Trading and Trade Management Techniques

What You Will Learn

1. Building wealth through "momentum trading"
2. The benefits of having large brokerage accounts
3. Why to trade uncovered short options and who can trade them
4. Why European expiration-style index options are used
5. More about "bracketed trades"
6. Why option traders use risk graphs and what they represent
7. Trading as a disciplined business
8. How to develop a trading routine
9. Why traders watch the overnight index futures
10. Some differences in trading small and large brokerage accounts
11. Why and how to roll a working trade out, up, or down
12. Why traders often leg into multiple-strike option trades
13. The ATR(14) shows a stock's average price range over the past 14 days.
14. The Bollinger Bands study plots trading volume.

Momentum Trading

Option traders who enter and exit several trades each week can often build their account values over time. For example, these traders typically sell several short-term vertical spreads on a variety of different stocks and receive a series of returns that, when added together, can amount to hundreds and even thousands of dollars per week. The amount of money within a trader's brokerage account governs the size and number of trades. When consistently successful, it is only a matter of time before the monthly income collected from this style of trading momentum adds up to tens of thousands of dollars in monthly premium income. Momentum traders conduct their trading in a business-like manner. They are disciplined in both their trading hours and the strategies they use. And thanks to the availability of the Internet and the versatility offered by today's modern trading applications, there is no need to dress up and drive to the office. Traders with relatively small accounts can sell several short-term bullish vertical spreads on stocks that are rallying; sell several short-term bearish spreads on stocks that are dropping; and perhaps sell a few short-term iron condors on stocks that are stuck within a narrow price range. Short-term includes option durations of one to perhaps six weeks. Some option traders regularly open and close one or more trades within the same trading day. These trades eliminate worry that can occur when traders are concerned about overnight market swings and price gaps. Gaps are caused by overnight price swings that occur with a stock closes at one price and then gaps up or down to another price when the market reopens the following morning.

When a trader's account grows to a sufficient size, he/she might buy a few long-term calls on growth stocks that expire in three or more months to perhaps two years. And, when the trader qualifies for trading uncovered options, he/she can begin trading far OTM uncovered short puts, short calls, and short strangles. These uncovered short options can only be traded by those who have been granted the highest option trading permission. And they choose safe OTM strikes that are unlikely to become ITM.

Uncovered (or naked) short call and put strategies are described in the next paragraph. And there are many option traders who have made millions of dollars in option premiums using these strategies.

Trading Uncovered Short Calls, Short Puts, and Strangles.

The short strangle simultaneously sells the same number of OTM puts and OTM calls that expire in a matter of days to perhaps a week. These trades work best on financial index options and high-priced stock options. But because the financial index options listed in the following table have the European-style expirations, they are somewhat safer.

Financial Index	Market Symbol
S&P 500	SPX
Nasdaq 100	NDX
Russell 2000	RUT

European-style expirations cannot be exercised if they are permitted to temporarily become ITM prior to expiration. But, like American-style expiration options, they will be automatically exercised by the Option Clearing Corporation (OCC) if the trader permits one of these European expiration style index option positions to expire ITM. However, the European-style expiration gives the option seller time to close or roll the trade.

When these uncovered calls, puts, and short strangles are initially sold, the strike prices used must be far enough OTM to remain OTM through expiration. Therefore, the trader would choose a strike price that is at or close to two standard deviations (95.5%) OTM. Choosing a strike price with a Delta value of 0.05 is common. This suggests that the selected strike price has a 95% probability of remaining OTM through expiration.

Experienced traders who specialize in selling index options also want their trades to be short term. This encourages them to choose options that expire in a matter of a few days to perhaps a week. Choosing a short time till expiration limits the amount of time that the strike price of the short options has to move ITM. Still a third value to check is volatility and the current value of the VIX. If the value of the VIX is in the mid teens to perhaps 20, the low volatility is an indication of price stability. This makes the short puts, short calls, or short strangle even safer. Combining the far OTM strike with a short time till expiration during a period of reasonably low volatility increases the probability for a profitable outcome. Despite all of these positive conditions, there are sometimes exceptions. If these uncovered index options begin to move closer to the ITM price, the trader MUST intervene. This can be done in several different ways.

1. The trader could enter a buy-to-close order. If trading the NASDAQ 100 index (NDX), the cost to close could exceed a hundred thousand dollars in premium. However, it is unlikely that an experienced option trader would choose to do this in isolation.
2. The trader could buy-to-close the option and sell another option for several thousand dollars at a strike that's farther OTM. This approach offsets a portion of the premium paid to close the initial trade. Consider the trader sold 10 SPX $3150 put options on Monday morning that expire at market close on Wednesday afternoon. When sold, the $3150 strike's Delta value was .05 and the premium was $5.00 per share. The trader collects $5,000 in premium less a few dollars in exchange fees. Early on Tuesday afternoon the SPX is dropping through $3,200. The SPX is now within $50 of the $3,150 strike price, and all indications are that the price will continue to drop. The trader would never permit the ten $3150 put options to expire ITM and be assigned because it would cost $3,150,000. The Mark of the $3150 SPX put has risen to $20.00 per share, which will only get worse. Buying to close ten contracts will cost $20,000 less the $5,000 originally received. What else can this trader do?
3. The trader could buy-to-close the current 3150 SPX put options and then sell ten $2900 SPX put options that reside farther OTM for a Mark value of $5.00 per share. This is still going to cost about $10,000, i.e., the $20,000 cost to buy back our initial $3150 SPX puts less the original $5,000 received and the $5,000 received from the sale of the $2900 SPX puts. Although the trader may be able to save $10,000, this action still suffers a $10,000 loss.
4. The trader decides to roll the short $3150 SPX puts to Friday's expiration. Rolling a trade out in time is a common way to reduce the current loss. In many instances, rolling to a later expiration can return a profit. Rolling includes buying to close the current option and selling another option that is either farther OTM or expires at a later date. This process is called a calendar spread because it buys the current trade and sells a new position one expiration farther out in time. This adds more time value to the position, which often reduces much of the loss in premium. The trader knows that $20,000 must be paid to close the $3150 SPX put options. The trader examines the cost to buy back the current $3150 puts and simultaneously sell ten $2900 SPX puts that expire on Friday. This trade returns $10 in premium per share. This reduces the trader's loss to $5,000, which includes the initial $5,000 credit and the $10,000 in premium received by selling the $2900 SPX puts that expire on Friday.
5. There are a few other considerations. For example, the trader examines the SPX put options that expire next Monday, which would add more time value. But this also increases the risk! Because the trader wants to avoid long-term short options, he decides to explore the call side of the SPX option chain.
6. By looking at the SPX call options, the trader checks how much premium can be collected by selling ten SPX calls. Because the SPX price is currently dropping, the calls appear to be reasonably safe, especially if the call options expire on the following day. The trader determines that ten short call options that expire tomorrow afternoon can be sold for around $2.00 per share. This earns another $2,000 in premium. Because these call options become part of a short strangle, the margin will be negligible. One of the benefits that accompany a short strangle is that the account

margin is applied to the most vulnerable position. Therefore, either the put side or the call side of a short strangle is used for the purpose of computing margin risk. Hence, it's unlikely that the ten short calls will be a factor in the margin calculation. Although the trader may still lose a few thousand dollars, the initial $20,000 loss has been substantially reduced. And the trader is confident that the loss will be recovered by selling more SPX short calls during the following week.

Using Profit Targets and Protective Stops (Bracketed Trades)

Bracketed trades were previously discussed in this book. Section 5 added a few brief examples of risk versus reward ratios. Many experienced stock, futures, and options traders include a profit target and protective stop with many, if not all, of their opening trade orders. When both a profit target and a protective stop is included, you now know that it is a *bracketed trade.* If the price of the stock or option drops, the protective stop is set to trigger. This ensures an acceptable loss. And if the price of a long stock or option position rallies sufficiently to achieve 50% to 70% in profit, the profit is taken. These stop triggers are submitted as a *one cancels other* (OCO) order. When one stop triggers, the other is automatically cancelled.

Most trading platforms permit the use of percentages, fixed price values, and trailing stops. Trailing stops follow price rallies. Let's assume that a 10% trailing stop is included in the purchase of a $100 stock. The stock price rallies to $120. A $12 price drop back to $108 would trigger the trailing stop. This leaves the trader with an $8.00 per share profit.

Protective stops prevent a trade from experiencing a major loss. It is important to determine normal price variations to prevent an unwanted stop trigger. Many traders use the ATR(14) study to determine a suitable trailing stop value. It's important to understand that when protective stops are too tight, say from 5% to 7%, it's possible to lose a trade prematurely from a normal price fluctuation. Protective stops should provide some working room to ensure the trade continues to work in the trader's favor without losing it from a minor price reduction.

How to Construct a Bracketed Trade

Because every trading platform works differently, there are variations in the way a bracketed trade is constructed. However, your brokerage employs a staff of customer support personnel who are more than happy to walk clients through these processes. For example, you may want to know how to set up one or more order closing triggers that are based on a price, a percentage, or perhaps a trailing stop. Once you learn how to use your trading platform, you will be able to save your trade setups as templates. If you are able to save your bracketed trades, stop losses, and profit targets as templates, you can recall the templates you like over and over. Using tried and true templates can also eliminates costly setup errors.

For example, a short vertical credit spread can be set up and submitted with a good till cancelled (GTC) limit order that triggers when the vertical spread's Mark value drops by perhaps 66%. A long call might use a template that is set to trigger when the call achieves a profit of 66%. Templates automate the trading process, save time, and as mentioned, eliminate errors. When a saved template is used, both the trade and the accompanying closing order are placed on the order bar with a click of the mouse. Saved templates can be reused over and over for a variety of option trading strategies.

Using Risk Graphs

Most long-time options traders examine risk graphs, also called *risk profiles,* prior to submitting new option trade setups. Risk graphs show traders how their option trade responds to price changes in the underlying equity. They also plot the theoretical time value. In addition, risk graphs show a trade's potential loss versus its potential profit. Being able to compare a trade's profit to loss potential quickly tells the trader whether the trade is worth the risk. Many traders look for a 2:1 profit-to-loss ratio before they enter a trade.

An example of a risk graph for a long call on Boeing stock, symbol BA, is shown first. Figure 7-1 shows a trade setup to buy a 205 BA long call. The corresponding risk graph is shown in Figure 7-2. The risk graph shows how an increase in the price of BA to $280 returns $35,000 in premium income.

Figure 7-1. A Long Call Shown on an Option Chain.

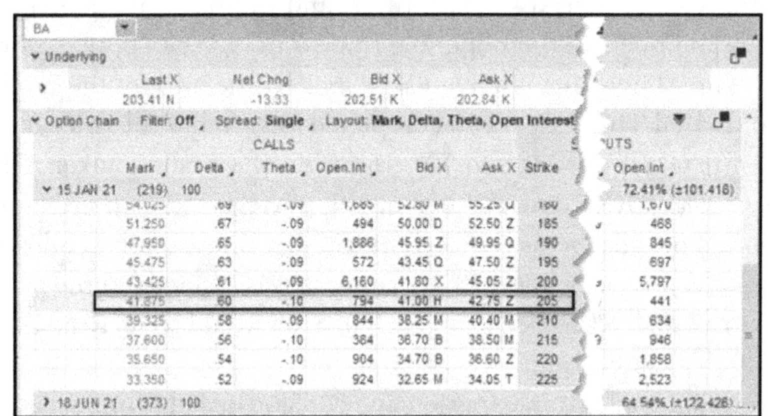

BA

Underlying

Last X	Net Chng	Bid X	Ask X
203.41 N	-13.33	202.51 K	202.84 K

Option Chain Filter: Off Spread: Single Layout: Mark, Delta, Theta, Open Interest

	CALLS						PUTS
Mark	Delta	Theta	Open.Int	Bid X	Ask X	Strike	Open.Int
15 JAN 21 (219) 100							72.41% (±101.418)
54.025	.69	-.09	1,665	52.80 M	55.25 Q	180	1,670
51.250	.67	-.09	494	50.00 D	52.50 Z	185	468
47.950	.65	-.09	1,886	45.95 Z	49.95 Q	190	845
45.475	.63	-.09	572	43.45 Q	47.50 Z	195	697
43.425	.61	-.09	6,160	41.80 X	45.05 Z	200	5,797
41.875	.60	-.10	794	41.00 H	42.75 Z	205	441
39.325	.58	-.09	844	38.25 M	40.40 M	210	634
37.600	.56	-.10	384	36.70 B	38.50 M	215	946
35.650	.54	-.10	904	34.70 B	36.60 Z	220	1,858
33.350	.52	-.09	924	32.65 M	34.05 T	225	2,523
18 JUN 21 (373) 100							64.54% (±122.426)

Figure 7-2. The Long Call Risk Graph.

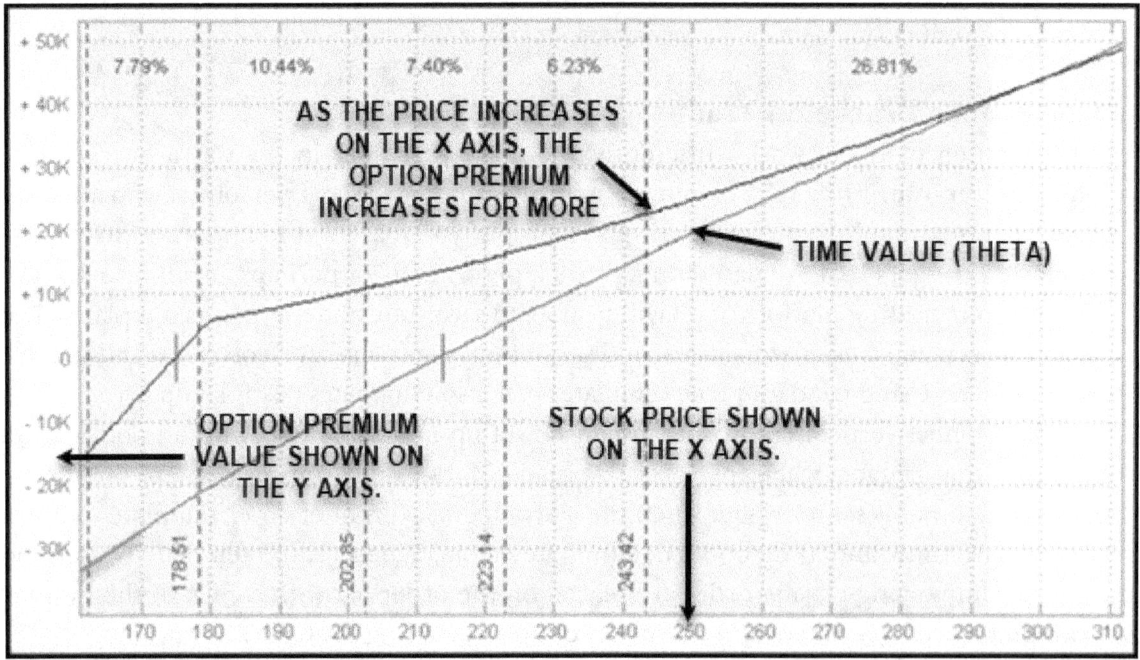

An example of an option chain and risk graph for an iron condor is next. Recall how the iron condor combines a bull put vertical spread and a bear call vertical spread. The iron condor is shown on an option

chain in figure 7-3. The iron condor's risk graph is shown in figure 7-4. The fact that it resembles a big bird with wings is probably where the name condor originated. If ten iron condor options are sold on Delta Airlines stock, symbol DAL, and the DAL stock price remains between $26 and $41, the iron condor returns approximately $900.

Figure 7-3. An Iron Condor Shown on an Option Chain.

DAL

Last X	Net Chng	Bid X	Ask X	Size	Volume	Open	High	Low
31.64 N	-2.53	30.90 P	30.91 Q	9 x 9	89,179,413	32.24	32.99	29.76g

Option Chain Filter: Off Spread: Single Layout: Mark, Delta, Theta, Open Interest

17 JUL 20 (37) 100 — 99.60% (±8.382)

CALLS							PUTS					
Mark	Delta	Theta	Open.Int	Bid X	Ask X	Strike	Bid X	Ask X	Mark	Delta	Theta	Open.Int
8.750	.79	-.05	867	8.40 X	9.10 X	24	.82 X	.89 B	.855	-.16	-.03	88
7.725	.78	-.05	1,323	7.60 N	7.85 X	25	1.04 X	1.10 P	1.070	-.19	-.03	1,311
7.025	.74	-.05	3,037	6.55 X	7.60 X	26	1.10 X	1.45 X	1.275	-.22	-.03	848
6.750	.71	-.08	2,837	6.25 X	7.25 X	27	1.60 X	1.81 X	1.705	-.27	-.04	1,041
5.725	.68	-.05	1,125	5.60 X	5.85 Q	28	1.99 Z	2.09 Q	2.040	-.31	-.04	782
5.125	.64	-.05	552	5.05 X	5.20 Q	29	2.39 B	2.48 P	2.435	-.36	-.04	337
4.575	.60	-.05	3,742	4.50 X	4.65 B	30	2.85 B	2.95 Q	2.900	-.40	-.04	1,578
4.075	.56	-.05	600	4.00 B	4.15 Q	31	3.35 X	3.50 X	3.425	-.45	-.04	513
3.625	.52	-.05	7,618	3.55 B	3.70 Q	32	3.90 X	4.20 X	4.050	-.49	-.05	529
3.275	.49	-.05	1,479	3.20 Q	3.35 Q	33	4.50 Q	4.65 B	4.575	-.54	-.04	948
2.850	.45	-.05	276	2.75 Q	2.95 B	34	5.15 X	5.30 Q	5.225	-.58	-.04	131
2.575	.42	-.05	6,566	2.52 X	2.63 Q	35	5.80 Q	6.00 Q	5.900	-.63	-.04	919
2.290	.38	-.05	619	2.24 Q	2.34 Q	36	6.55 X	6.80 X	6.675	-.66	-.04	94
2.030	.35	-.05	11,084	1.92 Q	2.14 Q	37	7.30 B	7.45 B	7.375	-.70	-.04	10,028
1.825	.32	-.05	1,049	1.78 X	1.87 B	38	8.05 Q	8.25 Q	8.150	-.74	-.03	5
1.590	.29	-.05	62	1.50 X	1.68 Q	39	8.70 X	9.30 X	9.000	-.78	-.03	112
1.455	.27	-.04	8,670	1.41 Q	1.50 B	40	9.70 Q	10.85 X	10.275	-.74	-.04	128
1.290	.25	-.04	398	1.15 X	1.43 X	41	10.05 X	11.45 X	10.750	-.80	-.03	95
1.160	.23	-.04	65	1.08 X	1.24 X	42	11.25 X	11.70 P	11.475	-.84	-.02	1
1.075	.21	-.04	152	1.00 X	1.15 B	43	12.30 Q	13.10 X	12.700	-.81	-.03	5

Position

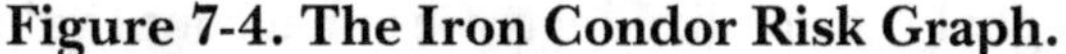

Figure 7-4. The Iron Condor Risk Graph.

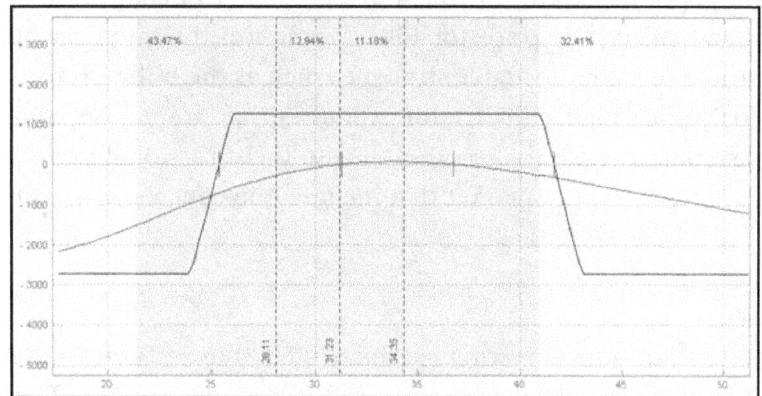

The Trading Routine

Most savvy traders treat their trading regime like a business because that is precisely what it is. They are disciplined and they establish a daily routine. They also create and use a series of watch lists of financial indexes, certain futures, and popular stocks. Many use investing services to assist in vetting and selecting stocks. These traders also examine the corresponding price charts to determine the current market bias for the related market sectors. And they monitor the underlying financial indexes including the Dow, NASDAQ, S&P 500, and the Russell 2000 to gage the current market sentiment. Many examine the three major financial index futures contracts both at night and in the early morning. This includes the Dow, Nasdaq, S&P 500, and Russell 2000, symbols /YM, /NQ, /ES, and /RTY. The price rallies and drops that occur in these indexes provide insight to the prevailing trading sentiment. But don't rely entirely on the overnight price swings, because they are not reliable. The market can and does change quickly. Looking at the overnight futures trading is a beginning, but it's not the end of the story. It does permit traders to consider the futures that fit the current mood and perhaps some of their own working trades on the financial indexes. Traders can even consider a handful of symbols and option strategies that fit the early morning market bias.

While a trader may have a good plan that fits his/her market observations, many experienced traders DO NOT trade during the first and last trading hour of the day, which opens at 9:30 a.m. and closes at 4:00 p.m. EST. They wait for the initial trading volatility to settle down into a more predictable trend once the opening volatility is over. Some traders also avoid trading during the lunch period when there is a slowdown in trading volume.

Trading Small Accounts

Those traders with limited account sizes of perhaps a few thousand dollars most often do better as short-term "premium collectors." They concentrate on selling credit spreads including bull puts, bear calls, iron condors, and perhaps a few covered calls if they happen to own the covering stock within their accounts.

These traders can also buy call or put options on inexpensive stocks and ETFs when the price charts and momentum studies predict that a strong price rally or drop is about to occur. Once their trade becomes profitable, they close these trades for profit and do it again. Making frequent trades on short-term options and taking small but reasonable profits in the 50% to 60% range can be quite rewarding. This high-frequency trading, sometimes referred to as "churning," can rapidly accrue excellent returns in premium income. The trader's goal is to realize increases in account value. Churning can achieve more profit than simply letting options expire worthless. It's possible to make three trades that each return profits of 50% rather than holding one trade for 100% profit over the same period.

Consider selecting three or four affordable strategies such as the bull put, bear call, and iron condor. Look for affordable stocks with high daily trading volumes that are accompanies by directional price moves. Consider buying a put or a call that corresponds to the directional move. And learn how to construct and send bracketed trades to the market that include one cancels other (OCO) profit targets and protective stops.

Trading Large Accounts

Only those traders who have account sizes that exceed $100,000 to $125,000 and have been granted the highest option trading level by their brokerages can sell uncovered options. These traders can make a fortune by selling high-priced index options on the NASDAQ 100 (NDX), the S&P 500 (SPX), and the Russell 2000 (RUT).

As discussed previously, many traders who are permitted to sell uncovered short puts, short calls, and short strangles often sell a high frequency of short-term options that exist roughly two standard deviations OTM (95.5% OTM). And they choose strikes between a Delta .04 and .06 that expire in one to three days. Their trades are reasonably safe because they initially exist far OTM with short times till expiration. Although this practice usually prevents these trades from becoming ITM, when the market begins to move against them, they take action. These responses were described at some length early in this section. Also recall that the NDX and SPX have European-style expirations. The European expiration style gives the trader time to either close or roll his or her position before the account is decimated.

While traders with small accounts are limited to the number and the size of the trades they can make, those with large accounts may have several dozen trades working at the same time. Although this diversification spreads their risk, it takes more time to enter, manage, and close that many trades. This can be avoided when the trader includes GTC profit targets and stop losses with each trade. But if these are not included when the order is entered, things can become tense. This is particularly true when the entire market makes a strong rally or drop, because managing a few dozen individual trades before they become exercised can be stressful. If the entire market is dropping, a trader may have to close a dozen or more short puts and bull put spreads to prevent them from becoming ITM and assigned. The opposite is true when the entire market experiences a strong rally and the trader must close several short calls and bear call vertical spreads.

Every experienced trader knows that the market can be fickle; it can turn quickly. So be prepared. Learn how to manage your working trades. Consider the use of bracketed trades. And be sure you know when it is time to close a losing position. And always consider a salvage operation by rolling a failing position. It's is definitely a part of your trading business.

Rolling Out, Up, and Down

Rolling options trades have been briefly described. Here, the discussion about rolling trades is expanded. It is the author's hope that rolling will become a normal part of your trade management and salvage routine. First, let's discuss rolling out in in time.

Rolling Out in Time

Several days ago, you traded a diagonal bull call spread. The market volatility was moderate, and the option premium was ideal for the bull call strategy. Your trade includes ten long-term ATM long calls that expire in nine months and ten short OTM calls eight strikes above and safely OTM. The ten short calls expire in three weeks. Based on the current ATR(14) — the 14-day average price range — you expect the short puts to remain safely OTM through expiration. You've included a GTC limit order that is set to close the short puts when the premium of the short calls drops by 65% — your profit.

An unplanned rally in the underlying stock moves your ten short calls within a few dollars of becoming ITM. Although your long calls are now ITM and profitable, you decide to hold the long calls for even more profit and roll the short calls to a later option expiration date and to a strike price that is farther OTM. To accomplish this, you place a rolling order on the short calls. This sets up a calendar spread with a buy-to-close order on your current short call and simultaneously sells an equal number of options five strikes farther OTM that expire in three more weeks. This returns a small credit of about 20-cents per share for a total credit of $200 for ten short calls—the difference between the cost of the buy-to-close order for your ten short call options and the farther OTM short calls that you are rolling into. This roll salvages the trade and provides the long calls with more time to return even more profit as they move deeper ITM with a rise in the price of the underlying stock. It also returns another $200 in premium from the sale of the ten short calls.

This roll example not only prevented the short calls from being exercised, it returned additional income. This may not always be the case, as there are defensive rolls that are used to minimize a potential loss. The short put trade on the SPX described earlier in this chapter was an example of a defensive roll that reduced a loss rather than achieving a profitable outcome. So don't expect that rolling is a magic bullet. Instead, it is a trade maintenance tool. You may wish to test your rolling skills in paper trading. Set up a short put, short call, or a vertical spread and practice a few rolls until you understand how they work when rolling into a different strike price and a later expiration date.

Rolling Down and Out

Rolling down is the inverse of rolling up. It is down rather than up because, unlike the short call options, rolling down is used with short put options. The rolling dynamics are identical, except rolling a put down and farther OTM and out to a later expiration date is used when the price of the underlying stock drops rather when it rallies. Be sure to use simulation when practicing these techniques on both the call and put sides of your option chains.

Legging into Option Trades

Consider a vertical spread as an option strategy that has two *legs*. For example, the bull call spread includes a long option leg at a strike that's either ATM or very close to it and an OTM short call option leg several strikes above. The iron condor has four legs. You can see an iron condor on an option chain in figure 7-3.

It is more difficult to fill multiple-leg trades like iron condors than it is to fill single-leg option trades. For example, buying ten long calls at the same strike price may fill within a few seconds, while trying to fill an iron condor or a three-leg butterfly may take more than an hour, or even expire unfilled at the end of the trading day. (The butterfly strategy is briefly discussed below and included in a trade example later in Section 8.)

To avoid a delay in order fulfillment, many traders break their strategies apart to expedite order execution. This method is referred to as *legging in*, which is well-suited for use with a brokerage that does not charge a brokerage fee for each trade.

Legging into a vertical bull put spread is accomplished by first buying the long put and then selling the short put above. Legging into a long call butterfly, which includes two long call wings at strike prices on either side of a central short call body, is accomplished by:

1. Buying the long calls that comprise the bottom wing.
2. When the long calls fill, simultaneously selling the short calls that comprise the body and the long calls that comprise the top wing.

One experienced trader calls this method her "caterpillars and butterflies." She begins by buying the long call options at the lowest strike price. Once filled, she then sells the short and long calls above to complete the butterfly trade.

Another option trader frequently sells one-day bull put options on the SPX index. She begins in the morning on expiration day, which is a Monday, Wednesday, or Friday. After the market has been open for 15 minutes, She locates the SPX put strike that has a Delta value of .05. Then she buys an OTM call that is $50 below. (The long OTM call reduces the use of account margin.) Once the long SPX put options order fill, she sells the same number of put options at the.05 Delta strike. If the short put remains safely OTM, she lets this trade expire at the end of the current trading day. This eliminates the usual concern about overnight risk.

According to the trader, this one-day SPX spread succeeds approximately 80% of the time. It can also include a protective stop to prevent the short puts from becoming ITM. Because indexes have frequent price transients, Mark-triggered stops often occur prematurely. Therefore, many traders prefer to use Delta-triggered stops which are more stable. Consider Delta-stop values around .10 to .20.

Section 7 Questions

1. What is a benefit of "momentum trading" versus buy-and-hold trading? ______________________ ______________________________
2. Why are uncovered, or "naked" short options vulnerable? ____________ ____________________ ____________________________________.
3. Why is it safer to trade European expiration-style index options? ______ ____________________ ____________________________________.
4. What is the VIX and why is it closely watched by traders? ____________ ____________________ ____________________________________.
5. Why do some traders sell short-term put and/or call options that exist at strike prices that are two standard deviations OTM? ________________________ ____________________________ __________________________.
6. A bracketed trade is created by adding a _____________ target and a protective _________________.
7. Why do option traders examine risk graphs? ______________________ ____________________ ____________________________________
8. The iron condor trade combines a short vertical put spread, called a bull put, and a short vertical call spread, called a ___________ __________.
9. Option traders with small accounts often focus on collecting option premium by trading a few different _____________ spreads
10. Uncovered short options are traded more often by option traders that have __________ brokerage accounts.
11. Why do option traders roll working trades to a farther OTM strike price with a later expiration date? ____ _____________.
12. Why do traders leg into multi-strike option trades? ______________________________________ ___________________________.

SECTION 8
OPTIONS TRADING PRACTICE

What You Will Learn

1. The steps used to simulate option trading (paper trading)
2. How to use price charts to develop a trading bias
3. Choosing a viable option strategy to match your trading bias
4. How to set up bullish, bearish, and neutral trades on option chains
5. Why it's better to "leg into" some multiple-strike option strategies
6. The use of stops and profit targets to manage option trades
7. Knowing when and why to keep or exit a working trade
8. When to use bracketed trades and trailing stops
9. Examining and understanding the use of risk graphs
10. Understanding how to use the option Greeks when setting up a trade
11. How to use the IV% (±$) with your option trades
12. The increase in risk that exists with AM-expiration options
13. How to set up and place single and multiple-strike option strategies

Trading in Simulation (*Paper Trading*)

If you are new to options, you should consider learning how to trade in simulation, also called *paper trading*. Most trading platforms support simulation. If your brokerage does not support this feature, you may wish to find one that does and open a small account. Some brokerages, such as Schwab-TD Ameritrade, permit the use of unfunded accounts for evaluation purposes. This provides access to the thinkorswim trading platform.

Be aware that simulated trade orders usually fill when they otherwise might not fill in the live market. As most traders know, the bid and ask prices are constantly changing and orders must often be adjusted to execute. Hence, simulations can be misleading with respect to order fulfilment. But the use of simulation for evaluating an option strategy is certainly useful. They must be set up, submitted, and monitored in the same way as if trading in the live market.

This chapter includes several option strategies that you may wish to test in simulation. This will require you to find a stock that matches the sample stock in value and price direction. Locating an appropriate bullish, neutral, or bearish stock also provides an important learning experience.

Compare price charts so that your simulated trade is similar to the suggested bullish, bearish, or neutral market bias contained in the corresponding exercise. Then you can test the trade in simulation by entering the option positions on an option chain. Be sure to examine your setup on a risk graph. Then submit it to see the trade's outcome.

Each practice session begins with a tradeable stock. This includes looking at the stock on a price chart, which is precisely what you should do when trading with real money. When you begin entering live trades of your own, be sure to determine the company's earnings per share (EPS) and the stock's current price trend and trading momentum. Also look at the ATR(14) and IV% to see how it influences option premium values. Finally, you'll use one or more option chains to select and set up one or more option trades.

Using a Watch List

Watch list development and use was described in Section 3, and a typical watch list was illustrated in figure 3-1. Many traders create multiple watch lists that include stocks and ETFs that belong to a particular market segment, such as including those symbols related to the travel industry (airlines, cruise lines, hotel chains, and casinos), another for pharmaceutical companies, and perhaps a third for energy exploration, production, storage, and transportation. Your watch lists can be linked to the corresponding price charts and option chains. Linking lets you select a symbol and then jump directly to the corresponding price charts and option chains. This eliminates the need to type the symbols when moving from one window to another. Except for searching watch lists to find a tradable stock or ETF, the remainder of this section guides you through the steps used by most experienced option traders to:

- Search a watch list to find an option trading opportunity.
- Examine the price chart to find or confirm a trading opportunity.
- Develop a bullish, bearish, or neutral bias.
- Examine the values within the corresponding option chains.
- Select a compatible option trading strategy.
- Configure and submit a trade order to the market.
- If filled, monitor the trade through expiration.
- Exit the trade or let it expire for profit, close it to minimize a loss, or roll and adjust the trade for a better outcome.

Exercise 1. The Covered Call

The covered call was introduced in Section 4. As mentioned, this is often the first option strategy that is attempted by investors who regularly buy and sell stocks and ETFs. They see selling one covered call for each 100 shares of stock held within their brokerage accounts as an opportunity to earn extra income.

The primary goal of the covered call is to collect additional income from the premium collected when sold. Covered calls are often sold multiple times for additional income in option premium. If the stock price rallies to the strike price of the short call, the trader may decide to close the short call and sell the underlying stock for the profit gained from the increase in the price of the stock. If the stock price happens to drop, the profit from the short call offsets a portion of the loss in stock value.

According to the trading rules described in Section 6, traders who understand how options work sell covered call options that expire within a matter of weeks and at strike prices that are safely OTM. Limiting the time to expiration can also reduce the time the price of the underlying stock has to increase sufficiently to reach the strike price of the short calls. To be safe, the option trader usually chooses a call strike price having a Delta .25 value — a 75% probability of remaining OTM through option expiration. As previously mentioned, some traders sell calls at strike prices that are at least one standard deviation (68.27%) OTM. And some traders choose a short call strike price having a Delta .30 value in order to collect a bit more credit, although they increase their risk by 5%.

Instead of owning the covering stock, some traders buy an ATM call for each OTM short call sold. This is called the "poor man's covered call," since buying the calls is much less expensive than buying the stock. This strategy typically combines long-term expiration long calls and short-term expiration short calls. To ultimately break even and move into profit, the short calls must be sold multiple times until the net premium becomes profitable.

Selling an OTM Call for Each 100 Shares of Stock

Because the covered call sells one short call for each 100 shares of stock, the stock completely covers the vulnerability of the short calls in the event they become ITM and are exercised. If exercised, the covering stock is immediately called away from the option seller by the option buyer on the other side of the trade. This is a popular short-term strategy that is used by traders who want to increase their return on a stock they own, particularly a stock that resides within a narrow price range. One OTM short call is sold for each 100 shares of the underlying stock or ETF held in a trading account. To produce additional premium income, some traders combine a bull put vertical spread with the covered call. This illustrates the flexibility offered by options. The bull put strategy is described in detail in Exercise 4.

As suggested above, the short calls are placed at a strike price that is at or very close to a 0.25 Delta value. The covered call setup example places the short call at the $45 strike. Notice the Delta value of .20 — even safer than the recommended .25.

Setup

Stock Symbol: LUV (Southwest Airlines)

Chart Description: Price trending upward with an occasional small price drop and a rally back to the original upward trendline. These pullbacks are called "bull flags."

Trader's Bias: Bullish

IV% or IV Rank; ±Price Movement: 83.92% (±7.604)

Trade Description: Sell 5 Options and receive a credit of $425 less exchange fees when the order fills.

Expiration Selection: Short-term; expires within 7 weeks or less.

Option Values:

Put/Call	*Strike*	*Bid*	*Ask*	*Mark*	*Delta*	*Theta*	*Open Int.*
-5 Calls	$45.00	$0.80	$0.90	$0.85	.20	$-.03	3,020

Figure 8-1. The Covered Call on an Option Chain.

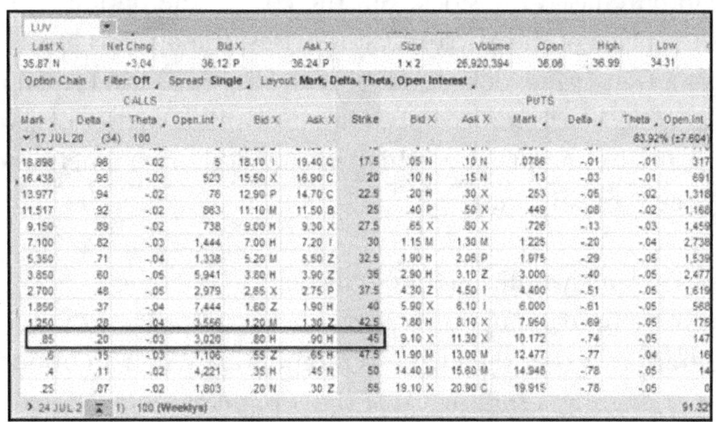

Exercise 8-1 Questions:

1. What is the goal of this trade? ____
2. What is the probability of the $42.50 short puts being ITM when this trade expires? ____________________________
3. If the trader doesn't own the covering stock, what could be substituted in place of the stock? ____.
4. Is this an example of "The Poor Man's Covered Call?" _______________.
5. How much premium will the trader collect by selling five $45 covered calls? ____.
6. How much premium would be received if the $42.50 strike price is used in place of the $45 strike price? ______________________________
7. What happens to this trade's risk if the $42.50 strike is used instead of the $45 strike? ____

Exercise 2. The Long Call

The long call is a bullish option trading strategy that buys one or more call options that expire in 90 days or more. The longer-term reduces the initial loss in daily time value. When buying long call options, the trader prefers a stock with a reasonably low IV%, which contributes to lower premium values when buying the calls.

The trader's bullish bias anticipates an increase in the price of Microsoft stock. The trader's goal is the same as if he/she had purchased the stock. But the cost of the options is slightly less than 12% of the cost of the stock. As the price of the Microsoft stock rises, the options move deeper ITM. If the long call's strike price achieves a Delta value of around .85, the long calls will return an excellent profit. This is especially true when the stock's price rallies substantially within a matter of several days to a few weeks. The increase in the long call's premium value is higher when a shorter timeframe reduces the daily time decay, which is shown by the value of Theta.

The Synthetic Stock—An Extremely Bullish Option Strategy
The long call is considered whenever an option trader sees an upward trending stock that he/she believes will continue its upward trajectory over the next several months. When an option trader is exceptionally confident in a long-term price rally, a slightly OTM short put can be combined with the long ATM call for even more profit. Of course, adding an uncovered short put requires the trader to have the highest option trading permission. Because the long call and the short put both return premium income, this option strategy can be exceptional. But if the trader's bullish bias is wrong, the synthetic stock trade can result in a substantial loss. Like most trades, whether buying stocks or trading options, being wrong can lead to a major financial loss.

For those traders who are not permitted to trade uncovered, or when trading in a rollover IRA or 401K account, an OTM long put can be added several strikes below the short put. This creates a vertical put spread, which is permitted because it eliminates the unlimited risk condition.

Setup

Stock Symbol: MSFT (Microsoft Corporation)

Chart Description: The price has been steadily trending upward for the past several months. The rally is a response to a series of increased quarterly earnings in conjunction with the recent receipt of a billion-dollar governmental cloud computing contract. Except for a few short-term price drops, Microsoft's stock price has consistently rallied back followed by a series of new highs and a return to the original upward trendline. The brief pullbacks are commonly referred to as *bull flags*, which are viewed by many traders as buy signals because they are almost always followed by a series of new highs.

Stock Symbol: MSFT (Microsoft Corporation)
Chart Description: A steady upward price trend with brief pullbacks and returns to the dominant upward trend.
Trader's Bias: Bullish
IV% or IV Rank; ±Price Movement: 35.91% (±56.474)
Buy five call options (Pay a debit).
Expiration Selection: Long-term; expires in 368 days.

Option Values:

Put/Call	*Strike*	*Bid*	*Ask*	*Mark*	*Delta*	*Theta*	*Open Int.*
+5 Calls	$190	$22.30	$22.95	$22.625	.54	$-.03	9319

Figure 8-2. The Long Call on an Option Chain.

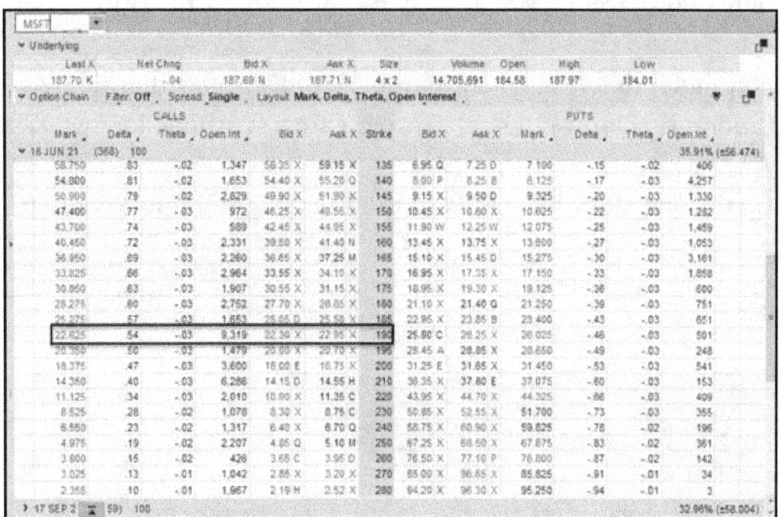

MSFT

Underlying

Last X	Net Chng	Bid X	Ask X	Size	Volume	Open	High	Low
187.70 K	-.04	187.69 N	187.71 N	4 x 2	14,705,691	184.58	187.97	184.01

Option Chain Filter: Off Spread: Single Layout: Mark, Delta, Theta, Open Interest

CALLS							PUTS					
Mark	Delta	Theta	Open.Int	Bid X	Ask X	Strike	Bid X	Ask X	Mark	Delta	Theta	Open.Int
18 JUN 21 (368) 100												35.91% (±56.474)
58.750	.83	-.02	1,347	56.35 X	59.15 X	135	6.95 Q	7.25 D	7.100	-.15	-.02	406
54.800	.81	-.02	1,653	54.40 X	55.20 Q	140	8.00 P	8.25 B	8.125	-.17	-.03	4,257
50.900	.79	-.02	2,829	49.90 X	51.90 X	145	9.15 X	9.50 D	9.325	-.20	-.03	1,330
47.400	.77	-.03	972	46.25 X	48.55 X	150	10.45 X	10.60 X	10.625	-.22	-.03	1,282
43.700	.74	-.03	589	42.45 X	44.95 X	155	11.90 W	12.25 W	12.075	-.25	-.03	1,459
40.450	.72	-.03	2,331	39.50 X	41.40 N	160	13.45 X	13.75 X	13.600	-.27	-.03	1,053
36.950	.69	-.03	2,260	36.65 X	37.25 M	165	15.10 X	15.45 D	15.275	-.30	-.03	3,161
33.825	.66	-.03	2,964	33.55 X	34.10 X	170	16.95 X	17.35 X	17.150	-.33	-.03	1,858
30.850	.63	-.03	1,907	30.55 X	31.15 X	175	18.95 X	19.30 X	19.125	-.36	-.03	600
28.275	.60	-.03	2,752	27.70 X	28.85 X	180	21.10 X	21.40 Q	21.250	-.39	-.03	751
25.275	.57	-.03	1,653	25.05 D	25.50 X	185	22.95 X	23.85 B	23.400	-.43	-.03	651
22.625	.54	-.03	9,319	22.30 X	22.95 X	190	25.80 C	26.25 X	26.025	-.46	-.03	501
20.350	.50	-.03	1,479	20.00 X	20.70 X	195	28.45 A	28.85 X	28.650	-.49	-.03	248
18.375	.47	-.03	3,600	18.00 E	18.75 X	200	31.25 E	31.65 X	31.450	-.53	-.03	541
14.350	.40	-.03	6,286	14.15 D	14.55 H	210	36.35 X	37.80 E	37.075	-.60	-.03	153
11.125	.34	-.03	2,010	10.90 X	11.35 C	220	43.95 X	44.70 X	44.325	-.66	-.03	409
8.525	.28	-.02	1,078	8.30 X	8.75 C	230	50.85 X	52.55 X	51.700	-.73	-.03	355
6.550	.23	-.02	1,317	6.40 X	6.70 Q	240	58.75 X	60.90 X	59.825	-.78	-.02	196
4.975	.19	-.02	2,207	4.85 Q	5.10 M	250	67.25 X	68.50 X	67.875	-.83	-.02	361
3.800	.15	-.02	426	3.65 C	3.95 D	260	76.50 X	77.10 P	76.800	-.87	-.02	142
3.025	.13	-.01	1,042	2.85 X	3.20 X	270	85.00 X	86.65 X	85.825	-.91	-.01	34
2.355	.10	-.01	1,967	2.19 H	2.52 X	280	94.20 X	96.30 X	95.250	-.94	-.01	3
17 SEP 2 (59) 100												32.96% (±58.004)

Exercise 8-2 Questions:

1. What is the goal of this trade? ____ ___________.
2. If the trader bought 500 shares of MSFT stock rather than 5 call options, how much would the stock cost? ______________.
3. Approximately how much must the trader pay for 5 MSFT 190 call options? ______________.
4. What could you add to this long call strategy to create a synthetic long stock strategy? _______ ______________________________.
5. Why can't a synthetic long stock be traded in qualified retirement accounts? ______________ ______________________________
6. How could the short put be protected to limit its risk? ______________________________ _________.

Exercise 3. The Long Put

The Boeing Company, symbol BA, is the world's largest aerospace company. Unfortunately, Boeing has been experiencing major problems from lawsuits and regulatory agency penalties. The FAA required Boeing to shut down the assembly line used to produce their top selling 737 Max aircraft coupled to the layoff of thousands of production workers. Moreover, Boeing's airline customers have suspended scheduled payments and cancelled orders for aircraft purchases until Boeing's problems are resolved and the 737 Max has been recertified to resume passenger service. As a result of these issues, the price of Boeing's stock has been in free-fall.

Stock Symbol: BA (The Boeing Company)

Chart Description: A steady downward price trend due to the loss of 737 Max aircraft sales, the suspension of scheduled payments, and related lawsuits.

Trader's Bias: The trader has a strong bearish bias and anticipates a major price drop in the price of Boing's stock.

IV% or IV Rank; ±Price Movement: 33.67% (±6.009)

Trade Description: Buy five 185 puts and pay a debit of $39.75 per share, or $1,987.50 for all 500 shares when this option trade fills.

Expiration Selection: Long-term; expires in 216 days or approximately 7 months.

Option Values:

Put/Call	*Strike*	*Bid*	*Ask*	*Mark*	*Delta*	*Theta*	*Open Int.*
+5 Puts	$185	$39.45	$40.05	$39.75	-.37	$-.09	456

Figure 8-3. The Long Put on the Option Chain.

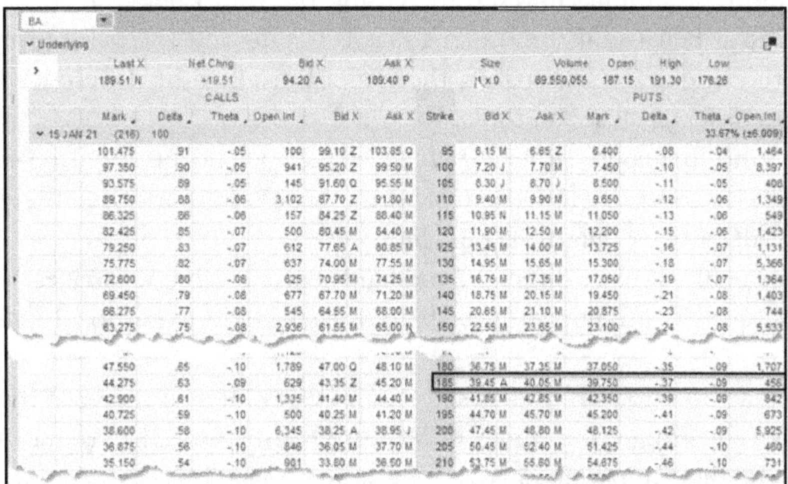

BA

Underlying

Last X	Net Chng	Bid X	Ask X	Size	Volume	Open	High	Low
189.51 N	+19.51	94.20 A	189.40 P	1 x 0	89,550,055	187.15	191.30	178.26

CALLS							PUTS					
Mark	Delta	Theta	Open Int	Bid X	Ask X	Strike	Bid X	Ask X	Mark	Delta	Theta	Open Int
15 JAN 21 (216) 100											33.67% (±6.009)	
101.475	.91	-.05	100	99.10 Z	103.85 Q	95	6.15 M	6.65 Z	6.400	-.08	-.04	1,464
97.350	.90	-.05	941	95.20 Z	99.50 M	100	7.20 J	7.70 M	7.450	-.10	-.05	8,397
93.575	.89	-.05	145	91.60 Q	95.55 M	105	8.30 J	8.70 J	8.500	-.11	-.05	408
89.750	.88	-.06	3,102	87.70 Z	91.80 M	110	9.40 M	9.90 M	9.650	-.12	-.06	1,349
86.325	.86	-.06	157	84.25 Z	88.40 M	115	10.95 N	11.15 M	11.050	-.13	-.06	549
82.425	.85	-.07	500	80.45 M	84.40 M	120	11.90 M	12.50 M	12.200	-.15	-.06	1,423
79.250	.83	-.07	612	77.65 A	80.85 M	125	13.45 M	14.00 M	13.725	-.16	-.07	1,131
75.775	.82	-.07	637	74.00 M	77.55 M	130	14.95 M	15.65 M	15.300	-.18	-.07	5,366
72.600	.80	-.08	625	70.95 M	74.25 M	135	16.75 M	17.35 M	17.050	-.19	-.07	1,364
69.450	.79	-.08	677	67.70 M	71.20 M	140	18.75 M	20.15 M	19.450	-.21	-.08	1,403
66.275	.77	-.08	545	64.55 M	68.00 M	145	20.65 M	21.10 M	20.875	-.23	-.08	744
63.275	.75	-.08	2,936	61.55 M	65.00 N	150	22.55 M	23.65 M	23.100	-.24	-.08	5,533
47.550	.65	-.10	1,789	47.00 Q	48.10 M	180	36.75 M	37.35 M	37.050	-.35	-.09	1,707
44.275	.63	-.09	629	43.35 Z	45.20 M	185	39.45 A	40.05 M	39.750	-.37	-.09	456
42.900	.61	-.10	1,335	41.40 M	44.40 M	190	41.85 M	42.85 M	42.350	-.39	-.09	842
40.725	.59	-.10	500	40.25 M	41.20 M	195	44.70 M	45.70 M	45.200	-.41	-.09	673
38.600	.58	-.10	6,345	38.25 A	38.95 J	200	47.45 M	48.80 M	48.125	-.42	-.09	5,925
36.875	.56	-.10	846	36.05 M	37.70 M	205	50.45 M	52.40 M	51.425	-.44	-.10	460
35.150	.54	-.10	901	33.80 M	36.50 M	210	53.75 M	55.60 M	54.675	-.46	-.10	731

Exercise 8-3 Questions:

1. How can put options be used when the price of a stock, ETF, or financial index is expected to drop over an extended period? ________________________________.
2. What does the trader expect the 185 strike price to do over the life of this trade? ________________________________.
3. What should the trader do if the price of Boeing stock begins to rally? ________________________________.
4. If the trader buys ten contracts and the Theta value is .09, how much value is expected to exit this option trade today? __________ ________________________________.

Exercise 4. The Bull Put (Vertical Spread)

The bull put vertical spread was described in substantial detail in Section 4. There, you learned it is a bullish strategy that expects the price of the underlying equity to either rally or move sideways. This option strategy includes a short put above a long put that's typically two or more strikes farther OTM. The short put returns more premium than the long put below because the short put is closer to the money with a higher Delta value. The number of strikes between the short and long puts, called the *strike width*, can be increased to collect more premium. However, increasing the width between the short and long strikes also increases risk. This is because if the trader's bias is wrong and the price of the underlying equity drops through both the long and short strikes, the trader must pay the difference in premium between the two strike prices in order to close the trade.

If both the short and long puts expire ITM, the trader would be required to pay the difference between strike prices. Five contracts (500 shares) with a $5.00 strike width between the short and long puts would cost the trader $2,500 plus brokerage fees.

If the price unexpectedly reverses direction and lands between the two strikes, the short put becomes subject to being exercised, which requires the seller of the short put to pay for the stock at the short put's strike price.

Seasoned option traders who sell options seek high IV% values to increase the corresponding premium values. This also encourages the trader to be more conservative, i.e., reduce risk, by reducing the strike width between the short and long puts.

Stock Symbol: SPY (ETF for the S&P 500 Financial Index)

Chart Description: Price trending upward with small price drops and recoveries commonly referred to as "bull flags."

Trader's Bias: Bullish

IV% or IV Rank; ±Price Movement: 33.67% (±6.009)

Trade Description: Buy ten contracts (Collect more credit for selling Pay a Debit) and Sell ten (Receive a Credit): Receive a net $3.00 per share credit by selling ten $308 puts and buying ten $305 puts for a total credit of $470 less a few dollars in exchange fees.

Expiration Selection: This trade expires at the end of the day; this limits the amount of time that the price of the SPY has to move against the $308 short strike with its.23 Delta value. This is especially true when the VIX volatility index is below 20.

Option Values:

Put/Call	*Strike*	*Bid*	*Ask*	*Mark*	*Delta*	*Theta*	*Open Int.*
-10 Puts	$308	$1.05	$1.08	$1.065	.23	$-.60	3,687
+10 Puts	$305	$.59	$.60	$.595	-.14	$-.46	10,440

Figure 8-4. The Bull Put Vertical Spread on an Option Chain.

SPY

Underlying

Last X	Net Chng	Bid X	Ask X	Size	Volume	Open	High	Low
313.60 Q	+6.55	313.58 Q	313.59 P	16 x 1	84,608,815	315.48	315.64	307.67

CALLS Mark	Delta	Theta	Open.Int	Bid X	Ask X	Strike	PUTS Bid X	Ask X	Mark	Delta	Theta	Open.Int
17 JUN 20 (1) 100 (Weeklys)												33.67% (±6.009)
9.945	.89	-.31	4,653	9.82 Q	10.07 Q	304	.47 X	.49 P	.480	-.12	-.41	7,266
9.100	.86	-.39	7,456	9.01 P	9.19 Q	305	.59 P	.60 P	.595	-.14	-.46	10,440
8.240	.84	-.48	6,276	8.14 P	8.34 Q	306	.71 O	.73 Z	.720	-.17	-.50	4,453
7.385	.81	-.52	11,377	7.32 P	7.45 Q	307	.87 N	.89 P	.880	-.20	-.55	5,238
6.555	.77	-.58	8,644	6.49 Q	6.62 Q	308	1.05 O	1.08 P	1.065	-.23	-.60	3,687
5.810	.73	-.66	11,534	5.74 P	5.86 Q	309	1.28 P	1.30 P	1.290	-.27	-.64	4,148
5.070	.69	-.72	15,762	5.04 Q	5.10 P	310	1.55 N	1.57 P	1.560	-.31	-.68	2,382
4.715	.67	-.75	3,349	4.69 P	4.74 P	310.5	1.68 P	1.71 P	1.695	-.34	-.69	861
4.355	.64	-.77	5,620	4.33 P	4.38 P	311	1.86 E	1.87 P	1.865	-.36	-.71	1,880
4.035	.62	-.79	1,979	4.01 Z	4.06 P	311.5	2.01 P	2.04 P	2.025	-.39	-.71	788
3.715	.59	-.80	4,309	3.69 P	3.74 P	312	2.19 N	2.22 P	2.205	-.41	-.72	1,753
3.410	.56	-.81	4,106	3.39 Q	3.43 P	312.5	2.38 N	2.42 P	2.400	-.44	-.72	371
3.120	.54	-.82	5,888	3.10 P	3.14 P	313	2.59 P	2.63 P	2.610	-.46	-.73	1,558
2.840	.51	-.82	3,004	2.82 P	2.86 P	313.5	2.81 P	2.85 P	2.830	-.49	-.72	876
2.570	.48	-.81	3,251	2.55 P	2.59 N	314	3.04 N	3.08 P	3.060	-.52	-.72	1,010
2.320	.45	-.79	3,455	2.30 P	2.34 N	314.5	3.29 P	3.33 P	3.310	-.55	-.71	900
2.080	.42	-.77	9,722	2.07 P	2.09 P	315	3.55 P	3.60 Z	3.575	-.58	-.69	2,427
1.860	.39	-.75	2,602	1.85 P	1.87 Z	315.5	3.82 P	3.88 Z	3.850	-.61	-.68	818
1.660	.36	-.72	3,549	1.64 Z	1.68 P	316	4.10 P	4.18 P	4.140	-.63	-.66	3,043
1.470	.34	-.68	3,962	1.46 P	1.48 P	316.5	4.43 P	4.49 P	4.460	-.66	-.64	1,054
1.290	.31	-.64	5,622	1.28 P	1.30 I	317	4.73 P	4.81 Z	4.770	-.69	-.61	3,235
1.125	.28	-.60	2,299	1.11 P	1.14 W	317.5	5.06 Q	5.20 Q	5.130	-.71	-.59	539
.990	.25	-.56	5,116	.98 N	1.00 Q	318	5.40 Q	5.58 Q	5.490	-.74	-.56	1,181
.865	.23	-.52	5,767	.86 P	.87 P	318.5	5.79 Q	5.95 P	5.870	-.76	-.53	462
.745	.21	-.47	5,628	.74 P	.75 Q	319	6.16 Q	6.35 Q	6.255	-.79	-.50	772
[illegible]55	.19	-.43	4,212	.65 P	.66 W	319.5	6.56 Q	6.73 Q	6.645	-.81	-.47	244

Exercise 8-4 Questions:

1. How many days exist until this trade expires? ______________.
2. If the trader successfully sells ten bull put spreads, about how much premium is received? ____________________.
3. Based on the Delta value of the short call, what is the probability of this bull put spread remaining OTM through expiration? ________%
4. If the price of the SPY ETF drops below the $305 long put, how much will this trade lose? ____ ________________________.
5. What can be done to the strike width to increase the amount of premium this trade can earn? ________________________________
6. How is this trade's risk affected if its strike width is increased? _______ __________________ ______________.
7. Explain the reason for your answer to question 6. _____________ ______________________ ________________________?

Exercise 5. The Long Straddle

A long straddle is a costly debit spread that buys a long-term call and a long-term put. The strategy is called a straddle because the put and the call options use the same strike price, i.e., they straddle the strike column. A long-term expiration option chain in excess of 90 days is typically used to provide ample time for the price of the underlying stock to make a large directional move, either up or down.

Once the trader determines that a sustained directional price move has begun, the losing option is closed for what value in premium remains and the appreciating option is retained as it moves deeper ITM and increases in value. The trader would determine when to sell the remaining long call or put when sufficient profit is returned. This could be a 50% to 70% increase. However, the trader would not want to hold the long option so long as to permit the daily time value (Theta) to begin reducing the premium value as the long option begins to approach expiration.

Stock Symbol: BA
Chart Description: Price moving sideways (called *basing*) with small rallies and drops. Expect a strong directional breakout.
Trader's Bias: Presently neutral.
IV% or IV Rank; ±Price Movement: 76.26% (±$103.136)
Trade Description: Buy (Pay a Debit) Pay a debit of approximately $8,400 for one contract when filled.

Expiration Selection: This trade expires in 216 days to reduce the effect of Theta which is reasonably small with several months till expiration remaining.

Option Values:

Put/Call	*Strike*	*Bid*	*Ask*	*Mark*	*Delta*	*Theta*	*Open Int.*
+1 Call	$185	$43.35	$45.20	$44.275	.63	$-.09	629
+1 Put	$185	$39.45	$40.05	$39.75	-.37	$-.09	456

Figure 8-5. The Long Straddle on an Option Chain.

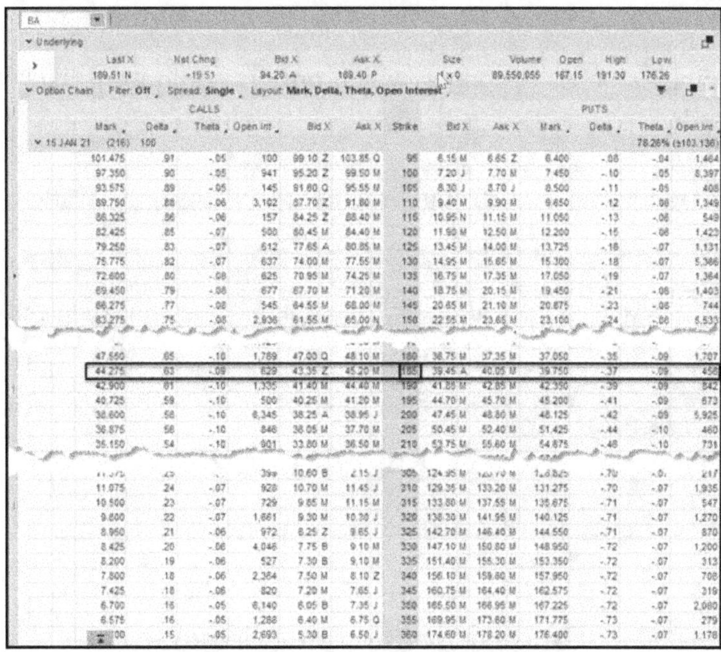

BA

Underlying

Last X	Net Chng	Bid X	Ask X	Size	Volume	Open	High	Low
189.51 N	+19.51	94.20 A	189.40 P	1 x 0	89,550,055	167.15	191.30	176.26

Option Chain Filter: Off Spread: Single Layout: Mark, Delta, Theta, Open Interest

CALLS							PUTS					
Mark	Delta	Theta	Open Int	Bid X	Ask X	Strike	Bid X	Ask X	Mark	Delta	Theta	Open Int
15 JAN 21 (216) 100											78.26% (±103.136)	
101.475	.91	-.05	100	99.10 Z	103.85 Q	95	6.15 M	6.65 Z	6.400	-.08	-.04	1,464
97.350	.90	-.05	941	95.20 Z	99.50 M	100	7.20 J	7.70 M	7.450	-.10	-.05	8,397
93.575	.89	-.05	145	91.60 Q	95.55 M	105	8.30 J	8.70 J	8.500	-.11	-.05	408
89.750	.88	-.06	3,102	87.70 Z	91.80 M	110	9.40 M	9.90 M	9.650	-.12	-.06	1,349
86.325	.86	-.06	157	84.25 Z	88.40 M	115	10.95 N	11.15 M	11.050	-.13	-.06	549
82.425	.85	-.07	500	80.45 M	84.40 M	120	11.90 M	12.50 M	12.200	-.15	-.06	1,423
79.250	.83	-.07	612	77.65 A	80.85 M	125	13.45 M	14.00 M	13.725	-.16	-.07	1,131
75.775	.82	-.07	637	74.00 M	77.55 M	130	14.95 M	15.65 M	15.300	-.18	-.07	5,366
72.600	.80	-.08	625	70.95 M	74.25 M	135	16.75 M	17.35 M	17.050	-.19	-.07	1,364
69.450	.79	-.08	677	67.70 M	71.20 M	140	18.75 M	20.15 M	19.450	-.21	-.08	1,403
66.275	.77	-.08	545	64.55 M	68.00 M	145	20.65 M	21.10 M	20.875	-.23	-.08	744
63.275	.75	-.08	2,936	61.55 M	65.00 N	150	22.55 M	23.65 M	23.100	-.24	-.08	5,533
47.550	.65	-.10	1,789	47.00 Q	48.10 M	180	36.75 M	37.35 M	37.050	-.35	-.09	1,707
44.275	.63	-.09	629	43.35 Z	45.20 M	185	39.45 A	40.05 M	39.750	-.37	-.09	456
42.900	.61	-.10	1,335	41.40 M	44.40 M	190	41.85 M	42.85 M	42.350	-.39	-.09	842
40.725	.59	-.10	500	40.25 M	41.20 M	195	44.70 M	45.70 M	45.200	-.41	-.09	673
38.600	.58	-.10	6,345	38.25 A	38.95 J	200	47.45 M	48.80 M	48.125	-.42	-.09	5,925
36.875	.56	-.10	846	36.05 M	37.70 M	205	50.45 M	52.40 M	51.425	-.44	-.10	460
35.150	.54	-.10	901	33.80 M	36.50 M	210	53.75 M	55.60 M	54.675	-.46	-.10	731
[illegible]	[illegible]	[illegible]	399	10.60 B	[illegible]	305	124.95 M	[illegible]	[illegible]	-.70	[illegible]	217
11.075	.24	-.07	928	10.70 M	11.45 J	310	129.35 M	133.20 M	131.275	-.70	-.07	1,935
10.500	.23	-.07	729	9.85 M	11.15 M	315	133.80 M	137.55 M	135.675	-.71	-.07	547
9.800	.22	-.07	1,661	9.30 M	10.30 J	320	138.30 M	141.95 M	140.125	-.71	-.07	1,270
8.950	.21	-.06	972	8.25 Z	9.65 J	325	142.70 M	146.40 M	144.550	-.71	-.07	870
8.425	.20	-.06	4,046	7.75 B	9.10 M	330	147.10 M	150.80 M	148.950	-.72	-.07	1,200
8.200	.19	-.06	527	7.30 B	9.10 M	335	151.40 M	155.30 M	153.350	-.72	-.07	313
7.800	.18	-.06	2,364	7.50 M	8.10 Z	340	156.10 M	159.80 M	157.950	-.72	-.07	708
7.425	.18	-.06	820	7.20 M	7.65 J	345	160.75 M	164.40 M	162.575	-.72	-.07	319
6.700	.16	-.05	6,140	6.05 B	7.35 J	350	165.50 M	166.95 M	167.225	-.72	-.07	2,080
6.575	.16	-.05	1,288	6.40 M	6.75 Q	355	169.95 M	173.60 M	171.775	-.73	-.07	279
[illegible]00	.15	-.05	2,693	5.30 B	6.50 J	360	174.60 M	178.20 M	176.400	-.73	-.07	1,178

Exercise 8-5 Questions:

1. Why do you think this option strategy is referred to as a long straddle? ____________________
2. Why does the option trader select a long-term expiration for this long straddle? ____________
3. Why might the trader look for and select a different stock with a lower IV% for this long straddle option strategy? ____________
4. If the price of Boeing's stock is dropping, which option would most likely be kept and which one would be closed? ____________
5. Would most option traders having a strong directional bias avoid this trade? ____________ Why? ____________
6. If the price begins to make a strong directional move, how should the trader respond? ____________?

Exercise 6. The Long Strangle

The long strangle essentially works like the preceding long straddle, except that the strikes are both a few strikes OTM where premium values are slightly less. Hence, the debit paid for a long strangle is less than that paid for the long straddle. When there is a directional price move, one side of the long strangle moves ITM while the other side is sold to recover whatever premium remains.

Like the preceding long straddle option strategy, the trader must monitor the trade and sell the losing option(s) and keep the rallying calls or puts as long as the underlying stock sustains either a rally or a drop and moves deeper ITM and increases in value. If the stock's directional move stops, the trader should close the trade to retain the accrued profit.

Stock Symbol: SPY (ETF for the S&P Financial Index)
Chart Description: Price trending upward with small price drops and recoveries (called bull flags)
Trader's Bias: Bullish
IV% or IV Rank; ±Price Movement: 36.39% (±69.906)
Trade Description: Buy one long put and one long call and pay a debit of $5,094.50 plus a few dollars in exchange fees.

Expiration Selection: Long-term; expires in 216 days.

Option Values:

Put/Call	*Strike*	*Bid*	*Ask*	*Mark*	*Delta*	*Theta*	*Open Int.*
+1 Call	$305	$23.37	$24.36	$23.865	.01	-$.05	17,999
+1 Put	$302	$26.51	$27.65	$27.08	-.05	-$.07	3,625

Figure 8-6. The Long Strangle on An Option Chain.

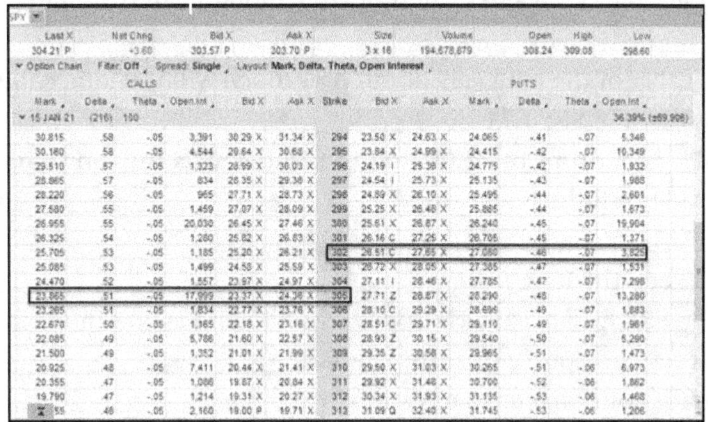

SPY

Last X	Net Chng	Bid X	Ask X	Size	Volume	Open	High	Low
304.21 P	+3.60	303.57 P	303.70 P	3 x 16	194,678,679	308.24	309.08	298.60

Option Chain Filter: Off, Spread: Single, Layout: Mark, Delta, Theta, Open Interest

15 JAN 21 (216) 100 — 36.39% (±69.908)

CALLS Mark	Delta	Theta	Open.Int	Bid X	Ask X	Strike	PUTS Bid X	Ask X	Mark	Delta	Theta	Open Int
30.815	.58	-.05	3,391	30.29 X	31.34 X	294	23.50 X	24.63 X	24.065	-.41	-.07	5,346
30.180	.58	-.05	4,544	29.64 X	30.68 X	295	23.84 X	24.99 X	24.415	-.42	-.07	10,349
29.510	.57	-.05	1,323	28.99 X	30.03 X	296	24.19 I	25.38 X	24.775	-.42	-.07	1,932
28.865	.57	-.05	834	28.35 X	29.38 X	297	24.54 I	25.73 X	25.135	-.43	-.07	1,988
28.220	.56	-.05	965	27.71 X	28.73 X	298	24.89 X	26.10 X	25.495	-.44	-.07	2,601
27.580	.55	-.05	1,459	27.07 X	28.09 X	299	25.25 X	26.48 X	25.865	-.44	-.07	1,673
26.955	.55	-.05	20,030	26.45 X	27.46 X	300	25.61 X	26.87 X	26.240	-.45	-.07	19,904
26.325	.54	-.05	1,260	25.82 X	26.83 X	301	26.16 C	27.25 X	26.705	-.45	-.07	1,371
25.705	.53	-.05	1,185	25.20 X	26.21 X	302	26.51 C	27.65 X	27.080	-.46	-.07	3,625
25.085	.53	-.05	1,499	24.58 X	25.59 X	303	26.72 X	28.05 X	27.385	-.47	-.07	1,531
24.470	.52	-.05	1,557	23.97 X	24.97 X	304	27.11 I	28.46 X	27.785	-.47	-.07	7,298
23.865	.51	-.05	17,999	23.37 X	24.36 X	305	27.71 Z	28.87 X	28.290	-.48	-.07	13,280
23.265	.51	-.05	1,834	22.77 X	23.76 X	306	28.10 C	29.29 X	28.695	-.49	-.07	1,883
22.670	.50	-.05	1,165	22.18 X	23.16 X	307	28.51 C	29.71 X	29.110	-.49	-.07	1,981
22.085	.49	-.05	5,786	21.60 X	22.57 X	308	28.93 Z	30.15 X	29.540	-.50	-.07	5,290
21.500	.49	-.05	1,352	21.01 X	21.99 X	309	29.35 Z	30.58 X	29.965	-.51	-.07	1,473
20.925	.48	-.05	7,411	20.44 X	21.41 X	310	29.50 X	31.03 X	30.265	-.51	-.06	6,973
20.355	.47	-.05	1,086	19.87 X	20.84 X	311	29.92 X	31.48 X	30.700	-.52	-.06	1,862
19.790	.47	-.05	1,214	19.31 X	20.27 X	312	30.34 X	31.93 X	31.135	-.53	-.06	1,468
[illegible]	.46	-.05	2,160	18.00 P	19.71 X	313	31.09 Q	32.40 X	31.745	-.53	-.06	1,206

Exercise 8-6 Questions:

1. Why is a long strangle less expensive than a long straddle? ________________________________ ____________________________________
2. Why does the option trader select a long-term expiration for the long strangle? _____________ ____________________________________.
3. Why do traders prefer low IV% values when buying a long-term strangle? __________________ ____________________________________.
4. Based on the Delta value of the long call, about how much will the long call's premium increase with a $1.00 increase in the SPY ETF?_______.
5. The price of the SPY ETF drops by $5.00 and the trader sells the long call and keeps the long put. Why did the trader sell the long call? __________ ______________________________ ____________________
6. Why did the trader keep the long put? ______________________________________
7. A few weeks later the SPY ETF price has dropped by $45 and is now more than $40 ITM. Would selling the long put return a profit or suffer a loss? ________________________________.
8. Explain the reason for your answer to question 7. ______________ _________________________ _________________________?

Exercise 7. The One-Day Bull Put Vertical Spread

This bull put vertical spread is a low-risk premium collection strategy that is traded shortly after the market opens on the option's expiration day. Traders with sufficiently large accounts typically trade S&P 500 Index (symbol SPX) put options. Traders with small accounts may choose to trade the more affordable QQQ (Nasdaq ETF), SPY (S&P 500 ETF), or the IWM (Russell 2000 ETF). However, be advised that these ETFs have American-style expirations.

This trade includes a short SPX put at a strike having a Delta .05 value and a long put 50 points below. An example might include a short put at the $3,000 strike and the long put below at the $2,950 strike. Because this trade expires at market close on the same day it is entered, there is no overnight risk.

The short put should include a protective stop at a strike price having approximately 50% less premium value than the short put above. For example, if the per-share premium collected is 50 cents per share, then a protective stop limit should be included. The short stop triggers if and when the Mark of the short put reaches 75 cents or more. The long put should also be sold to recover all premium that remains.

According to one option trader that uses this strategy several times each week, approximately 80% of her one-day bull put trades succeed. She also considers the fact that she doesn't need to worry about overnight risk a major benefit.

This trade is typically entered in two steps, which is an example of legging in. Begin about 15 to 30 minutes after the market opens in the morning. Your goal is to evaluate the current market sentiment, which includes checking the VIX volatility index mentioned below. Of course, this can change during the day, but seeing the overall direction is somewhat useful. Once the long puts fill, sell an equal number of short puts at the Delta .05 strike (50 points above) and include a good till canceled (GTC) protective stop with the short puts. The goal is for the trade to expire worthless for profit at the end of the current trading day.

Another benefit that accompanies QQQ, SPX, SPY, and IWM options is they are extremely liquid with above average open interest values. The liquidity increases the likelihood of filling the option orders quickly.

Chart Description: Price of the index moving sideways or rallying. The recent trend has been neutral to upward. Small reversals are followed by returns to the upward price trend.

Note: If you are not familiar with the addition of protective stop losses, be sure to have your brokerage's technical support staff walk you through the setup. Learn how to set up both market limit protective stops and trailing stops. Also learn how to save your working setups as templates that can be recalled and used with a few keystrokes, and recall both of these stop types. This will speed up the process as well as eliminating setup errors.

Trader's Bias: Neutral to bullish

IV% or IV Rank; ±Price Movement: 13.40% (±30.928)

Trade Description: Buy ten put options 50 points below the Delta .05 strike. When filled, leg into an equal number of put options at the Delta .05 strike and include a protective stop at a 50% higher Mark value. Receive a credit when filled.

Expiration Selection: A short-term bull put vertical spread trade that is entered and expires on the same day.

Trade Description: On an SPX option expiration day of Monday, Wednesday, or Friday, Buy ten long SPX puts 50 points below the put that has a .05 Delta value. When filled, sell ten short puts at the SPX strike price that has the .05 Delta value. Include a protective stop set to trigger at a 15 – to 20-percent loss. When both options fill, this trade returns a credit of $730 less a few dollars in exchange fees. As long as the trade remains OTM throughout the day, permit it to close worthless in order to retain the credit in premium.

Option Values:

Put/Call	*Strike*	*Bid*	*Ask*	*Mark*	*Delta*	*Theta*	*Open Int.*
-10 Puts	$3110	$15	$30	$.225	-.01	$.28	366
+10 Puts	$3060	$.85	$105	$.95	.05	$.78	258

Figure 8-8. The One-Day Bull Put Vertical Spread Option Chain.

SPX (0) - EXPIRES TODAY PUTS

Strike	Bid X	Ask X	Mark	Delta	Theta	Open.Int
						13.40% (±30.928)
3020	.05 C	.20 C	.125	-.01	-.18	586
3025	.10 C	.20 C	.150	-.01	-.21	751
3030	.10 C	.20 C	.150	-.01	-.21	112
3035	.10 C	.20 C	.150	-.01	-.21	160
3040	.10 C	.20 C	.150	-.01	-.21	256
3045	.10 C	.25 C	.175	-.01	-.24	98
3050	.15 C	.25 C	.200	-.01	-.26	1,450
3055	.15 C	.30 C	.225	-.01	-.29	194
3060	.15 C	.30 C	.225	-.01	-.28	366
3065	.20 C	.35 C	.275	-.01	-.33	369
3070	.20 C	.35 C	.275	-.01	-.33	725
3075	.25 C	.40 C	.325	-.02	-.37	536
3080	.30 C	.45 C	.375	-.02	-.41	309
3085	.35 C	.50 C	.425	-.02	-.45	165
3090	.40 C	.55 C	.475	-.03	-.49	165
3095	.50 C	.65 C	.575	-.03	-.56	145
3100	.60 C	.80 C	.700	-.04	-.64	941
3105	.70 C	.90 C	.800	-.04	-.70	216
3110	.85 C	1.05 C	.950	-.05	-.78	258
3115	1.00 C	1.25 C	1.125	-.06	-.87	613
3120	1.25 C	1.50 C	1.375	-.07	-.99	199
3125	1.55 C	1.75 C	1.650	-.08	-1.11	361
3130	1.80 C	2.10 C	1.950	-.10	-1.22	305
3135	2.20 C	2.55 C	2.375	-.11	-1.36	309
3140	2.70 C	3.00 C	2.850	-.14	-1.50	366
3145	3.20 C	3.60 C	3.400	-.16	-1.63	192

Notice the short SPX puts are sold at the 3110 strike with a Delta .05 value and the long SPX puts are placed 50 points below at the 3060 strike. This returns a net credit of 73 cents per share or $73 per option contract. The ten 3060 long puts also offset the amount of account margin being used by the ten short 3110 puts.

If the trade succeeds, ten options return $730 in a single day. Successfully trading this strategy three time each week on the SPX returns $2190 per week assuming all trades succeed and ten contracts each average $730. If the protective stop triggers for a small loss, one successful trade will more than offset the amount spent on the stop loss. It's important to note that when volatility is unusually high, avoid this trade due to the increase in risk from large price swings.

Checking the VIX

Before submitting this trade, check the value of the volatility index (VIX). When the VIX value approaches 20, the risk increases. This is typically a result of a drop in the value of many of the stocks listed within the SPX index—the reason the VIX is referred to as the fear index. If a stop loss is not included when this trade is entered, a high VIX value can quickly drop the original .05 Delta strike price ITM, which can be punishing.

Legging In

Many traders prefer to leg into this trade by first buying the long puts 50 points below the SPX strike that has the Delta 0.05 value. The orders typically fill much faster when trading the option contracts separately.

Including a Stop Loss or Trailing Stop

The inclusion of a stop loss or a trailing stop should always be considered to limit the amount of money this trade can lose. Regardless of the stop type, whether a trailing stop or a percentage-based stop limit, be sure to use something in the 15% to 25% range to prevent the stop loss from triggering prematurely from a brief downward price swing. When stops are too conservative, especially when held overnight, many trades that would otherwise succeed are stopped out and lost.

However, when the price of the SPX does decline in value, when a reasonable stop loss triggers it will prevent a major loss and it will also keep the short SPX put options from becoming ITM.

The ten long options located 50-points below may increase in value and offset a portion of the short put's loss. This would be despite Theta's rapid loss in the option's time value. Be aware that when approaching option expiration at the end of the final trading day, it becomes much more difficult, if not impossible, to sell the ten long puts prior to market close.

Some traders may prefer to roll the vertical spread rather than using a stop loss. As you read earlier in Section 6, this is done by rolling the vertical spread to farther OTM strike prices and at a later expiration date. However, it is just as wise and certainly requires less effort to use a reasonable stop loss and let it trigger according to plan. Then monitor the VIX value. When it drops back into the teens, consider repeating this one-day SPX vertical put spread.

Exercise 7 Questions

1. How long does this short vertical spread remain in effect? ______________________ ______________________
2. What are two reasons to include the long put?
   (1) ______________________________________
   (2) ______________________________________.
3. If this trade's short put is placed at the 3050 strike price, which strike price would be chosen for the long put? ______________________
4. When legging into this trade, which option is traded first? ____________ ____________.
5. Why would a trader avoid the use of a $5.00 stop-loss with this trade? ______________________ ______________________
6. When does it become more difficult to sell the long put? ______________________ ______________________
7. What two things can a trader do to prevent the short puts from becoming ITM?
   1) ______________________________________
   2) ______________________________________
8. How many trades must succeed to offset the option premium lost when a stop loss buys too close the working short put? ______________________________________

Exercise 8. The Short Put
(Trader must have highest option trading level.)

Far OTM short-term puts are frequently sold on rallying stocks, ETFs, and financial indexes. This is a premium collection strategy. It is frequently used by experienced option traders who are permitted to trade uncovered short put and call options.

Using short-term options that expire within a matter of days to perhaps a few weeks is common, although there are some traders who consider selling far OTM short puts that expire as far out in time as eight weeks (56 days). This is an extremely simple strategy that sells one or more OTM short-term puts for a credit in premium. However, the risk is substantially increased with longer times till expiration. And increased risk is synonymous with increased reward. Longer times till expiration also increases the credit in premium that the trader receives when the short put trade order is filled. The difference in premium can be substantial, but it is often not worth the stress of worrying about the short put's strike price becoming ITM.

Because most option traders prefer to reduce risk, they choose short options that expire within days to a few weeks. To collect more premium income, they often sell short-term puts on high priced financial indexes and stocks having premiums that sell for several dollars per share. Their short puts are often sold at strike prices that are at least two standard deviations OTM with a Delta value of no more than 0.05. These traders often check the VIX volatility index to make sure it is in the teens. If the VIX rises above 20, the risk begins to increase. When this happens, some traders cover the short put with a long put several strikes farther OTM. This has two benefits. First, it reduces exposure to an uncovered short put. And it also reduces the amount of margin in use to avoid a margin call.

This strategy in addition to the short call and the short strangle strategies described in exercises 9 and 10 that follow, all use similar risk-avoidance rationales. The short put, short call, and short strangle strategies are frequently traded on the NDX, SPX, and RUT financial indexes. These indexes are chosen because all three have European expiration styles, which cannot be exercised prior to option expiration. But you can also use these three strategies on $1,000+ stock such as AMZN, GOOG, and SHOP. You might also consider several other European expiration-style options having the following symbols.

OEX, OIX, RMN, RUI, RUT
RVX, SML, SPL, VIX, VXN
XEO, XSP, BYT, FUM, HHO
HSX, HVY, IXK, IXX

You can view the option chains that correspond to these symbols on your trading platform. You will find limited Open Interest values on several of these. Without sufficient Open Interest values of at least 10 to 20 per option contract, look elsewhere. Low Open Interest makes it more difficult to fill your opening and closing orders, which is frustrating when trying to open a trade and even worse, dangerous when trying to close a trade.

Like any uncovered short option trade, the short puts, calls, and strangles must all be closely monitored. Be prepared to roll a working trade or leg into a vertical spread by adding a protective long option to prevent a major loss.

Many traders that use this strategy in addition to the short call and short strangle prefer the NDX and SPX option indices because they expire on Monday, Wednesday, and Friday afternoons. Shorter times to expiration also increase the impact of Theta, which is a primary goal when selling put and call options and credit spreads.

AM Expirations

Rather than always expiring at market close on Friday afternoon, the NDX also has AM expirations as do the SPX monthly options. Many traders avoid AM expiration due to a concern about an overnight price gap. Although the strike price of a short put may be safely OTM at market close on Thursday afternoon, a major overnight gap can result in a major loss. For this reason, many traders are hesitant to sell AM expiration options.

As mentioned above, the strike price of these short options on expensive stocks and indexes should be at strike prices that are two standard deviations OTM. However, do not confuse the two-standard deviation rule when setting up a conventional vertical spread. Recall that the strike prices of the short puts and short calls are considered reasonable when the Delta value is close to the mid .20s.

Stock Symbol: RUT (Russell 2000 Financial Index)

Chart Description: Price experiencing small daily increases with an occasional reversal. The long-term trend is slightly upward. Small reversals are followed by returns to the upward price movement.

Trader's Bias: Neutral to bullish

IV% or IV Rank; ±Price Movement: 43.58% (±96.729)

Trade Description: Sell ten put options: Receive a $3,700 credit less a few dollars in exchange fees when this trade fills.

Expiration Selection: Short-term; expires in 5 days.

Option Values:

Put/Call	*Strike*	*Bid*	*Ask*	*Mark*	*Delta*	*Theta*	*Open Int.*
-10 Puts	$1970	$3.10	$4.30	$3.70	0.05	-$1.34	282

Stock quote and option quote for RUT on 2/28/21 12:47:00

LAST	Net Chng	BID	ASK	Size	Open	High	Low
2201.051	0	N/A	N/A	0 x 0	2201.298	2232.287	2165.8589

5 MAR 21 (5) 100 (Weeklys) CALLS PUTS 43.58% (±96.729)

Mark	Delta	Theta	Open.Int	BID	ASK	Strike	BID	ASK	Mark	Delta	Theta	Open.Int
233.85	1	0	0	228.3	239.4	1965	2.85	4.1	3.475	-0.05	-1.28	220
228.9	1	0	3	223.4	234.4	1970	3.1	4.3	3.7	-0.05	-1.34	282
224.1	1	0	0	218.6	229.6	1975	3.3	4.6	3.95	-0.06	-1.4	365
219.35	1	0	1	213.8	224.9	1980	3.5	4.8	4.15	-0.06	-1.45	148
214.6	1	0	2	209.1	220.1	1985	3.8	5.1	4.45	-0.06	-1.52	134
209.85	1	0	2	204.3	215.4	1990	4	5.4	4.7	-0.07	-1.58	104
205.2	1	0	0	199.6	210.8	1995	4.3	5.7	5	-0.07	-1.65	275

Figure 8-9. The Short Put on an Option Chain.

Exercise 8 Questions:

1. Why can't the short put be traded by new and inexperienced option traders? ______________ ______________________________
2. What is an option trader's primary goal when selling the short put? ____________________ ______________________________
3. How much premium did the trader receive, excluding exchange fees, when the ten $1970 short put options were originally sold? ______________
4. What happens to the value of Theta as an option approaches expiration? ________________ ______________________________
5. What happens to the value of Gamma if it approaches the ATM strike price? (Hint: See Gamma Risk in Section 4.) ____________________ ______________________________ ____________
6. How does Theta affect the value of the short put's premium as this trade nears expiration? ___ ______________________________.
7. What two things could the trader do to prevent the short puts from becoming ITM?
   1) ______________________________
   2) ______________________________
8. Explain how the short 1970 put option might be rolled to the 1800 short put that expires on the following Friday. ______________________________

Exercise 9. The Short Call
(Trader must have highest option trading level.)

The short call is almost identical to the short put, except it is located on the opposite side of the option chain. The goal is to collect and retain the premium when one or more short-term uncovered call options are sold. By short term, the options should expire within a matter of days to perhaps eight weeks (56 days). The trade example shown below expires in five weeks.

Many option traders use much shorter times till expiration. Selling short call options that expire inside two or three days increases the benefit provided by Theta. It also limits the amount of time the underlying equity's price has to move against the trade.

The strike price of these short call options should be sufficiently far enough above the equity's price to remain OTM through expiration. Many traders choose call strike prices having Delta values at or below .25, like the one shown in the example trade. When selling uncovered calls on expensive index options, consider choosing a strike price at or very close to Delta .05.

Stock Symbol: RUT (Russell 2000 Financial Index)

Chart Description: Price has been trending down with a few small daily increases only to return to the gradual downward trajectory. The EMA(20) plot is currently negative, but it has not yet crossed below the SMA(50) plot. Small positive rallies are consistently followed by a return to the downward price trend.

Trader's Bias: Mildly neutral to bearish

IV% or IV Rank; ±Price Movement: 43.58% (±96.729)

Trade Description: Sell ten call options: Receive a credit of $1.82 per option for a total of $182 in premium income per option contract or $1,820 for ten contracts less a few dollars in exchange fees when this trade fills.

Expiration Selection: Short-term; expires within 5 days.

Option Values:

Put/Call	*Strike*	*Bid*	*Ask*	*Mark*	*Delta*	*Theta*	*Open Int.*
-10 Calls	$2350	$1.2	$2.45	$1.82	-.05	$-0.7	208

Figure 8-10. The Short Call on an Option Chain.

Stock quote and option quote for RUT on 2/28/21 12:47:00

LAST	Net Chng	BID	ASK	Size	Open	High	Low
2201.051	0	N/A	N/A	0 x 0	2201.298	2232.287	2165.8589

5 MAR 21 (5) 100 (Weeklys) CALLS PUTS 43.58% (±96.729)

Mark	Delta	Theta	Open.Int	BID	ASK	Strike	BID	ASK	Mark	Delta	Theta	Open.Int
233.85	1	0	0	228.3	239.4	1965	2.85	4.1	3.475	-0.05	-1.28	220
228.9	1	0	3	223.4	234.4	1970	3.1	4.3	3.7	-0.05	-1.34	282
224.1	1	0	0	218.6	229.6	1975	3.3	4.6	3.95	-0.06	-1.4	365
219.35	1	0	1	213.8	224.9	1980	3.5	4.8	4.15	-0.06	-1.45	148
214.6	1	0	2	209.1	220.1	1985	3.8	5.1	4.45	-0.06	-1.52	134
209.85	1	0	2	204.3	215.4	1990	4	5.4	4.7	-0.07	-1.58	104
205.2	1	0	0	199.6	210.8	1995	4.3	5.7	5	-0.07	-1.65	275
2.8	[illegible]	-0.96	[illegible]	[illegible]	3.5	[illegible]	[illegible]	[illegible]	[illegible]	[illegible]	[illegible]	[illegible]
2.425	0.06	-0.86	158	1.75	3.1	2340	140.9	152.8	146.85	-0.87	-2.12	14
2.1	0.06	-0.77	42	1.5	2.7	2345	145.7	157.5	151.6	-0.87	-2.09	0
1.825	0.05	-0.7	208	1.2	2.45	2350	150.5	162.5	156.5	-0.87	-2.08	5
1.6	0.05	-0.63	111	1	2.2	2355	155.3	167	161.15	-0.88	-2.03	0
1.45	0.04	-0.59	174	0.85	2.05	2360	160.8	171.8	166.3	-0.88	-2.08	6
1.25	0.04	-0.52	128	0.65	1.85	2365	165.6	176.6	171.1	-0.88	-2.05	1
1.125	0.03	-0.48	53	0.55	1.7	2370	170.4	187.4	178.9	-0.86	-2.64	0
1	0.03	-0.44	70	0.4	1.6	2375	175.3	186.2	180.75	-0.89	-2	1
0.9	[illegible]	-0.4	[illegible]	0.3	[illegible]	[illegible]	[illegible]	[illegible]	[illegible]	[illegible]	[illegible]	[illegible]

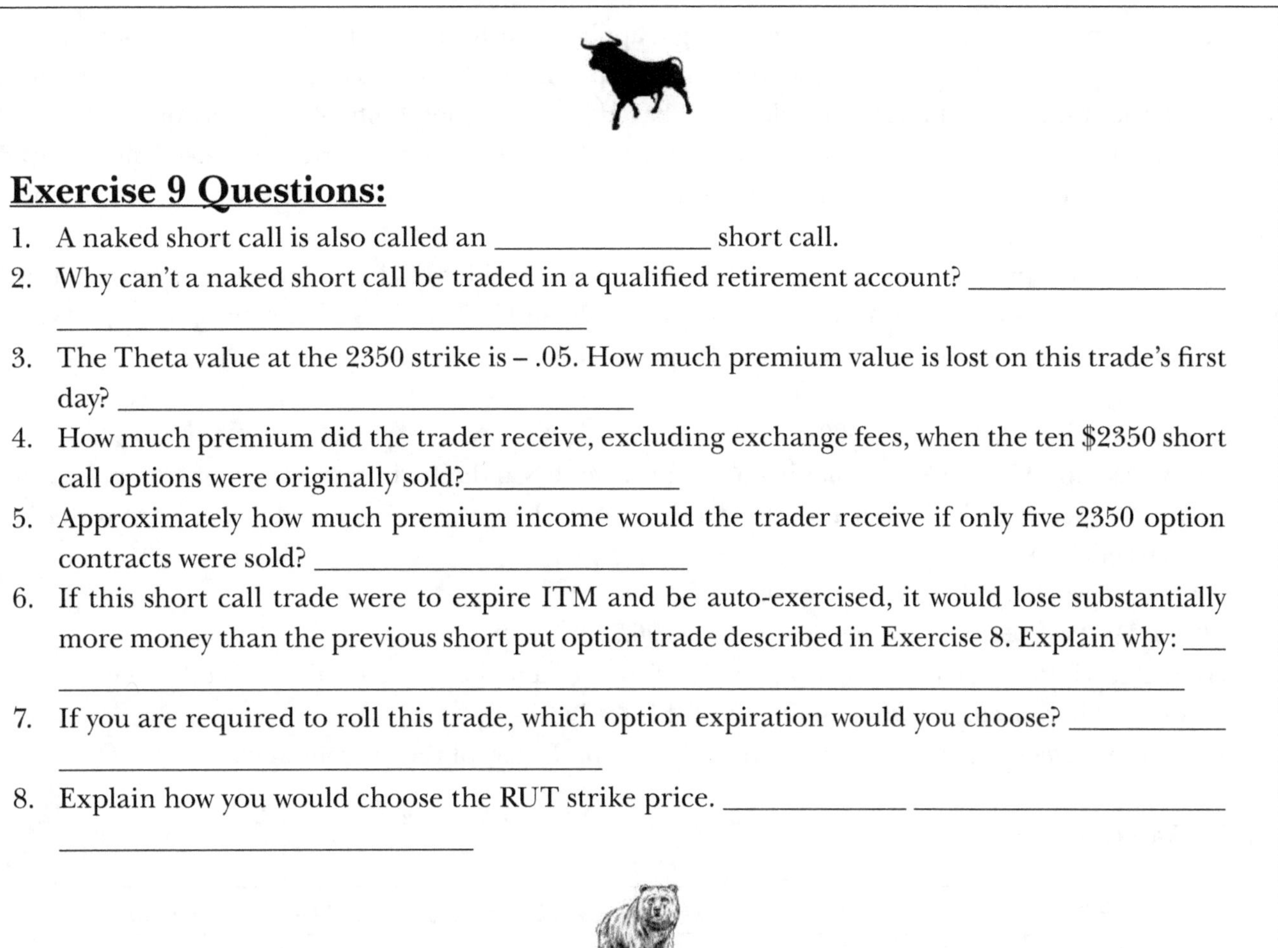

Exercise 9 Questions:

1. A naked short call is also called an ______________ short call.
2. Why can't a naked short call be traded in a qualified retirement account? ________________ ________________________________
3. The Theta value at the 2350 strike is – .05. How much premium value is lost on this trade's first day? ______________________
4. How much premium did the trader receive, excluding exchange fees, when the ten $2350 short call options were originally sold?______________
5. Approximately how much premium income would the trader receive if only five 2350 option contracts were sold? ________________
6. If this short call trade were to expire ITM and be auto-exercised, it would lose substantially more money than the previous short put option trade described in Exercise 8. Explain why: ___ ____
7. If you are required to roll this trade, which option expiration would you choose? __________ ________________________________
8. Explain how you would choose the RUT strike price. ___________ ___________________ ________________________

Exercise 10. The Short Strangle
(Trader must have highest option trading level.)

The short strangle strategy combines the short put and the short call strategies, both of which were just described in exercises 8 and 9. Combining the short put with the short call option strategy collects premium income from both the put and call sides of the option chain. This trade works best and can be extremely profitable when the price of the underlying equity remains within a narrow price range.

The strangle works well with high-priced financial indexes, index ETFs like the QQQ, SPY, and RUT, and expensive stocks such as AMZN, GOOG, and perhaps SHOP to name just three. A high-priced index or stock permits the trader to choose far OTM strike prices that have low Delta values. This increases the probability of remaining OTM through option expiration. And by using high-value indexes, ETFs, and stocks, the premium credit received when the trade is sold can be significant.

The account margin used by the short strangle applies only to the most vulnerable half of this trade, i.e., either the put or call side of the strangle. For example, if the short put is closer to the money than the short call, the trade's use of margin is calculated based on the vulnerability of the short put.

This is a popular short-term option strategy for traders who have been granted permission to trade uncovered short options. And having a comparatively large account balance is likely required to underwrite the margin necessary to enter this trade.

Notice the risk profile shown in figure 8-12. The vertical sides of the square plot shows the trader where the trade loses value. These are located at the 1970 and 2350 strikes. The cone-shaped plot in the center of the square represents the value of Theta.

Stock Symbol: RUT (Russell 2000 Financial Index)

Chart Description: RUT's price has been moving sideways and remaining within a narrow price range for the past week, although a short-term spike in trading volume occurred just prior to yesterday's market close.

Trader's Bias: Neutral to slightly bearish

IV% or IV Rank; ±Price Movement: 43.58% (±96.729)

Trade Description: Sell ten short strangles consisting of ten puts and ten calls and collect a total credit of $5,525 in premium when both legs of this trade fills.

Expiration Selection: Short-term; expires in 5 days on Friday of the current week.

Option Values:

Put/Call	*Strike*	*Bid*	*Ask*	*Mark*	*Delta*	*Theta*	*Open Int.*
-10 Puts	$1970	$3.1	$4.3	$3.7	.05	$1.34	282
-10 Calls	$2350	$1.2	$2.45	$1.825	-.05	$-0.7	208

Figure 8-11. The Short Strangle on an Option Chain.

Stock quote and option quote for RUT on 2/28/21 12:47:00

LAST	Net Chng	BID	ASK	Size	Open	High	Low
2201.051	0	N/A	N/A	0 x 0	2201.298	2232.287	2165.8589

5 MAR 21 (5) 100 (Weeklys)			CALLS						PUTS			43.58% (±96.729)
Mark	Delta	Theta	Open.Int	BID	ASK	Strike	BID	ASK	Mark	Delta	Theta	Open.Int
233.85	1	0	0	228.3	239.4	1965	2.85	4.1	3.475	-0.05	-1.28	220
228.9	1	0	3	223.4	234.4	1970	3.1	4.3	3.7	-0.05	-1.34	282
224.1	1	0	0	218.6	229.6	1975	3.3	4.6	3.95	-0.06	-1.4	365
219.35	1	0	1	213.8	224.9	1980	3.5	4.8	4.15	-0.06	-1.45	148
214.6	1	0	2	209.1	220.1	1985	3.8	5.1	4.45	-0.06	-1.52	134
209.85	1	0	2	204.3	215.4	1990	4	5.4	4.7	-0.07	-1.58	104
205.2	1	0	0	199.6	210.8	1995	4.3	5.7	5	-0.07	-1.65	275
2.8	[illegible]	-0.96	[illegible]	[illegible]	[illegible]	[illegible]	[illegible]	[illegible]	[illegible]	[illegible]	[illegible]	[illegible]
2.425	0.06	-0.86	158	1.75	3.1	2340	140.9	152.8	146.85	-0.87	-2.12	14
2.1	0.06	-0.77	42	1.5	2.7	2345	145.7	157.5	151.6	-0.87	-2.09	0
1.825	0.05	-0.7	208	1.2	2.45	2350	150.5	162.5	156.5	-0.87	-2.08	5
1.6	0.05	-0.63	111	1	2.2	2355	155.3	167	161.15	-0.88	-2.03	0
1.45	0.04	-0.59	174	0.85	2.05	2360	160.8	171.8	166.3	-0.88	-2.08	6
1.25	0.04	-0.52	128	0.65	1.85	2365	165.6	176.6	171.1	-0.88	-2.05	1
1.125	0.03	-0.48	53	0.55	1.7	2370	170.4	187.4	178.9	-0.86	-2.64	0
1	0.03	-0.44	70	0.4	1.6	2375	175.3	186.2	180.75	-0.89	-2	1
0.9	[illegible]	-0.4	[illegible]	0.3	[illegible]	[illegible]	[illegible]	[illegible]	[illegible]	[illegible]	[illegible]	[illegible]

Figure 8-12. The Short Strangle Risk Profile.

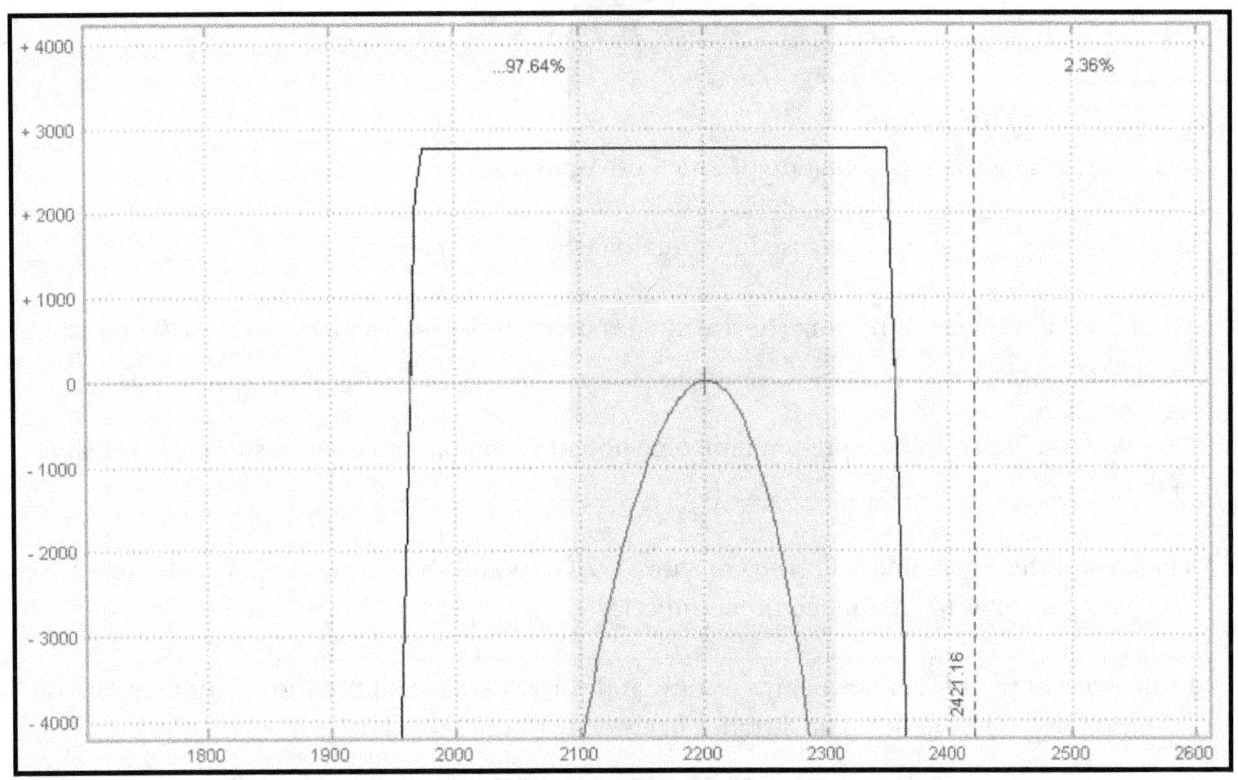

Exercise 10 Questions:

1. The short strangle is a combination of which two option strategies? ____________________ and the ____________________.
2. Why can't the short strangle be used in a qualified retirement account? ____________________ ____________________
3. What is an advantage of trading short strangles on high-priced financial indexes, ETFs, and/or stocks? ____________________ ____________________
4. How does the short strangle premium income potential compare to either a short call or a short put? ____________________ ____________________
5. The sum of the Theta values for the ten short 1970 puts and the ten short 2350 calls are – 1.34 and – 0.7 respectively. How much premium is lost on the first day of this trade? ____________________ ____________________
6. If the price of the RUT index begins to rally and you decide to roll the short calls to expire on Friday of next week, what would a trader likely do with the short put? ____________________ ____________________
7. Explain why the expiration date and strike prices were chosen. ____________________ ____________________
8. A risk profile for the short strangle is shown in figure 8-12. What do the vertical sides of the graph represent? ____________________ ____________________
9. In the risk profile, what does the cone-shaped plot in the middle of the square plot represent? ____________________ ____________________

Exercise 11. The Butterflies

Many option traders regularly use a variety of short-term butterfly strategies. These strategies are called butterflies because their risk profiles include a central body and external wings on each side. There are a variety of butterfly strategies that are used according to the trader's bullish or bearish bias. As you can see in the risk profile illustrations in figures 8-14, 8-15, and 8-16, the plots vary according to the selected butterfly strategy. Figure 8-14 is typical of a long call balanced butterfly with long call wings and a short call between. The inverted V-shaped body is often referred to as a witch's hat or a tent. Figure 8-14 is typical of the balanced long call butterfly in which the exterior long call wings have the same number of contracts and identical strike widths from the central body. When the body is sold and the wings are bought, the witch's hat resembles an inverted V on the risk profile.

To qualify as a butterfly, the same number of long and short calls or long and short puts must always be included. If the central body sells four call options, the wings must include a total of four long options. A +2, – 4, +2 butterfly that buys two wing options and sells the central body options is a balanced long call butterfly. A +1, – 4, +3 butterfly that buys the wings and sells the body is an unbalanced long call butterfly. There are also broken wing butterflies. The broken wing butterfly plots shows one wing drooping below the other, resembling a broken wing. These butterflies are created by varying the strike widths between the body and exterior wing options.

A broken wing butterfly example might include a strategy that separates the two exterior wings from the central body by five strikes below and one strike above. Adding the broken wing butterflies brings the total to 16 different butterfly configurations.

A list of eight different butterfly configurations follows:

Balanced Long Call Butterfly: +2 –4 +2 (equal-distant strike widths)
Unbalanced Long Call Butterfly: 3 –4 +1 (equal-distant strike widths)
Balanced Long Put Butterfly: +2 –4 +2 (equal-distant strike widths)
Unbalanced Long Put Butterfly: 3 –4 +1 (equal-distant strike widths)
Balanced Short Call Butterfly: –2 +4 –2 (equal-distant strike widths)
Unbalanced Short Call Butterfly: –3 +4 –1 (equal-distant strike widths)
Balanced Short Put Butterfly: –2 +4 –2 (equal-distant strike widths)
Unbalanced Short Put Butterfly: –3 +4 –1 (equal-distant strike widths)

All eight of the above configurations can be converted to broken wing or "skip strike" butterflies by simply varying the widths between strikes. This brings the total to 16 different butterfly option strategies mentioned above. A few others exist, such as the Delta 20-40-60 butterfly and the double-butterfly. The Delta 20-40-60 butterfly is discussed immediately following the balanced long call butterfly description.

Finally, a double butterfly is described. The double butterfly is configured to straddle the current ATM price of the underlying. It includes a long put butterfly below and a long call butterfly above. The double butterfly is designed to earn a profit from either a price rally or a price drop. The double butterfly example is placed on the Russell 2000 ETF, symbol IWM, which is shown trading at $227.20. The IWM options have $1.00 strike widths, while each of the two double butterfly trade examples use $2.00 spread widths. The long put butterfly costs $25.40 and has a maximum profit potential of $176.00. The long call butterfly costs $36.40 with a maximum profit potential of $185.00. Butterflies rarely return their maximum profits as they are usually closed when they achieve a profit that approaches 65% to 70% of their potential. Of course, only one of the butterflies will succeed. And more options could be purchased to increase the somewhat meager return, although many would see it being worthwhile since the return is achieved in two days. If a limit stop order is used to return 65% from the profitable butterfly, the opposite butterfly would be simultaneously closed for a small debit which sell the long wings and buys-to-close the short body.

The risk graphs for each of the butterflies is similar to the one shown on the right in the next illustration. The first peak represents the long put butterfly's profit potential, while the second peak represents the long call butterfly's profit potential.

LONG PUT BUTTERFLY BELOW:
Buy 1 222 Put
Sell 2 224 Puts
Buy 1 226 Put

LONG CALL BUTTERFLY ABOVE:
Buy 1 228 Call
Sell 2 230 Calls
Buy 1 232 Call

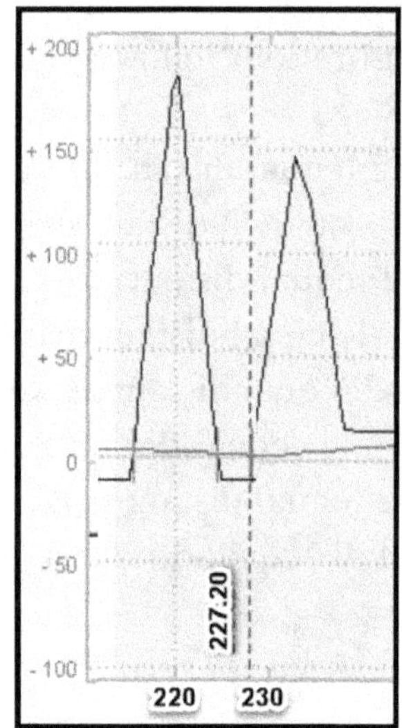

New option traders should test this strategy in simulation. Once comfortable with the trade and satisfied with its return, consider taking it live.

There is also the Delta 20-40-60 butterfly. This strategy is commonly used on financial index options such as the SPX. This is a short-term bearish strategy that is discussed immediately following the balanced long call butterfly example described next.

The Balanced Long Call Butterfly

A balanced long call butterfly setup is displayed on the option chain in figure 8-13. Notice the two long calls form the wings and the short calls form the body. This is a debit spread that relies on a rally in the price of Disney (DIS) stock. The trader must pay a debit of $148.80 when this trade is filled. If the price of Disney stock rallies to $120, this long call butterfly has a maximum profit potential of $854 while it can lose about $148.00. The risk profile for this long call butterfly is shown in figure 8-14. This is quite typical of a butterfly option chain.

Stock Symbol: DIS (Walt Disney Company)

Chart Description: DIS's price has begun to rally after a long period below $100. The trader expects a reasonably strong price rally over the next few weeks.

Trading momentum study in use suggests a brisk increase in DIS stock buying activity.

Trader's Bias: Bullish

IV% or IV Rank; ±Price Movement: 48.19% (±9.192)

Trade Description: Buy the wings and sell the body: This trade includes +5 calls in each wing and – 10 calls in the body. A small debit in Premium is paid when this butterfly trade fills.

Expiration Selection: Short-term; expires in 28 days.

Option Values:

Put/Call	*Strike*	*Bid*	*Ask*	*Mark*	*Delta*	*Theta*	*Open Int.*
+5 Calls	$115	$4.90	$5.20	$5.05	.51	$.10	9,534
-10 Calls	$120	$2.70	$3.15	$2.925	.36	$-.09	14,866
+5 Calls	$125	$50	$1.40	$1.525	.22	$.07	13,498

Figure 8-13. A Balanced Long Call Butterfly on an Option Chain.

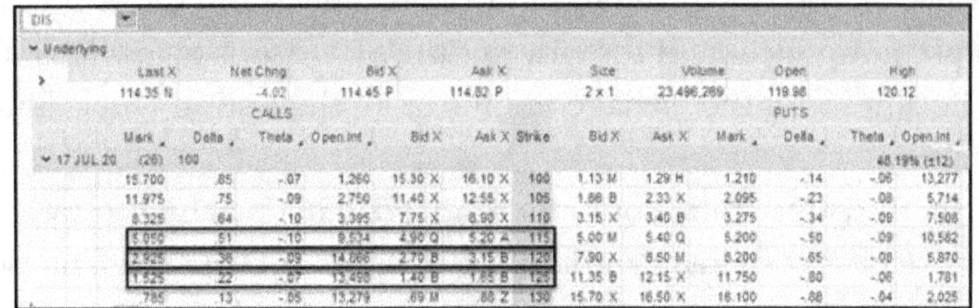

DIS

Underlying

Last X	Net Chng	Bid X	Ask X	Size	Volume	Open	High
114.35 N	-4.02	114.45 P	114.82 P	2 x 1	23,496,269	119.98	120.12

17 JUL 20 (28) 100 — 48.19% (±12)

CALLS Mark	Delta	Theta	Open.Int	Bid X	Ask X	Strike	PUTS Bid X	Ask X	Mark	Delta	Theta	Open.Int
15.700	.85	-.07	1,260	15.30 X	16.10 X	100	1.13 M	1.29 H	1.210	-.14	-.06	13,277
11.975	.75	-.09	2,750	11.40 X	12.55 X	105	1.88 B	2.33 X	2.095	-.23	-.08	5,714
8.325	.64	-.10	3,395	7.75 X	8.90 X	110	3.15 X	3.40 B	3.275	-.34	-.09	7,508
5.050	.51	-.10	9,534	4.90 Q	5.20 A	115	5.00 M	5.40 Q	5.200	-.50	-.09	10,582
2.925	.36	-.09	14,866	2.70 B	3.15 B	120	7.90 X	8.50 M	8.200	-.65	-.08	5,870
1.525	.22	-.07	13,498	1.40 B	1.65 B	125	11.35 B	12.15 X	11.750	-.80	-.06	1,781
.785	.13	-.05	13,279	.69 M	.88 Z	130	15.70 X	16.50 X	16.100	-.88	-.04	2,025

Figure 8-14. The Balanced Long Call Butterfly Risk Profile.

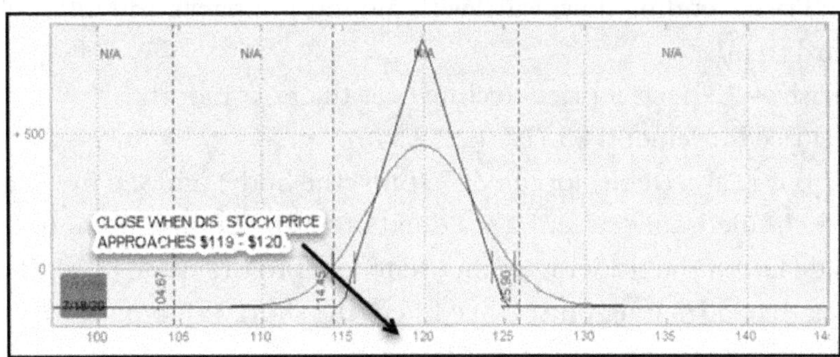

The Delta 20-40-60 Short Put Butterfly

Only experienced traders with sufficiently large accounts should consider the following short put butterfly trade. The SPX is used because it has a European expiration style which prevents it from being vulnerable to early exercise. If bullish, traders can use this strategy on the call side of the option chain. Consider setting up a Delta 20-40-60 short call butterfly on an option chain and checking its risk graph to determine how it responds to changes in the price of the SPX. Regardless of your options trading experience, be sure to test this trade in simulation a few times until you know how it works. Also consider the use of back trades, i.e., trade in simulation using historical data. This is a good way to determine how this strategy responds to changes in the price of the SPX index.

Sell 5 SPX puts at the Delta .20 strike (OTM)
Buy 10 SPX puts at the Delta .40 strike (OTM)
Sell 5 SPX puts at the Delta .60 strike. (ITM)

The S&P Index, symbol SPX, is used because it has a European-expiration style and cannot be exercised unless one or more options expire ITM. This gives the trader time to either roll or close the trade if the SPX doesn't drop in price according to the trader's bearish bias. As you should know, and with only the rare exception described in the Uncovered (or Naked) Short Options paragraph of Section 4, option traders do not permit a short option to expire ITM. Just for grins, let's examine a 20-40-60 butterfly on the SPX. This trade is an example of an unbalanced broken wing butterfly. It sells five option contracts at the strikes that include a Delta value of .20 and .60 and buys ten contracts at the strike having a Delta value of .40. These happen to be located at the $2,890, $3,075, and $3,185 strike prices as can be seen on the option chain in figure 6-13. Notice on the risk graph in figure 6-14. The graph shows how this trade could potentially return $37,675 in premium income if the price of the SPX drops below $2,900 within a short period of time. This potential declines with the passage of time as all the option *Greek* values change each day.

NOTE: When bullish, the same trade could be reversed. This is achieved by buying five puts at Delta .20 and another five puts at Delta 60 and selling ten puts at Delta .40. The risk graph in figure 8-16 would plot the profit to the right of the butterfly's V-shaped body.

Stock Symbol: SPX (S&P 500 Financial Index)
Chart Description: Price trending downward with modest pullbacks and followed by price drops back to the downward trend.
Trader's Bias: Bearish — Expects a price decline over the next month.
IV% or IV Rank; ±Price Movement: 33.11% (±237.548)
Trade Description: Buy (Pay a Debit) for ten 3075 puts (the body) and sell five each 2890 and 3185 puts (the wings). When filled, the trader pays a debit of $2,102.50 plus a few dollars in exchange fees. (To fill this trade faster, the trader may choose to leg into the trade by selling the five $2890 short puts and buying the $3075 long puts. Once filled, the short $3185 puts are bought independently.
Expiration Selection: Short-term; expires in 29 days.

Option Values:

Put/Call	*Strike*	*Bid*	*Ask*	*Mark*	*Delta*	*Theta*	*Open Int.*
-5 Puts	$2890	$37.10	$37.70	$37.40	.20	$1.47	1,084
+10 Puts	$3075	$75.50	$76.50	$76.00	-.40	$1.61	4,183
-5 Puts	$3185	$117.00	$119.00	$118.05	.60	$1.35	140

Figure 8-15. The Delta 20-40-60 Put Butterfly on an Option Chain.

Figure 8-16. The Delta 20-40-60 Short Put Butterfly Risk Profile.

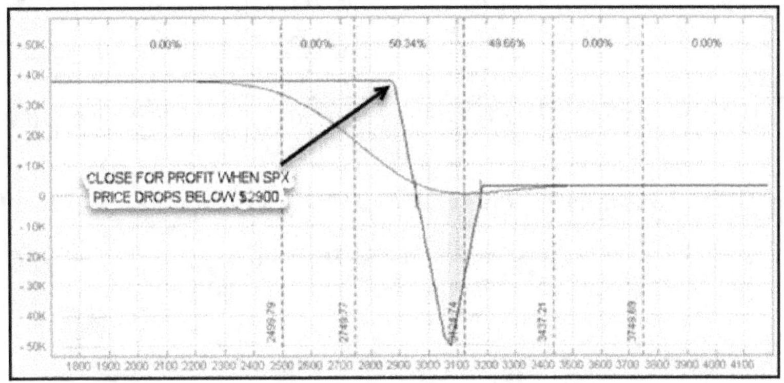

A Long Call Broken Wing Butterfly Example

The broken wing butterfly is reasonably popular among those traders who are familiar with how the butterfly strategy works. It is also a reasonably inexpensive trade, so those with small brokerage accounts can use this trade.

The example assumes the trader has a bullish bias. The example trade has a short term duration and expires in just three days. However, it may be closed much earlier if the IWM stock price rallies according to the trader's bullish bias. Once the price moves close to $225 per share, which is inside the tent, also called a witch's hat of the butterfly, the trade would be closed for a profit of approximately $250. The entire process from trade entry to exit is often achieved in a single day.

Traders often automate the closing order by including a good till canceled (GTC) profit target that is set to trigger once this trade achieves a 60% to 65% profit. Since this trade only requires a small debit when entered, traders with small brokerage accounts can consider its use.

If the trader is bearish and expects a price to drop, the same trade could be placed on the put side of the option chain. The bearish version of this trade would buy one $226 put, sell five $222 puts, and buy four $220 puts.

Stock Symbol: IWM (Russell 2000 Financial Index ETF)

Chart Description: The IWM stock price is currently trending upward in response to numerous small businesses experiencing increases in sales in addition to several national chains reopening after being closed for several months.

Trader's Bias: Bullish — Expects the price of IWM stock to continue its upward trend.

IV% or IV Rank and ±Price Movement: 34.52% (±6.334)

Trade Description: Buy (Pay a Debit) for ten 3075 puts (the body), and sell five each 2890 and 3185 puts (the wings). When filled, the trader pays a debit of $11.00 plus a few dollars in exchange fees. (To fill this trade faster, the trader may choose to leg into the trade by buying one $222 ITM long call and selling five $226 short puts. Once the order fills, the remaining four $227.50 long calls are bought to complete the long call broken-wing butterfly.

Option Values:

Put/Call	*Strike*	*Bid*	*Ask*	*Mark*	*Delta*	*Theta*	*Open Int.*
+1 Call	$222	$3.64	$3.71	$3.68	0.57	$-0.4	1399
-5 Calls	$226	$1.53	$76.50	$-1.55	0.34	$-0.33	2678
+4 Calls	$227.5	$0.99	$119.00	$1.00	0.26	$-0.27	2522

Figure 8-17. Unbalanced Long Call Butterfly Trade on an Option Chain

5 MAR 21 (3) 100 (Weeklys)				CALLS							PUTS			34.52% (±6.334)
Mark	Delta	Theta	Vega	Open.Int	BID	ASK	Strike	BID	ASK	Mark	Delta	Theta	Vega	Open.Int
8.96	0.83	-0.28	0.06	482	8.89	9.03	215	0.8	0.82	0.81	-0.17	-0.28	0.06	35292
8.13	0.8	-0.3	0.06	348	8.02	8.23	216	0.95	0.97	0.96	-0.2	-0.31	0.06	6450
7.32	0.77	-0.33	0.07	269	7.23	7.4	217	1.14	1.16	1.15	-0.23	-0.33	0.07	7957
6.91	0.75	-0.34	0.07	233	6.87	6.95	217.5	1.24	1.26	1.25	-0.24	-0.35	0.07	3683
6.52	0.74	-0.35	0.08	395	6.47	6.57	218	1.34	1.37	1.355	-0.26	-0.36	0.08	7965
5.76	0.7	-0.37	0.08	1009	5.71	5.81	219	1.58	1.61	1.595	-0.3	-0.38	0.08	17152
5.02	0.66	-0.39	0.09	3081	4.97	5.06	220	1.85	1.87	1.86	-0.34	-0.39	0.09	23958
4.34	0.61	-0.4	0.09	1278	4.28	4.39	221	2.14	2.18	2.16	-0.39	-0.4	0.09	1868
3.68	0.57	-0.4	0.09	1399	3.64	3.71	222	2.46	2.52	2.49	-0.43	-0.4	0.09	12543
3.35	0.54	-0.4	0.09	391	3.32	3.38	222.5	2.66	2.7	2.68	-0.46	-0.4	0.09	2643
3.05	0.51	-0.4	0.09	3057	3.02	3.08	223	2.86	2.91	2.885	-0.49	-0.4	0.09	2688
2.48	0.46	-0.38	0.09	1536	2.46	2.5	224	3.27	3.34	3.305	-0.54	-0.38	0.09	5076
1.98	0.4	-0.36	0.09	4646	1.96	1.99	225	3.77	3.87	3.82	-0.6	-0.36	0.09	5977
1.55	0.34	-0.33	0.09	2678	1.53	1.56	226	4.34	4.42	4.38	-0.66	-0.33	0.09	5097
1.17	0.29	-0.29	0.08	4069	1.16	1.18	227	4.9	5.09	4.995	-0.72	-0.29	0.08	5688
1	0.26	-0.27	0.08	2522	0.99	1.01	227.5	5.23	5.42	5.325	-0.74	-0.27	0.08	661
0.86	0.23	-0.25	0.07	2665	0.85	0.86	228	5.59	5.77	5.68	-0.77	-0.25	0.07	663
0.62	0.18	-0.21	0.06	5800	0.61	0.62	229	6.39	6.53	6.46	-0.82	-0.21	0.06	697
0.44	0.14	-0.17	0.05	9861	0.43	0.44	230	7.21	7.36	7.285	-0.86	-0.17	0.05	3907
0.3	0.1	-0.13	0.04	6060	0.29	0.31	231	8.07	8.23	8.15	-0.9	-0.13	0.04	189

Figure 8-18. Unbalanced Long Call Butterfly Risk Graph

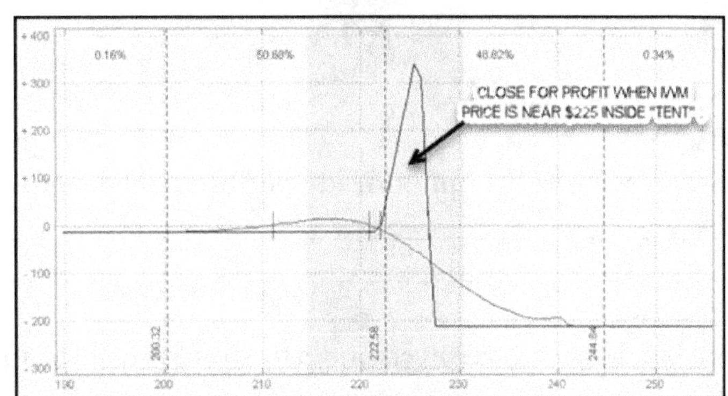

The Double Butterfly Example

The double butterfly, described in some detail above, is shown on an option chain in figure 8-19. The long put and long call butterflies use long wings and short bodies. The examples both have one long option in each wing and two short options in the bodies. The number of options could be increased to achieve more profit potential, which would also increase the debit required when this trade is filled.

The double butterfly shown on the following option chain in figure 8-19 is an interesting butterfly strategy. Before taking it live, be sure to test this trade in simulation a few times in order to become familiar with the set up and exit routines. You should also test +2, – 4, +2 and perhaps +4, – 8, +4 versions of this trade. The external values of 2 and 4 represent the number of options used in each long wing and the central values of 4 and 8 represent the number of options to include in the central bodies. Be sure to check the risk profiles for each of these trade setups. Finally, you will also be able to view both the cost and the profit potential of each of the trade simulations in the order confirmation dialogs.

Figure 8-19. The Double Butterfly on an Option Chain.

Stock quote and option quote for IWM on 3/10/21 16:28:02														
LAST	LX	Net Ch	BID	BX	ASK	AX	Size	Volume	Open	High	Low			
227.2	P	3.88	228	P	227.97	P	3 x 1	4E+07	226	228.97	225.2			
UNDERLYING EXTRA INFO														
Last Si	Yield	PE	Div	Div.Freq	Ex Div.Da	52High	52Low	Shares		Beta				
0	1.04%	136.9	0.59	Q	12/14/20	230.3	95.69	218600000		1.294				
12 MAR 21 (2) 100 (Weeklys)					CALLS						PUTS		30.99% (±4.802)	
Mark	Delta	Theta	Vega	Open.Int	BID	ASK	Strike	BID	ASK	Mark	Delta	Theta	Vega	Open.Int
8.075	0.86	-0.17	0.04	2627	7.96	8.19	220	0.46	0.52	0.49	-0.13	-0.3	0.04	6711
7.23	0.83	-0.22	0.05	2632	7.13	7.33	221	0.57	0.65	0.61	-0.16	-0.3	0.05	1093
6.32	0.82	-0.25	0.05	1703	6.2	6.44	222	0.69	0.79	0.74	-0.19	-0.3	0.06	2341
5.88	0.8	-0.26	0.05	840	5.78	5.98	222.5	0.76	0.85	0.805	-0.21	-0.3	0.06	624
5.465	0.75	-0.28	0.06	1619	5.36	5.57	223	0.91	0.94	0.925	-0.23	-0.4	0.06	6390
4.665	0.69	-0.32	0.07	5535	4.57	4.76	224	1.06	1.14	1.1	-0.27	-0.4	0.07	1963
3.905	0.63	-0.35	0.07	4612	3.81	4	225	1.34	1.38	1.36	-0.32	-0.4	0.07	837
3.195	0.56	-0.37	0.08	4605	3.11	3.28	226	1.58	1.68	1.63	-0.38	-0.4	0.08	2531
2.57	0.53	-0.39	0.08	2505	2.51	2.63	227	1.92	2.03	1.975	-0.44	-0.4	0.08	1194
2.265	0.49	-0.39	0.08	1413	2.21	2.32	227.5	2.12	2.23	2.175	-0.48	-0.4	0.08	3743
2	0.41	-0.38	0.08	2318	1.94	2.06	228	2.33	2.49	2.41	-0.51	-0.4	0.08	1046
1.46	0.33	-0.35	0.08	1856	1.44	1.48	229	2.81	3	2.905	-0.58	-0.4	0.08	222
1.075	0.26	-0.32	0.07	4151	1.04	1.11	230	3.37	3.58	3.475	-0.65	-0.4	0.08	241
0.73	0.19	-0.27	0.07	1201	0.69	0.77	231	4.03	4.26	4.145	-0.72	-0.3	0.07	74
0.495	0.16	-0.22	0.06	1906	0.47	0.52	232	4.76	5.01	4.885	-0.78	-0.3	0.06	29
0.41	0.14	-0.19	0.05	1256	0.38	0.44	232.5	5.17	5.42	5.295	-0.8	-0.3	0.06	9
0.325	0.1	-0.17	0.05	1039	0.3	0.35	233	5.59	5.85	5.72	-0.83	-0.2	0.05	34

Exercise 11 Questions:

1. What tool can you use to see how an option trade performs relative to price changes in the underlying equity? ____________
2. Describe the structure of a long call balanced butterfly strategy like the first butterfly example that used the DIS stock ____________
3. In the risk profile, the exterior options are called wings. What is the cone-shaped plot in the middle of the plot called? ____________
4. What is the difference between a balanced and an unbalanced butterfly? ____________
5. How is a broken-wing or "skip-strike" butterfly created? ____________
6. Looking at the risk graph in figure 8-14, where does the DIS stock price achieve the strategy's maximum profit? ____________
7. The risk graph in figure 8-14 shows the long call butterfly trade suffers a financial loss as the price of Disney stock rises above $125. Explain where else the risk graph begins to show a loss based on the stock price. ______. ____________
8. What would a put butterfly be called if the wings are bought and the body is sold? ____________
9. Is the 20-40-60 Delta short put butterfly a credit spread or a debit spread? ____________
10. When the Delta 20-40-60 short put butterfly is entered, the ITM Delta 60 short put is ITM. Why can't this ITM short put be exercised? ____________

Exercise Questions with Answers

Section 1 Questions with Answers

1. Olive oil futures were traded in ancient Greece.
2. As early as the 12th century agricultural debts were bought and sold in the country of France.
3. Many believe that the first stock market system was developed in Antwerp, Belgium.
4. The East India Company became the world's first publicly traded company in the year 1602.
5. One out of three ships sailing from the East Indies were often lost to pirates.
6. Why did the London Stock Exchange initially prohibit the sale of stocks? Because of the rampant fraud.
7. Which U.S. Stock Exchange was founded in 1817? New York Stock Exchange.
8. The New York Stock Exchange is the world's largest stock exchange.
9. The NASDAQ stock exchange, which includes numerous tech stocks, was created in 1971.
10. The Secretary of the Treasury Alexander Hamilton, who served from 1789 to 1795, encouraged the creation of American Stock exchanges.
11. The Dow Jones Industrial Average (DJIA) was created by Charles Dow and originally listed a total of 12 different stocks.
12. Today, the DJIA lists the 30 largest U.S. companies based on their market capitalization.
13. The TSX stands for the Toronto Stock Exchange.
14. The TSX's high market capitalization is due to the number of large oil companies listed on that exchange.
15. SPX is the symbol used for the S&P 500 financial index.
16. The VIX is the S&P 500 volatility index, which is a tradeable index.
17. The first major stock market crash in the U.S. occurred in 1929.
18. What is the purpose of stock market "circuit breakers?" To reduce the likelihood of a market crash.
19. CBOE is an abbreviation for the Chicago Board of Options Exchange.
20. The CBOE provides oversight for the U.S. options market.

Section 2 Questions with Answers

1. Can option trading provide a steady income? Yes (with an understanding of how options work).
2. Name three well-known brokerages: 1)Fidelity 2)Vanguard 3)Charles Schwab-TD Ameritrade, 4) Interactive Brokers, 5)E*Trade, 6)Merrill, 7) Trade Station, 8) Robin Hood.
3. Do brokerages permit their clients to transfer and manage their retirement accounts? Yes.
4. What does the SEC prohibit within a retirement account? Unlimited Risk Trades.
5. Do all brokerages charge their clients trading commissions? No. Many have suspended trading commissions.
6. How are trades financed within a brokerage account? With cash, stocks, and other equities deposited and held within an individual's brokerage account.
7. Why would a brokerage issue a margin call? When the account value becomes insufficient to finance the account holder's working trades.
8. Who do margin calls protect? Both the account holder and the brokerage.
9. What causes a Regulation-T Margin Call to be issued? When a margin account makes a transaction that exceeds its available buying power. (or when not enough equity exists to cover a loss).
10. Do both stock and cash held within a margin account have identical values? Explain: Cash is credited at 100% of its value while stocks are typically credited at a percentage of their value depending on brokerage policy.
11. How does an increase in the value of the VIX index affect account margin? An increase in the VIX increases risk and simultaneously increases the amount of account margin being used.

Section 3 Questions with Answers

1. What is a *scalper*? A scalper looks for short-term price rallies and drops and closes the trades for relatively small profits.
2. Can day trading be stressful? The excessive action and demanding attention can result in stress.
3. Why do you think swing trading would be less stressful than day trading? Swing trading is not as intense, takes less time, and is less demanding.
4. What is a *pattern day trader*? A trader that makes four or more trades over five consecutive business days. Day traders are pattern day traders.
5. A "trading ladder" is well suited to which trading style? Day trading.
6. Day traders use templates that include three elements. First is the entry price. The other two are a protective stop limit and a profit target.
7. Swing traders also bracket trades with stop limits and profit targets.
8. Three terms are used to describe a company's capitalization, including large cap, mid cap, and small cap.
9. List the "four pillars of wealth": equities, options, futures, and foreign exchange.
10. Call and put options are traded on stocks, ETFs, financial indexes, and futures contracts.
11. Spending $50 on a $1,000 stock is referred to as financial leverage.
12. The abbreviation CME stands for the Chicago Mercantile Exchange.
13. Futures contracts are negotiated between producers and processors.
14. Currency pairs are traded on the Foreign Exchange.
15. The abbreviation GTC stands for Good Till Canceled.
16. Name two types of financial analysis used by traders: Fundamental and Technical.
17. Watch lists are often linked to price charts for further analysis.
18. What do the abbreviations SMA and EMA stand for? Simple Moving Average and Exponential Moving Average.
19. A moving average crossover is seen as a buy or sell signal.
20. Portfolio margin is available to experienced option traders.

Section 4 Questions with Answers

1. An option is a time-limited derivative of an equity such as a stock, ETF, financial index, futures contract, etc.
2. There are two kinds of options: call options and put options.
3. The abbreviations for in the money and out of the money are ITM and OTM.
4. Financial leverage is a major advantage of trading options.
5. Most option contracts on stocks represent 100 shares of stock.
6. The remaining time value of an option is also referred to as extrinsic value.
7. Changes in market volatility affects the price of an option.
8. Each option chain has a vertical column of option strike prices.
9. .The prices of both put and call options increase as they become deeper in the money.
10. Option values are examined on a mathematical table called an options chain.
11. You can buy and short stocks, ETFs, and even futures contracts on an options chain.
12. Out of the money options do not have any intrinsic value.
13. The difference between an option's market price and its intrinsic value is called the option's extrinsic value.
14. Open interest shows the number of option contracts that existed when the market opened in the morning of the current trading day.
15. Gamma risk increases as an option approaches its expiration date.
16. Long refers to buy while short refers to sell.
17. Trades that contain four different option strikes are often difficult to fill.
18. The incremental values between strike prices is called the strike width.
19. The acronym ATM stands for at the money.
20. Call strike prices that are greater than the ATM strike price are OTM.
21. Name three variables that affect option prices: volatility, time, price changes.
22. The Mark is midway between the Bid and the Ask.
23. Delta is the amount the option premium changes in response to a $1.00 change in the underlying.
24. Delta is also used as a measure of probability.
25. A trader might buy call options when bullish on a stock.
26. When bearish on a stock, the trader might buy a put option.
27. Another word for an uncovered short option is a naked short option.
28. A trader owns 500 shares of stock and sells five OTM call options. This is a covered call strategy.
29. The bull put vertical spread is a credit spread that sells OTM put options and buys an equal number of puts options farther OTM.
30. An iron condor combines a bull put spread and a bear call spread.
31. Diagonal and calendar spreads use two different expiration dates.
32. Credit spreads collect premium when entered. Traders are required to pay for debit spreads.
33. A Delta value of .25 has approximately a 75% probability of remaining OTM through option expiration.
34. The European expiration style option cannot be exercised prior to expiration.
35. The abbreviation IV stands for Implied Volatility. HV is Historical volatility.
36. IV Rank ranges from 0.0% to 100%.

Section 5 Questions with Answers

1. To see what is currently happening to the overall market or to a specific stock, traders examine Price Charts.
2. Japanese candlestick charts were first used in the early 1700s with rice futures.
3. The candlestick chart is among the most popular in use today.
4. Tick charts measure s specific number of trades.
5. The top and bottom of a candlestick's shadow, also called its wick, measures the high and low value for the established time duration.
6. A green candle body indicates an increase in price.
7. A double bottom chart pattern is a bullish chart pattern.
8. A demand zone is located at a price chart's support level.
9. Supply zone and price resistance are both located near the top of a price chart.
10. A demand zone is an indication of the underlying stock being oversold.
11. Exponential moving averages are weighted toward the most recent price points.
12. The abbreviation for the 50-period simple moving average is SMA(50).
13. When the 50-period SMA crosses below the EMA(20), traders see this as a sell signal.
14. The ATR(14) measures the average daily price change over the most recent 14 trading days.
15. The EMA(20) is used as the central plot for both the Bollinger bands and the Keltner Channel studies.
16. Bollinger bands plot trading volatility over time while the Keltner channel tracks a stock's average daily price change.
17. The TTM_Squeeze is used to a signal a price breakout.
18. Momentum studies such as the RSI, CCI, MACD, etc. are used to determine whether a stock is oversold or overbought.
19. The Awesome Oscillator and Stochastics Oscillator are two more momentum oscillators.
20. How many momentum studies should you place on your price charts at the same time? one.

Section 6 Questions with Answers

1. Every experienced option trader uses trading rules.
2. The rules dictate which option strategy to use based on the current market conditions.
3. Developing and using one or more watch lists is a useful practice.
4. Some traders subscribe to stock market advisories such as Investor's Business Daily.
5. Dividend distributions often produce a small price drop in the underlying stock.
6. Earnings reports are sometimes accompanied by a brief price decrease or increase.
7. Stocks included on your watch lists should have an average trading volume of at least one million shares per day.
8. A narrow Bid-to-Ask spread is an indication of high trading volume.
9. Traders check the IV% on an option chain before selecting a compatible bullish, bearish, or neutral option strategy.
10. Low IV% values or ranks reduce premium values.
11. Option trades fill faster when Open Interest values are high.
12. Expiration of long options should be greater than 90 days.
13. LEAPS stands for Long-Term Equity Anticipation Security.
14. Short put Mark values decrease as the price of the underlying stock increases.
15. Short option's Delta value should be at or below ±0.25 for a 75% probability of remaining OTM through expiration.

Section 7 Questions with Answers

1. What is a benefit of "momentum trading" versus buy-and-hold trading? High-volume (momentum) trading creates a steady income stream.
2. Why are uncovered, or naked short options vulnerable? If they become ITM they are subject to being exercised.
3. Why is it safer to trade European expiration-style index options? European-expiration style options cannot be exercised prior to option expiration.
4. What is the VIX and why is it closely watched by traders? The VIX is the S&P 500 volatility index; it increases risk when it rises in value.
5. Why do some traders sell short-term put and/or call options that exist at strike prices that are two standard deviations OTM? Far OTM strike prices are safer; a shorter time till expiration limits the amount of time the price of the underlying has to move against the trade.
6. A bracketed trade is created by adding a profit target and a protective stop.
7. Why do option traders examine risk graphs? To determine how option premium responds to price changes in the underlying.
8. The iron condor trade combines a short vertical put spread, called a bull put, and a short vertical call spread, called a bear call.
9. Option traders with small accounts often focus on collecting option premium by trading a few different credit spreads
10. Uncovered short options are traded more often by option traders that have large brokerage accounts.
11. Why do option traders roll working trades to a farther OTM strike price with a later expiration date? Rolling is a trade management technique used to salvage a losing trade.
12. Why do traders leg into a multi-strike option trade? To achieve faster order execution.

Section 8 Exercise 8-1 Questions with Answers

1. What is the primary goal of a covered call? To collect additional income by selling stock-covered call options.
2. What is the probability of the $42.50 short puts being ITM when this trade expires? 72%.
3. If the trader doesn't own the covering stock, what could be substituted in place of the stock? Buy ATM long calls.
4. Is this an example of "The Poor Man's Covered Call?" Yes.
5. How much premium will the trader collect by selling five $45 covered calls? $425.00.
6. How much premium would be received if the $42.50 strike price is used in place of the $45 strike price? $625.00.
7. What happens to this trade's risk if the $42.50 strike is used instead of the $45 strike? It decreases by 8%.

Section 8 Exercise 8-2 Questions with Answers

1. What is the goal of this trade? An increase in the value of the call options so they can be sold for profit.
2. If the trader bought 500 shares of MSFT stock rather than five call options, how much would the stock cost? $93,850.
3. Approximately how much must the trader pay for five MSFT 190 call options? $11,312.50.
4. What could you add to this long call strategy to create a synthetic long stock strategy? Sell five slightly OTM put options.
5. Why can't a synthetic long stock be traded in qualified retirement accounts? The synthetic stock is an unlimited risk option strategy.
6. How could the short put be protected to limit its risk? Buy a put a few strikes below the short put.

Section 8 Exercise 8-3 Questions with Answers

1. How can put options be used when the price of a stock, ETF, or financial index is expected to drop over an extended period? Long puts are bought and increase in value when the price underlying stock drops in value.
2. What does the trader expect the 185 strike price to do over the life of this trade? The trader expects the 185 strike price to increase in value by moving deeper ITM.
3. What should the trader do if the price of Boeing stock begins to rally? Close the trade to limit a loss; the trader might consider buying some ATM call options.
4. If the trader buys ten contracts and the Theta value is .09, how much value is expected to exit this option trade today? $90.

Section 8 Exercise 8-4 Questions with Answers

1. How many days exist until this trade expires? One day.
2. If the trader successfully sells ten bull put spreads, about how much premium is received? $470.00.
3. Based on the Delta value of the short call, what is the probability of this bull put spread remaining OTM through expiration? 77%.
4. If the price of the SPY ETF drops below the $305 long put, how much will this trade lose? $300.
5. What can be done to the strike width to increase the amount of premium this trade can earn? Increase the strike width.
6. How is this trade's risk affected if its strike width is increased? Increasing the strike width increases risk.
7. Explain the reason for your answer to question 6. Increasing the strike width of a vertical spreads increases the amount of money that can be lost.

Section 8 Exercise 8-5 Questions with Answers

1. Why do you think this option strategy is referred to as a long straddle? Both the long ATM calls and puts straddle the strike column.
2. Why does the option trader select a long-term expiration for this long straddle? To reduce the initial loss in time value.
3. Why might the trader look for and select a different stock with a lower IV% for this long straddle option strategy? A lower IV% reduces the debit in premium that must be paid when buying long options.
4. If the price of Boeing's stock is dropping, which option would most likely be kept and which one would be closed? Keep the long puts and sell the long calls.
5. Would most option traders having a strong directional bias avoid this trade? This is a neutral-bias trade rather than a directional trade. Why? Buying the losing options would be a waste of money.
6. If the price begins to make a strong directional move, how should the trader respond? Close the losing put or call options and keep the profitable put or call options.

Section 8 Exercise 8-6 Questions with Answers

1. Why is a long strangle less expensive than a long straddle? The premium is less expensive at OTM strike prices.
2. Why does the option trader select a long-term expiration for the long strangle? To reduce initial loss in time value.
3. Why do traders prefer low IV% values when buying a long-term strangle? Low IV% values reduce the debit in premium that must be paid to open this trade.
4. Based on the Delta value of the long call, about how much will the long call's premium increase with a $1.00 increase in the SPY ETF? 51 cents.
5. The price of the SPY ETF drops by $5.00 and the trader sells the long call and keeps the long put. Why did the trader sell the long call? The long call declines in value when the long put increases in value.
6. Why did the trader keep the long put? The long put is ITM and profitable.
7. A few weeks later the SPY ETF price has dropped by $45 and is now more than $40 ITM. Would selling the long put return a profit or suffer a loss? Selling the long put would return a profit.
8. Explain the reason for your answer to question 7. The SPY ETF options would begin to lose premium value from the passage of time. The trader should check Theta prior to closing this trade to determine if the trade has additional profit potential.

Section 8 Exercise 8-7 Questions with Answers

1. How long does this short vertical spread remain in effect? Less than a day.
2. What are two reasons to include the long put? (1) Reduce the amount of risk. (2) Reduce the amount of margin required.
3. If this trade's short put is placed at the 3050 strike price, which strike price would be chosen for the long put? The 3000 strike price.
4. When legging into this trade, which option is traded first? The long 3000 put.
5. Why would a trader avoid the use of a $5.00 stop-loss with this trade? A $5.00 stop-loss would likely trigger and close the trade prematurely.
6. When does it become more difficult to sell the long put? Near option expiration at the end of the trading day.
7. What two things can a trader do to prevent the short puts from becoming ITM?
   1) Include a stop loss or trailing stop to buy-to-close the short put.
   2) Roll the trade to a safer strike price and a later expiration date.
8. How many trades must succeed to offset the option premium lost when a stop loss buys to close the working short put? One successful trade should recover the loss.

Section 8 Exercise 8-8 Questions with Answers

1. Why can't the short put be traded by new and inexperienced option traders? Uncovered short options can only be traded by experienced option traders.
2. What is an option trader's primary goal when selling the short put? Premium collection.
3. How much premium did the trader receive, excluding exchange fees, when the ten $1970 short put options were originally sold? $3,700.
4. What happens to the value of Theta as an option approaches expiration? Theta's value increases rapidly as an option approaches expiration.
5. What happens to the value of Gamma if it approaches the ATM strike price? (Hint: See Gamma Risk in Section 4.) Gamma's value increases as the option approaches the ATM strike and as the trade approaches expiration. This is called "Gamma Risk."
6. How does Theta affect the value of the short put's premium as this trade nears expiration? Theta values rise rapidly causing option premium values decline near zero as an option approaches expiration.
7. What two things could the trader do to prevent the short puts from becoming ITM?
   1) Include a protective stop limit or trailing stop order.
   2) Roll the short put to a later expiration date and farther OTM strike price.
8. Explain why the short 1970 put option might be rolled to the 1800 short put that expires on the following Friday. To salvage the short RUT put trade and to prevent the short put from becoming ITM from an unexpected price drop.

Section 8 Exercise 8-9 Questions with Answers

1. A "naked short call" is also called an uncovered short call.
2. Why can't a naked short call be traded in a qualified retirement account? An uncovered short option is an unlimited risk trade which is not permitted in qualified retirement accounts.
3. The Theta value at the $2350 strike is – .05. How much premium value is lost on this trade's first day? $50.00.
4. How much premium did the trader receive, excluding exchange fees, when the ten $2350 short call options were originally sold? $1,825.
5. Approximately how much premium income would the trader receive if only five 2350 option contracts were sold? $912.
6. If this short call trade were to expire ITM and be auto exercised, it would lose substantially more money than the previous short put option trade described in Exercise 8. Explain why: OTM call strike prices have higher premium values than OTM put strike prices.
7. If you are required to roll this trade, which option expiration would you choose? The next expiration date to retain the shortest possible term short option.
8. Explain how you would choose the RUT strike price. I would choose a strike price that is two standard deviations OTM to increase my odds for success.

Section 8 Exercise 8-10 Questions with Answers

1. The short strangle is a combination of which two option strategies? The short call and the short put.
2. Why can't the short strangle be used in a qualified retirement account? An uncovered short option is an unlimited risk trade which is not permitted in qualified retirement accounts.
3. What is an advantage of trading short strangles on high-priced financial indexes, ETFs, and/or stocks? The higher prices favor short-term options and increase premium values.
4. How does the short strangle premium income potential compare to either a short call or a short put? It sums the premium collected from both the short put and the short call options.
5. The sum of the Theta values for the ten short 1970 puts and the ten short 2350 calls are – 1.34 and – 0.7 respectively. How much premium is lost on the first day of this trade? $2,040. $1,795.60.
6. If the price of the RUT index begins to rally and you decide to roll the short calls to expire on Friday of next week, what would a trader likely do with the short put? Hold the short put through expiration as long as it safely OTM.
7. Explain why the expiration date and strike prices were chosen. The far OTM strike prices were chosen to increase the odds for successfully expiring OTM. The short-term expiration limits the amount of time the price has to move against one of the option strike prices.
8. A risk profile for the short strangle is shown in figure 8-12. What do the vertical sides of the graph represent? The vertical sides of the plot are immediately above the strike prices of the short puts and the short calls.
9. In the risk profile, what does the cone-shaped plot in the middle of the square plot represent? The values of Theta relative to the price of the underlying index.

Section 8 Exercise 11 Questions with Answers

1. What tool can you use to see how an option trade performs relative to price changes in the underlying equity? A risk profile.
2. Describe the structure of a long call balanced butterfly strategy like the first butterfly example that used the DIS stock? Two long call options (the wings) on each side of a short call (the body) separated by the same number of strikes above and below the body. The sum of the long call options used in the wings is equal to the number of central short call options that form the body.
3. In the risk profile, the exterior options are called wings. What is the cone-shaped plot in the middle of the plot called? The tent or the witch's hat.
4. What is the difference between a balanced and an unbalanced butterfly? Balanced butterflies have the same number of options in each wing; unbalanced butterflies have a different number of options in each wing.
5. How is a broken-wing or "skip-strike" butterfly created? The broken-wing butterfly has different strike widths between the body and the exterior wings.
6. Looking at the risk graph in figure 8-14, where does the DIS stock price achieve the strategy's maximum profit? When the DIS stock price is at $120.
7. The risk graph in figure 8-14 shows the long call butterfly trade suffers a financial loss as the price of Disney stock rises above $125. Explain where else the risk graph begins to show a loss based on the stock price. When the price of the DIS stock drops below $115.
8. What would a put butterfly be called if the wings are bought and the body is sold? A long put butterfly.
9. Is the 20-40-60 Delta short put butterfly a credit spread or a debit spread? The 20-40-60 short put butterfly is a debit spread.
10. When the Delta 20-40-60 short put butterfly is entered, the ITM Delta 60 short put is ITM. Why can't this ITM short put be exercised? SPX index options have European-style expirations which cannot be exercised prior to expiration.

Glossary

There are many common terms that option traders use. A good many have already been used within the pages of this book. If you ran across an unfamiliar, option-specific term, perhaps the definition within this glossary would be useful.

Alert. A trader-established notification based on a preset value sent to inform the trader by e-mail and/or text messaging when a specified condition occurs. For example, if the price of the underlying security pierces an established price, the trader receives an alert either for information or in order to take action.

Ask Price. The buying price, or option premium, in dollars and cents, to be paid for each share of the underlying optionable security within an option contract (most often 100 shares per option contract). When trading shares of stock, Ask is used to sell, and Bid is used to buy.

At the money (ATM). An option strike price (or *exercise* price) that is closest to the current price of the underlying optionable security.

Backwardation (or Normal Backwardation). See *Contango.*

Base or Basing. A term used to describe a sideways movement on a price chart. Rally, base, and drop describe a sequence of upward, sideways, and downward price moves.

Bearish. A negative bias held by a trader who expects a security or market to decline in value.

Bearish Spread. An option spread designed to be profitable if the underlying security declines in price. A common bearish spread consists of buying an in the money put and selling an out of the money put. This is called a *bear put spread.*

Beta. A measure of how closely the movement of the market price of a stock corresponds to the movement of the financial index to which it belongs. For example, the beta value of AAPL stock is a comparison of its market price volatility with that of the S&P 500 financial index.

Bid Price. Option sell orders are initiated using the Bid cell on the selected strike price row of an option chain. The default price is the Mark, which is midway between the Bid and Ask prices.

Bid-to-Ask Spread. The difference in price between the Bid and Ask values on an option chain. An option chain's Mark value is midway between the Bid and Ask values. Narrow Bid-to-Ask spreads reflect brisk trading activity and minimize *slippage* in the premium paid or received for a trade.

Bracketed Trade. A trade that includes a limit entry, a protective stop, and a profit target. It is typically used when buying shares of stock or exchange traded funds (ETFs).

Breakout. As applied to market price, a breakout refers to a strong price rally or drop. Traders look for entry opportunities when their analysis signals a possible price breakout.

Brokerage Account. An account held by the client of a brokerage firm that includes securities and cash. The value of the account may be used as collateral (or *margin*) to finance the purchase of stocks, options, futures contracts, and other marketable securities.

Bullish. A positive bias held by a trader who expects a security or market to increase in value.

Bullish Spread. An option spread designed to be profitable if the underlying security rises in price. A common bullish spread consists of buying an ATM call and selling an out of the money call. This spread is called a *bull call spread.*

Buy to Close Order. A buy order placed by an option trader who originally sold one or more option contracts. The buy to close order requires the option trader to pay premium to close an active position.

Calendar (or Time Spread). An option spread created by selling one option and buying another on the same security. The option sold expires sooner than the option bought. This spread is named *calendar spread* because the two contracts have different expiration dates. The goal of a calendar spread is to receive more income from the sold option compared with the option that is purchased. If sufficient time remains in the option bought, another option may be sold for additional premium income.

Call. A call option contract entitles the buyer to acquire (or "call away") 100 shares per contract of the underlying security from the seller, who is contractually obligated to deliver the stock to the buyer if the call's strike price becomes in the money and is exercised. This transaction must occur prior to contract expiration.

Called Away. The buyer of a call option may call the optioned security away from the seller if the option becomes in the money (ITM) by one cent. (See *in the money.*) The seller must deliver the stock to the buyer, who must pay the seller the option price. If the seller does not own the called stock, he or she must purchase and deliver the stock to the buyer for a loss. If the sold options expire ITM by one penny, they are auto-exercised by The Options Clearing Corporation.

Candlestick Chart. A price chart that uses red and green rectangles that resemble the bodies of candles. The candles have lines above and below, called *shadows* or *wicks.* The bottom and top of each candle body represents the opening and closing price for the selected time interval, i.e., week, day, hour, and so on. A green candle body represents a rally (a higher closing price than that of the opening price). Red candle bodies represent a drop candle, i.e., a lower closing price than the opening price.

Cash Settlement Option. Option contracts on financial indexes are cash settled rather than stock settled. In the case of either a call or a put, the seller must pay the buyer the difference between the option price and the current ITM price.

Charm is a minor Greek value that reflects the rate at which the Delta of an option changes with the passage of time. The value of Theta is a derivative of Charm. Hence, Charm is a measure of *Delta decay.*

Chart Interval. Any of several chart time intervals used on price charts. Examples are weekly, daily, hourly, and minute charts. Most traders look across several time intervals to determine the characteristics of price movements across time. Experienced chart analysts use candlestick charts beginning with weekly intervals and working their way to shorter time intervals to develop an understanding of price characteristics. Chart studies are often applied to enhance a trader's expectation relative to future price movements.

Chart Study. A mathematical indicator used on security price charts to show price averages, overbought/oversold conditions, trading volume, average price movements, and much more.

Chicago Board of Exchange (CBOE). The company responsible for providing live options data used by client brokerages throughout the world.

Closeout Date. A predetermined date on which a contract should be closed to preserve the value that remains within an option position.

Closing Price. The final price at which a security traded at the end of the trading day. When applied to an option contract, this is the premium paid or received when a buy to close or sell to close transaction is processed.

Closing Purchase. A buy to close transaction conducted by the holder of a short option (the option writer) to liquidate an option position.

Closing Sale. A sell to close transaction conducted by the holder of a long option (the option buyer) to liquidate an option position.

Contango. This is a term related to a comparison between the spot price of a future and the current contract price. Some option traders borrow and misapply the term, in spite of the fact that options do not have *spot prices.* When the price of an option or futures contract is either rising or falling in value, it is said to be either contango or in normal backwardation. Contango is when the contract price exceeds the expected future spot price. In options, contango implies the current premium at the strike price of a short position has lost value, profiting the holder of a short option. Normal backwardation relates to the loss in the premium value of a long option.

Contract (or Option Contract). An agreement to relinquish an underlying security if the agreed upon option price either exceeds the contracted call price by one cent or falls below the contracted put price by one cent. Contracts are managed by The Options Clearing Corporation.

Covered Option. A call option position that is collateralized by a security, such as shares of stock or a put option contract that is collateralized by cash. When a covered call option contract is exercised by the option buyer, the seller must deliver the optioned securities to the buyer at the option price agreed upon.

Crossovers. On price charts, a crossover is the point at which one element or line crosses another. This can be the crossover of two moving average plots, a crossover of two study envelope lines, as when a Bollinger band envelope crosses inside the Keltner channel envelope, or when one or more price plots cross a standard moving average plotline.

Day Order. A limit or protective stop order that automatically expires at the end of the trading day. (See *good till canceled* order).

Delta. A mathematical value that determines the change in option premium value resulting from a $1.00 change in the market price of the underlying option security, such as a stock or ETF. Call Delta values are positive and increase from 0.0 to 1.0 as calls drop deeper ITM. Put Deltas are negative and range from 0.0 to –1.0. Put Deltas move closer to –1.0 as the put strike prices increase.

Discount Brokerage. A brokerage that offers unusually low commission and exchange fees.

Distal. A line drawn on a price chart at the bottom of a demand zone near support or the top of a supply zone near resistance to represent the location of a protective stop. Distal lines are the most distant from the current price.

Diversification. An investing strategy that spreads risk across a variety of companies, industry sectors, or both to reduce exposure to a single industry.

Drawing Tools. A toolset contained on most trading platforms that permits the user to draw trend lines, price lines, symbols, text, and other marks on the price chart.

Drop. A term used to describe a downward price movement.

E-mini Future. A futures derivative of a financial index such as the S&P 500 index. The e-mini futures are traded directly in the futures market or indirectly through options on futures. The e-mini financial index symbols are: S&P 500 = ES, NASDAQ = NQ, DJIA = YM, Russell 2000 = RTY, and S&P 400 =

EMD. The thinkorswim trading platform inserts a slash sign in front of the symbol, such as /ES for S&P 500 index futures.

Electronic Communication Exchange Networks (ECNs). ECNs are also called alternative trading networks. The ECNs support stock and currency trading outside the traditional stock exchanges. They are computer-driven networks designed to match limit orders.

Exchange Fees. An options exchange originated fee charged by an option exchange for each option contract bought or sold.

Exchange Traded Fund (ETF). A security comprised of several stocks or a market index. ETFs are frequently made up of stocks belonging to the same market sector or geographical region. For example, an ETF may bundle several Asia-Pacific or European stocks.

Execution. The completion of a buy or sell order. This is transacted by market makers or, to a lesser extent, on the floor of a stock exchange.

Exercise. Option buyers may execute (or "exercise") their contractual rights when the price of the underlying pierces an option price prior to contract expiration. Call buyers pay the option price for receipt of the optioned security (call stock away from the seller). Put buyers put stock to the option seller. The underlying optioned securities and cash are transferred between buyer and seller accounts.

Exercise (or Strike) Price. The agreed upon option price (or strike price) per share of the underlying security. The call buyer pays the call seller, and the put seller pays the put buyer. The underlying optionable security and cash are transferred between buyer and seller accounts.

Expiration Day (or Maturity Date). The final day of an option contract. Once an option contract expires, the option contract is null and void. The goal of an option seller is to have the option contract expire worthless, at which time the option can no longer be exercised.

Extrinsic Value. An ITM option's current premium value. When a long option is exercised, its value consists of an option's intrinsic value (the distance from the current price of the underlying security) less the extrinsic value (the option's remaining time value).

Foreign Currency Exchange (Forex). The forex market is the largest security market in the world, trading in trillions of dollars each day. Traders speculate on the increase and decrease in one currency, such as the dollar, against another currency, such as the British pound or Euro. They buy currency pairs comprised of a base and a quote currency. Forex buyers buy a base currency against the quote currency if the buyer expects the base currency to increase against the quote currency. If correct, the buyer sells the pair for a profit once the base currency has rallied to his or her satisfaction.

Full-Service Broker. A brokerage firm that provides a full array of products and services. This may include banking, market research, investment counseling, and a variety of investment quality securities. Full-service brokerages usually charge higher transaction fees to cover the higher cost of their services.

Futures Contracts. A contract between a producer and a processor for the production and delivery of a product by the producer to the processor at a contract price agreed upon. The processor pays the processor in advance of delivery. Each futures contract has an expiration date and must be fulfilled prior to expiration. Futures speculators buy and sell futures contracts with an expectation of making profit margins from the difference between the buying and selling prices.

Gamma. Gamma is an option *Greek*. The value of Gamma controls the sensitivity of Delta to a change in the market price of the underlying optionable security. A 0.15 change in Gamma causes the value of Delta to change by 0.15 with a $1.00 change in the underlying. Experienced option traders are sensitive to the effect of Gamma, particularly near option expiration, where option premiums are most sensitive to changes in the values of Gamma.

Gamma Risk. Since Gamma has a strong influence on option premium values, option traders are sensitive to *gamma risk.* This phenomenon occurs when an option contract approaches expiration at strikes that are at or close to the ATM strike.

Good Till Canceled (GTC) Order. A limit or a stop order that remains in force for a sustained period. The amount of time a GTC order continues to work depends on the brokerage. Some limit GTC order to 60 or 90 days. Others allow their clients to specify GTC expiration dates.

Greeks. Greek letters used on several of the option chain column headings. The Greeks are found in the formulas used to compute option premium values. Some represent English words such as Delta (difference), Rho (rate of interest), Theta (time value), Vega (volatility). The Greek letter Gamma is used to determine the rate of change in Delta. (Although Vega is not a Greek letter, it was adopted to represent volatility.)

Hedge. A financial position designed to offset losses suffered by the failure of a secondary investment. It can be thought of as insurance against an unlimited loss. A perfect hedge returns 100 percent of the value of a secondary investment in the event it fails to produce the intended results.

Index Option. An option whose underlying security is a stock index. Three popular index option symbols are the SPX (S&P 500), NDX (NASDAQ), the RUT (Russell 2000), all of which are heavily traded.

In the Money (ITM). A call option is ITM when the market price of the underlying security is greater than the option's strike (exercise) price. A put option is ITM when the market price of the underlying security is less than the put option's strike (exercise) price.

Intrinsic Value. The difference between the current market value of the underlying security that is ITM and an option's strike price. A call that is $5 ITM has an intrinsic value of $5. Intrinsic value applies to the value of the underlying security. *Extrinsic* value applies to an ITM option's current premium value.

Inverted. Used as a maintenance technique to either offset a loss or receive a limited profit when one leg of a short strangle is jeopardized by becoming in the money. Becoming inverted occurs when a trader either buys a put above a short call or buys a call below a short put. The trader's goal is to minimize loss, and in some cases the inversion may return a small profit. (A short strangle is constructed by selling the same number of option contracts of out of the money calls and out of the money puts that both expire on the same date.)

IV Rank. Used in place of IV% by many long-term option traders, IV Rank compares current IV% with its yearly high and low values. IV Rank values range from 0% to 100%.

Kappa. An option *Greek* constant used to compare a change in option premium value with a 1% change in current option volatility.

Lambda. A minor option *Greek* that measures the ratio of the dollar price change of an option to a 1% change in the expected price volatility (or the *implied volatility* of the underlying equity. Lambda measures how much an option's price changes compared to a given change in implied volatility. Lambda's value is higher when more time remains until the option's expiration, and declines in value as the option approaches expiration. When lambda is high, the option value is much more sensitive to small changes in volatility.

Last Sale Price. The final price of an equity security (stock, ETF, option, etc.) when last sold or purchased. (Last is available on option chains to show the last premium amount paid at the strike prices of all call and put options.)

LEAPS. The acronym used for **L**ong-term **E**quity **A**ntici**P**ation **S**ecurities. LEAPS are typically used with call option contracts in anticipation of a strong price rally over one to three years. Many option contracts have expiration dates as far out as three years.

Legging In. Entering one or more options at different times when two or more strikes are included in an option strategy. One example could be to buy a long put and then sell a short put that is closer to the money to reduce the amount of account margin. A trader can also leg a long call into a bull call spread to create a butterfly spread for maintenance purposes. "Legging" a long call into a butterfly adds a bull put credit spread. This can be done to recover from what would otherwise be a losing trade.

Leverage, Financial. An investment instrument that provides a higher rate of return using a smaller amount of money.

Limit Order. An order to purchase or sell at a specified price. When buying, the limit order requires the price of the underlying security to be at or below the limit price. When selling, the price of the underlying security must be at or above the specified price. Limit orders are transacted as either DAY or GTC orders.

Limited Risk. A risk management strategy. An example is buying an option contract in which the maximum risk is the premium paid at entry.

Liquid (or Liquidity). The speed at which a security can be traded. In options, a high level of Open Interest signifies an acceptable level of liquidity.

Liquidity and Liquidity Risk. Market liquidity is required for trades to execute in a reasonable amount of time. A low-liquidity level indicates a lack of interest on the part of market traders. An illiquid security can languish unbought and unsold for months and years. Traders are advised to avoid entry into low-liquidity securities. Funding liquidity is a concern of corporate treasurers who must find sufficient funds to keep the company afloat, i.e., pay bills and make payroll to sustain normal business operations.

Listed Options. Actively traded options that are listed on an options exchange, such as the CBOE.

Long Order. Buying a security is said to be taking a long position in that security.

Longer-Term Options. Option contracts with long-term expiration dates, typically those contracts that expire in more than 90 days. Some longer-term options are classified as LEAPS. These expire in one year or more. Some option contracts remain active for up to three years.

Market Depth. The resistance to price change based on trading volume. Market depth is a measure of the trading volume required to move the price of the underlying security. A 100-share trade is not sufficient to impact the price when market depth is high. A trade of one million shares typically exceeds the market depth and moves the market price of the underlying security.

Market Order. An order to purchase or sell a security at the current listed market price. The price is established by an authorized *market maker,* who represents the security exchange responsible for the selected security. Market orders are executed immediately and have priority over limit orders. Market orders are used with protective stops.

Market Sector. A market category that includes a specific type of business. Categories include basic materials, capital goods, consumer discretionary, consumer staples, energy, financial, health care, technology, telecommunications, transportation, and utilities.

Maturity Date. Also called *contract expiration date,* the maturity date is the final trading day of an option contract. Upon contract expiration, all open positions cease to exist.

Minor Greeks. Some Greeks that are used within the mathematical pricing model equations are rarely, if ever, discussed. These include, but are not limited to lambda, epsilon, vomma, vera, speed, zomma, color, ultima. A handful of these; including lambda, vomma, ultima, charm, and zomma; are briefly described within this glossary. None of these minor Greeks are available within the thinkorswim trading platform. These *minor* Greeks are used as variables within the option pricing models. They affect things such as the change in delta with a change in volatility. Brief descriptions of five of the minor Greeks are included within this glossary for information purposes.

However, none of these minor Greeks will ever be used in your daily trading activities.

Moving Average. A mathematical average of data points over a specified period. Moving averages are used on financial price charts to show the average price over a selected interval of time. Examples are the SMA(9), SMA(20), SMA(50), or SMA(200), referring, respectively, to 9-, 20-, 50-, or 200-period simple moving averages. Other types of moving averages also exist, such as exponential moving average (EMA) and triangular moving averages (TMA). The EMA places more emphasis on the most recent data points. The TMA places more emphasis on the center data points of the specified range, i.e., 9, 20, 50, 200, and so on.

Naked Writing (or *Uncovered Short Puts or Calls*). Selling an uncollateralized call option or a *cash covered* put option. The naked call or put seller does not have a position in the underlying security, nor is it *covered* by a long option position as in a bull put spread strategy, which "covers" a farther out of the money (OTM) short call.

Neutral Option Strategy. An option strategy, such as the Gamma-Delta-Neutral spread, used to profit from a small fluctuation in the market price of the underlying stock. Neutral spreads are typically *ratio spreads.* An example is the purchase of a number of call option contracts at one strike price and the sale of a greater number of call contracts at a higher strike price to achieve Gamma neutrality. The sum of Deltas is used to determine how many shares of the underlying stock must be shorted, where each share of stock has a Delta value of 1.0. **Neutral Spread.** An option spread in which the trader believes the price of the underlying security will move sideways, without either a strong price rally or drop. A common neutral spread consists of simultaneously selling an OTM call and an OTM put to collect premium. This spread is called a *short strangle.* The trader believes the market price of the underlying security will remain between the strike prices of the call and put through contract expiration.

Novice Trader. An amateur trader who is both uneducated and inexperienced in the dynamics of financial markets. Novice traders typically buy high and sell low and are rarely familiar with account management or risk management strategies.

Odds Enhancer. Any one of hundreds of mathematical studies used by traders to enhance the statistical probability of their trading success. Odds enhancers are used on charts and tables to indicate such metrics as trader sentiment, trading volume, price breakouts or reductions, and so on.

Open Interest. The number of working option contracts at each *strike price* listed on an option chain.

Opening Price. The first price at which a security or option is traded when the market initially opens.

Option. A derivative of a security that conveys a term-limited contract between a buyer and a seller. The buyer of a call option pays a contract premium for the right to buy call shares of the underlying security from a call seller, i.e., to call away shares at the option price. The buyer of a put option pays a contract premium for the right to put shares of the underlying security to the put seller, i.e., to put shares to the seller at the option price. However, the option contract can be exercised by the option buyer only if the market price of the underlying security exceeds the option price by at least one cent. This is called being in the money (ITM). If the option contract expires before the price of the underlying security becomes ITM, the option contract *expires worthless* and all contract obligations terminate.

Option Chain. A financial table used by option traders to buy and sell call and/or put option contracts at *strike prices* above, at, and below the current market price of the underlying security. Each option chain has a specific contract expiration date. Columns include essential information such as the Bid (sell) and Ask (buy) prices, current Open Interest, mathematical probabilities, time values, implied volatility, and so on.

Options Clearing. An issuer of tradable option contracts. Examples include the Chicago Board of Exchange, American Stock Exchange, Pacific Stock Exchange, Philadelphia Stock Exchange, International Securities Exchange, and so on.

Options Exchange. A for-profit company that transacts options trades. Examples include the Chicago Board Options Exchange, American Stock Exchange, and International Securities Exchange.

Option Selling (or Option Writing). Clicking the Bid cell of a selected strike price row within an option chain is used to sell (or *write*) one or more option contracts. Most option contracts represent 100 of an underlying security. (See *covered writing, naked writing*).

Option Spread. An option trading strategy that includes two or more *legs* on the same security at different strike prices. A spread may simultaneously buy a call and sell a farther OTM call (a *bull call spread*). Some option strategies, such as *butterfly* and *iron condor* spreads, include two puts and two calls at different strike prices.

Option Strategy. Any one of many option strategies for buying, selling, or buying and selling option call and/or put contracts.

Order. An offer to buy or sell a financial security, including equities, option or future contracts, or foreign exchange currency pairs. Orders are transmitted by traders to brokerage companies who submit orders to one or more governing securities exchanges. Once received, buy and sell orders are matched by a market maker. Option market makers are contracted by exchanges to fulfill option buy and sell orders. Once orders are matched, electronic records of the order fulfillment are returned to the originating brokerages, who in turn notify the trader. Option orders include call and/or put option contracts at one or more strike prices. Some option spreads may also include the purchase of underlying shares of stock.

Order Bar. A horizontal row containing order information, including buy and/or sell instructions, number of contracts, option price(s), option expiration date(s), order duration, order type (limit, market, stop, etc.).

One Cancels Other (OCO). A bracketed order that includes two or more stops. When one stop triggers, all orders that may remain are automatically canceled. For example, when a protective stop is executed, the companion profit target stop is simultaneously canceled.

Order Confirmation Dialog. A dialog containing an order description and pricing information on a queued order ready for submission.

Order Duration. Order durations vary with the type of trade required to accomplish the trader's goal. There are DAY (expires at the close of normal trading hours), GTC (good till canceled orders), EXT (remains open during the day's extended trading hours), and GTC_EXT (an extended hours order that is good till canceled).

Order Rules Dialog. A dialog used to establish automated order triggers based on a price, an *option chain* value, or a chart study.

Out of the Money (OTM). A call option strike price that is higher than the market price of the underlying optionable security. A put option strike price is lower than the market price of the underlying optionable security. The value of an OTM option contract is the available premium at the option strike price(s). The premium value, i.e., the Mark, is typically midway between an option's Bid and Ask price.

Portfolio Margin. A margin account originally promulgated by the Securities and Exchange Commission (SEC). A portfolio margin account grants additional credit to brokerage clients on the basis of a minimum account balance (typically between $100,000 and $125,000) and the client's trading experience. While standard margin accounts are typically granted the use of 50% of their account equity, portfolio margin account holders may collateralize up to 85% of their account equity. This expands the ability of portfolio margin account holders to extend their trading activity.

Position. The position of a working trade is the number of shares, or option contracts, that are either bought or sold in anticipation of a profit. Option contracts often include two or more *legs* (or *spreads*) comprised of simultaneous buy (long) and sell (short) orders.

Premium. The value of each optioned share of an underlying security at the specified strike price. The premium value is typically midway between the Bid (sell) and Ask (buy) price and is called the Mark (market price). Premium is highest when an option is initially traded. Premium values erode as the underlying option contract approaches the contract expiration date.

Professional Trader. A knowledgeable, experienced trader who makes a full-time living buying and selling securities listed on one or more financial markets is considered a professional trader.

Proximal. A line drawn on a price chart at the top of a demand zone near support or the bottom of a supply zone near resistance to represent a location near the entry point of a trade. Proximal lines are the closest to the current price.

Put. A put option entitles the buyer to *put* the optioned shares of the underlying security to the seller of the *put* option contract if the option price falls below the contract's strike price and becomes ITM. Each option contract typically includes 100 shares of stock.

Rally. A term used to describe an upward move in price.

Return if Called. The amount of income received by a covered call writer, expressed as a percentage. The return includes the original premium received when traded, the appreciation in the value of the underlying stock, and any dividends paid prior to exercise.

Rho. Rho measures the sensitivity to option premium caused by changes in the prevailing rate of interest. A Rho value of .050 causes a decrease in the value of option premiums by .050 if interest rates rise by 1.0.

Risk/Reward Management (also Trade Management). The management of a working trade. May be closed for profit or rolled into another option position. The goal of trade management is to either avoid or minimize a financial loss.

Rolling Down. Closing an option and opening another that expires on the same date but at a lower strike price when rolling down puts farther OTM; can also be used to move short calls closer to the money for more premium when the price of the underlying is dropping.

Rolling Out. Simultaneously closing a working option position and opening a new position expiring at a later date.

Rolling Up. Closing an option and opening another that expires on the same date but at a higher strike price when rolling up calls, or at a lower strike price when rolling up puts.

Rolling Out and Up or Down. Simultaneously closing a working option position and opening a new position at a new strike above or below and expiring at a later date.

Scalp or Scalping. The action of taking small profits from a small price increase in a long trade or a small decrease in a short trade. For example, a pattern day trader may buy 100 shares of a stock for $25/share and then sell it several minutes later for $25.20/share for a small $20 profit. This requires day traders who scalp throughout each day to use low-commission discount brokerages.

Sell to Close Order. A sell order placed by an option trader who originally bought one or more option contracts. If the sell to close order is filled, the option trader will receive option premium.

Sentiment (or Market Sentiment). The current prevailing aggressiveness or timidity of buyers and/or sellers toward one or more securities or the financial market as a whole.

Simulated (Paper) Trading. A feature provided on many trading platforms that permits traders to practice their trading skills or to test new trading strategies.

Short Position. Selling a security, such as a stock, option, or future, is said to be shorting that position. Shorting a stock happens when a *bearish* trader sells a stock in anticipation of a drop in the market price of that stock. A *buy to cover* order is placed to close the position and take profit from the loss.

Short-Life Option. A short-life option contract expires within 60 days or less. Many weekly options that expire within days to a few weeks are traded.

Skew. Skew occurs when option premiums become inverted owing to a temporary inversion in implied volatility values. *Horizontal skew* causes shorter expiration options to have higher premium values than longer expiration options. *Vertical skew* causes farther OTM options to have higher premium values than strikes that exist closer to the money.

Slippage. A change in the premium midpoint that exists between the Bid and the Ask price of the underlying. Slippage is greatest on illiquid securities that typically have large Bid-to-Ask spread widths. Slippage is small on actively traded securities having narrow Bid-to-Ask spreads that are often only a few cents.

Stock Capitalization Categories. Stock categories are divided by *market capitalization.* Large cap stocks are greater than ten billion dollars. Midcap stocks range from one to ten billion dollars. Small cap stocks are less than one billion dollars.

Stock Scanner. A computer-based tool used to establish specific parameters, such as price ranges, volumes, current volatilities, moving average crossovers, and so on. These parameters are used to find and list stocks meeting the established scan criteria.

Straddle. The straddle is an option strategy designed to profit from a strong price move in the underlying security in either direction. Strong trading volatility is desirable. A long straddle includes the simultaneous purchase of a put and a call on the same security having the same strike price and expiration date. A short straddle includes the simultaneous sale of a put and a call at the same strike price and expiration date. Many straddles are traded at the current ATM (at the money) strike price.

Strangle. The short strangle is a neutral trade strategy that profits from the sale of an equivalent number of put and call option contracts on the same underlying security and with the same expiration dates. The strike prices are far OTM to avoid exercise throughout the option contract life. The goal of the short strangle is to collect premium by selling one or more put and call contracts. The long strangle buys put and call contracts at different strike prices that expire on the same contract date. The buyer of a long strangle seeks a strong movement in the price of the underlying security. With a substantial move in the underlying, the profitable position can be sold for more premium than originally spent on both legs of the strangle option.

Strike Price. Strike prices are in a column at the center of an option chain. An ATM strike price is closest to the market value of the underlying security. OTM call strike prices are greater than the ATM strike price; OTM put strike prices are lower than the ATM strike price. Option traders evaluate premium, Open Interest, and other values at different strike prices when constructing an option strategy. An option's strike price is also referred to as *the exercise price.*

Swing Trader. A market trader that trades securities in anticipation of a *price swing* that returns a profit.

Tau. The absolute change in option price in response to a 1.0% change in volatility. Tau is also used to capture the sensitivity of an option's premium to a change in implied volatility.

Target Exit Point. A predetermined price to close a working order. The trader 1) buys an option contract for less than paid at entry, or 2) sells an option contract for more than paid at entry. (Buy for a dime and sell to close for a dollar, or sell for a dollar and buy to close for a dime.)

Time Premium. The reduction of an option's premium value, measured by the Greek Theta, caused by the passage of time. The decay of time premium is also referred to as *extrinsic value.* Premium value declines more rapidly as an option contract approaches the contract expiration date.

Time Spread. An option spread consisting of the purchase of an option and the simultaneous sale of a *different* option on the *same* security with a *nearer* expiration date. The purpose of a time spread is to profit from the accelerated loss in time value of the option that is written, relative to the option that is purchased. Time spreading is often a *neutral* strategy, but it can also be bullish or bearish, depending on the options involved (more often referred to as a *calendar spread*).

Trading Days. There are 252 trading days in the year. (Also see *trading hours.*)

Trading Floor. The main floor of a stock or options exchange where market makers fill sell and buy orders. Most trading floor activity is being replaced by automated, computer-based trading.

Trading Hours. Normal trading hours begin at 9:30 a.m. and close at 4:00 p.m. EST. Morning extended trading hours are from 4:00 a.m. till 9:30 a.m. EST. Evening extended trading hours are from 4:00 p.m. through 8:00 p.m. EST.

Trading Ladder. A trading interface on a computer with vertical green and red bars that look like ladders. Each bar represents a price point of the underlying security. Clicking a green bar is used to buy a security at the selected price; clicking a red bar is used to sell a security at the selected price. Multiple OCO-style orders with a limit buy order, a protective stop, and a profit target (a *bracketed order*) are often structured and sent on trading ladders. Trading ladders are popular for use by pattern day traders and futures speculators.

Trading Platform. A trading platform is a computer-based trading application, either installed directly on a brokerage client's computer or accessible through the Internet. Trading platforms provide an interface between a brokerage client and the brokerage for round trip order entry, processing, and confirmation.

Transaction Fees (Commissions and Exchange Fees). The cost of buying or selling a security. Commissions and exchange fees are charged by brokerage firms. The commissions paid are typically governed by a brokerage schedule. They can be a fixed fee per equity trade, such as $6.99 or $9.99 per trade or a per-share fee, such as $0.005 per share. Exchange fees originate at the options exchange, such as the CBOE. An exchange fee is charged for each option contract traded and can range from $0.50 per contract to $1.50 per contract. Financial index option exchange fees are among the highest exchange fees charged to brokerages, which pass exchange fees through to their client transactions. Exchange fees are paid round trip, i.e., on both trade entry and exit.

Trend Line. Trend lines are used on price charts to show price direction. An upward trend line is called a *rally*, whereas a downward trend line is called a *drop*. A sideways trend line is said to be *basing*. If a price is making a series of higher highs and higher lows, it is said to be on an uptrend; if it is making a series of lower lows and lower highs, it is said to be in a downtrend.

Truncated Risk. Risk can be *truncated* (or hedged) by entering a stop-loss or buying/selling a position to limit possible losses of a working position. When an option contract is purchased, it has limited risk and unlimited reward. The risk is the money originally spent on option premium. Unlimited reward is based on a movement in the underlying in the trader's favor. For example, buying a call that moves ITM can produce a profit that is many times greater than the original premium paid when the trade was entered.

Ultima is the rate at which the Vomma of an option responds to volatility in the underlying market.

Underlying. A stock, ETF, financial index, or futures contract. Option contracts are financial derivatives of an *underlying* security. This term is commonly used by traders who buy and sell equities, futures, and forex pairs.

Vega. Vega reflects a change in an option's price resulting from a change in the underlying security's *implied volatility*. Vega causes a change in premium value for every 1% change in implied volatility. A Vega value of 0.10 causes a premium change of $0.10 for each 1% change in implied volatility.

Vertical Spread. An option strategy comprised of two call or two put positions, one above the other, i.e., arranged vertically. A *bull call spread* is an example that includes buying a call and selling a call above, i.e., at a higher strike price. A *bear put spread* includes buying a put and selling a put below, i.e., at a lower strike price.

Volatility. A measure of the frequency at which trading is occurring; also a measure of trader sentiment. High current volatility indicates higher than usual trading activity. Historical volatility for a specific security is the average number of daily trades conducted over the past twelve months. Implied volatility compares current trading volume with historical volatility. Option traders make extensive use of implied volatility data. Volatility can have the greatest impact on the time value of option premium. High volatility causes greater price fluctuation, increasing risk, and corresponding option premiums and is most noticeable for ATM options.

Volume. For options, the number of contracts that have been traded within a specific period, usually a day or a week. For equity securities, futures, and forex, the volume represents the number of trades, typically in the millions, that are traded during each trading day.236 GLOSSARY.

Vomma is a second-order derivative for an option's value. Vomma is the rate at which the Vega of an option responds to market volatility. A positive value for vomma indicates that a percentage point increase in volatility results in an increase in an option's value. Although rarely discussed, vomma is like Vega, Delta, and Gamma in its use for options pricing.

VWAP. VWAP stands for volume-weighted average price. It is a measure of the underlying's price based on the number of shares or contracts traded at different prices. It is the weighted average price at which most of the trading has occurred.

Watch List. A table that lists tradable securities of interest to a trader, usually stocks, ETFs, and futures. Many traders have multiple watch lists that fall into different categories or market sectors.

Zeta. A rarely used option Greek constant that measures the sensitivity of an option.

Zomma is a minor Greek that is a measures of the degree to which the Gamma of an option is sensitive to changes in implied volatility. Zomma is also referred to as *DgammaDvol.* This minor Greek belongs to a group of measurements used to assess the price sensitivity of an option to other variables including changes in interest rates, volatility, or the spot price of the option's underlying equity.

As previously mentioned, there are a number of the rarely discussed, more obscure Greeks that long-time, experienced option traders have ever heard of.

However, experienced and successful option traders do understand how to use the values available to them on the thinkorswim option chains.

Alphabetical Index

www.ingramcontent.com/pod-product-compliance
Lightning Source LLC
LaVergne TN
LVHW080320110826
845155LV00026B/171

* 9 7 8 1 9 4 7 6 3 7 2 8 3 *